Storytelling, History, and the Postmodern South

*Southern Literary Studies* | Fred Hobson, Series Editor

# Storytelling, History, and the Postmodern South

*Edited by* Jason Phillips

*Louisiana State University Press* )|( *Baton Rouge*

Published by Louisiana State University Press
Copyright © 2013 by Louisiana State University Press
All rights reserved
Manufactured in the United States of America
First printing

Designer: Barbara Neely Bourgoyne
Typeface: Whitman
Printer: McNaughton & Gunn, Inc.
Binder: Dekker Bookbinding

Library of Congress Cataloging-in-Publication Data

Storytelling, history, and the postmodern South / edited by Jason Phillips.
    pages cm. — (Southern literary studies)
    Includes bibliographical references.
    ISBN 978-0-8071-5034-4 (cloth : alk. paper) — ISBN 978-0-8071-5035-1 (pdf) — ISBN
978-0-8071-5036-8 (epub) — ISBN 978-0-8071-5037-5 (mobi)  1. American fiction—20th
century—History and criticism.  2. Historical fiction, American—History and criticism.
3. Literature and history—Southern States—History—20th century.  4. Postmodernism
(Literature)—Southern States.  5. Storytelling in literature.  6. Southern States—In
literature.  7. Race in literature.  8. Autobiographical memory in literature.  I. Phillips,
Jason, 1973–
    PS261.S76 2013
    813.009'975—dc23

                                                                            2012039372

*In memory of Noel Polk*
*and Bertram Wyatt-Brown*

# CONTENTS

# ACKNOWLEDGMENTS

This book of essays evolved from a conference held at Mississippi State University that sought to "deconstruct" Dixie. Noel Polk deserves credit for first suggesting the conference over lunch while I bombarded him with questions about southern storytelling in history and fiction. The Office of Research and Economic Development at Mississippi State, then under the leadership of Vice President Kirk Schulz, generously sponsored the event. History Department head Alan Marcus deserves special thanks for encouraging this project and for hosting a delicious catfish fry for all conference participants.

This book would not exist without the brilliant essays each contributor submitted and resubmitted as we toiled together on a unique anthology. It was a pleasure working with all of them. Bert Wyatt-Brown was the first author to promise an essay, and his commitment helped the project immeasurably. I am especially grateful to Farrell O'Gorman for all his help as I tried to combine southern history and literature in this collection. Farrell's willingness to answer questions and critique my drafts made the task of bridging two disciplines much easier. Elizabeth Gratch did a superb job copyediting our essays. I thank series editor Fred Hobson and acquisition editors John Easterly and Margaret Lovecraft for their expert assistance in handling this book at Louisiana State University Press. Sadly, Noel Polk and Bert Wyatt-Brown died in 2012. They cannot receive a copy of this book, a project they encouraged from the beginning. I miss them and dedicate this book to their memory.

Storytelling, History, and the Postmodern South

# Introduction

## The Liars at the Jung Hotel

JASON PHILLIPS

On November 5, 1968, the day after a tumultuous election ended with Richard Nixon as president, Ralph Ellison stood before the Southern Historical Association at the Jung Hotel, New Orleans, and called the members gathered there "respectable liars." The time, place, and audience compelled Ellison to "be a little nasty" about how historians had obscured the "racial situation in the country." On the subject of race, Ellison argued, "our written history has been as 'official' as any produced in any communist country—only in a democratic way: individuals write it instead of committees." Ellison asserted that historians drew inspiration from "great tall tales" that promoted a romantic version of the past that masked the hypocrisy of America's self-image. The historian claims to be "dedicated to chronology" and professional standards of inquiry, Ellison contended, but "he can suppress, he can emphasize, he can project, and he can carve out his artifact; and this helps us to imagine ourselves, to project ourselves, to achieve certain goals, certain identities." For generations those goals and identities promoted white supremacy instead of the truth. Ellison thanked God that "there have been a few novelists who decided to tell the 'truth' in their own unique and devious ways." If his audience wanted to learn about the South, Ellison told them, "don't go to historians, not even to Negro historians"; instead, go to William Faulkner, Robert Penn Warren, and the Blues.[1]

Ellison branded scholarship "official" history to expose its affiliation with a dominant consciousness, but I prefer a term that evokes the southern dimensions of this issue: *master narratives*. In the South master narratives are stories masquerading as knowledge or truth that promote the interests of white patriarchy past and present. Whether or not master narratives deliberately empower and oppress groups is a complex question about historical motive and authors' intentions. Ellison deemed historians guilty of calculated censorship; he called them "liars." While his fellow panelists, William Styron, Robert Penn Warren, and C. Vann Woodward, stuck to the advertised topic, "The Uses of History in Fiction," Ellison inverted the discussion to reveal the abuses of fiction in history. Announcing, "We have reached a great crisis in American history," Ellison alluded to more than the troubles of 1968; he meant that American historiography had lost its credibility. By excluding or marginalizing large populations within history, master narratives left many people with "a high sensitivity to the ironies of historical writing and . . . a profound skepticism concerning the validity of most reports about what the past was like."

Still, there was hope. While Ellison's audience "altered" the story of the South "to justify racial attitudes and practices," African American storytellers preserved censored aspects of American history in oral traditions: "Historical figures continued to live in stories of and theories about the human and social dynamics of slavery, and about the effects of political decisions rendered during Reconstruction. Assertions of freedom and revolts were recalled along with triumphs of labor in the fields and on the dance floor; feats of eating and drinking and fornication, or religious conversion and physical endurance, and of artistic and athletic achievements. In brief, the broad ramifications of human life as Negroes have experienced it were marked and passed along." Ellison urged his audience to debunk official history by using these sources to write a richer story of the nation's past, a narrative that interwove white tall tales and black folklore. Glaring at a thousand southern historians, Ellison prophesied, "We are now going to have a full American history."[2]

I suspect that Ralph Ellison would have mixed feelings about the present condition of American historiography. As he foretold, historians have mined African American evidence, written about a host of subjects, and enriched our understanding of the United States' past. Nonetheless,

Ellison's "full American history" remains unrealized. For decades critics, including literary theorists, feminists, social historians, and linguists, have advanced Ellison's argument that historical narratives privilege a dominant ideology. As a result, they have buried master narratives beneath monographic analysis instead of crafting new stories. But as Nathan Irvin Huggins has explained, "In an important way the *story* is what history is all about. We all need to be calling for a new narrative, a new synthesis taking into account the new history" of African Americans and other oppressed groups. Until these scholars tell a story that fulfills Ellison's prophecy, Huggins warned, they will continue "to work in an eddy of the larger stream." Other historians and literary scholars have addressed master narratives directly to show how they sanctioned white supremacy. But much of this recent work impugns historical memory for promoting racial hierarchy, whereas Ellison accused historiography itself of whitewashing the past. It seems the liars at the Jung Hotel have shifted the blame and shame Ellison directed at them to the public. Finally, Ellison's assault on master narratives transcended binary thinking about black-white and fact-fiction, while most of his successors' attempts have not. In 1968, perhaps the most racially charged year of the century, Ellison praised white novelists and black musicians for telling the truth about the South and discredited all historians, white and black, for lying about it. When black members of the audience assailed William Styron for writing *The Confessions of Nat Turner* (1967) and called all white Americans racists, Ellison sighed, "I would suspect that all Americans, black and white, are racists."[3]

To face these difficult problems, this collection of essays showcases scholars who encounter master narratives from multiple, fresh perspectives. They cross boundaries, question dichotomies, and experiment with the form, not merely the content, of scholarship. Legions of scholars continue to challenge master narratives by adding oppressed perspectives and actors to history and literature. That important work is not the primary aim of *Storytelling, History, and the Postmodern South*. Instead, each essayist in this book heeds Huggins's advice that history is storytelling and explores the enduring dynamic between history, literature, and power in the American South. Like Ellison, the contributors to this volume look beyond ideology and race to explore how less visible, more basic elements of a work, such as its form, plot, aesthetics, or genre, can re- or deconstruct mastery. By mixing history and literature, these authors blend analysis with storytelling and professional with personal insights. They remind us that style *is* substance in writing. Achieving Ellison's full American history is beyond the reach of any anthology, but this one contributes to that goal by insisting that writing a full history means harnessing, not criticizing, the inherent power of narratives. In short they work at the crossroads of southern history and literature because neither discipline has a monopoly on truth, knowledge, or grace and because only a joint effort can grasp the power of master narratives in the South.

Using the tools of the master is risky business. As Anne Goodwyn Jones has shown, recent calls for poststructuralism in southern literary studies can reinforce rather than deconstruct southern mastery because Jacques Derrida's abstractions are homologous to southern traditions of dichotomy and patriarchy. She writes, "Derrida might have invented the South: the logic of dichotomy and its rigidly bounded and hierarchically organized categories have quite overtly characterized the dominant public written discourse of the region at least since the early nineteenth century." By applying poststructuralism to the South, Jefferson Humphries and others presuppose a monolithic region, privilege masculinity, and "reimplant southern ideology under the name of theory." In other words, scholars who use the tools of the master run the risk of thinking like him. To avoid this danger, Jones recommends "historically based theoretical practices" that deconstruct the South without reifying it. *Storytelling, History, and the Postmodern South* offers diverse examples of this method, yet, as Ellison showed us, historical approaches also borrow the master's tools. In historiography, fiction, and collective memory, masters used the past to empower themselves in the present. The "Lost Cause" is only the most obvious example of this practice. Fortunately, southernists have many models for applying historical approaches and telling stories that subvert mastery: William Faulkner, Robert Penn Warren, C. Vann Woodward, the Percy family, and others crafted strong traditions of internal criticism that deconstructed master narratives. As southern historian Timothy Tyson explains, "I grew up immersed in southern traditions of storytelling and insurgency, where we sometimes killed the master but always kept the narrative, thank you very much." Eschewing the poststructuralism of Stanley Fish, Tyson applied the critical approach honed by Warren and Woodward to craft *Radio Free Dixie: Robert F. Williams and the Roots of Black Power* (1999). Tyson and Jones followed Ellison's lead by locating the heart of southern mastery and insurgency in the same place, in stories. Jones provocatively asked how mastery has "translate[d] into writing practices and how does writing re- or deconstruct male power? That is a question that remains to be answered." *Storytelling, History, and the Postmodern South* offers many answers to this vexing question.[4]

Although these essays approach master narratives from diverse perspectives, they revolve around similar preoccupations. The first four essays explore the liminal zone between literature and history, the place where master narratives have been constructed and contested for centuries. In a brilliant reading of *Lanterns on the Levee: Recollections of a Planter's Son* (1941) Bertram Wyatt-Brown argues that William Alexander Percy's life and work blurred fact and fiction to negotiate between the anti-intellectual conventions of a rural, hierarchical South and Percy's own cosmopolitanism and homosexuality. This personal and artistic negotiation produced a masterful blend of myth and memoir in *Lanterns,* making the book neither fiction nor history exclusively but deserving of a place beside both the best southern literature and autobiography. In the second chapter about fact-fiction, Farrell O'Gorman crosses many more borders to upend dichotomies of North-South, East-West, white-black, Protestant-Catholic, mind-body, and modern-postmodern. O'Gorman's fresh historical reading of southern Gothic fiction by William Faulkner, Cormac McCarthy, and Walker Percy highlights the centrality of religion in these texts by placing them within a broader, hemispheric context. He boldly shows that these fantastical fictions should be required reading for historians because each tale exposes our inability to tell the whole truth, to author an autonomous, accurate narrative history. Anne Marshall explores this theme further by comparing the works of Robert Penn Warren and C. Vann Woodward. Focusing on *All the King's Men* (1946) and *The Burden of Southern History* (1960), Marshall studies how Warren and Woodward managed the troublesome and painful task of creating history that unburied brutal truths beneath the South's master narratives. According to Marshall, southern novelists and historians not only share similar subjects; they also employ similar mixtures of fact and fiction to approach the complexity of the South. K. Stephen Prince shows how Thomas Nelson Page jumbled fact and fiction to redefine mastery in the New South. While the responsibility of creating history paralyzed Warren's

Jack Burden, it invigorated Page. According to Prince, Page had a surprisingly modern take on the power of culture and public opinion and believed that his most popular stories were truer than facts. At a time when American historians dedicated themselves to professional objectivity, Page fused history and literature in ways that echoed Romantic historiography and anticipated postmodernism. Collectively, these four essays show us that fiction and nonfiction about the South differ in degree, not kind. Both tell stories that mix imagination and actuality to evoke and explore the region's past, present, and future. Likewise, both champions and critics of master narratives worked between history and literature to "tell about the South."

The five remaining essays examine how southern writers and scholars orient themselves and identify others as southern insiders or outsiders to establish authority and address mastery. Jewel L. Spangler's close reading of James Ireland's memoir refutes the standard portrait of Ireland, and early Virginia Baptists in general, as religious outsiders who were persecuted by southern neighbors. Spangler recasts Ireland as a slave-owning patriarchal insider who used language to wield mastery and order his household. Specifically, Spangler interprets neglected chapters of the memoir that detail an attempt to poison Ireland by his female hired servant and slave girl. In the process of retelling the story, Spangler reconsiders race and religion in Virginia. By interpreting neglected Confederate novels, Orville Vernon Burton and Ian Binnington show how the acts of reading and writing wartime literature helped to combine local and regional identities into a nationalism that outlasted the Confederacy. Novels by Sally Rochester Ford, Mary Jane Haw, and James Dabney McCabe galvanized binary traits for southerners and Yankee "others" that promoted mastery and presaged Lost Cause mythology. But Burton and Binnington wisely insist that regional identity and Confederate nationalism never erased local affiliations.

For many southerners, the county line—not the Mason-Dixon Line—divided insiders from outsiders. Jim Downs complicates the social construction of race after emancipation by finding a proliferation of color categories, instead of the "one-drop rule," in a host of sources from government documents to travelers' accounts in the United States and throughout the Atlantic world. By retelling the story of Rosina Downs, a slave girl who could pass as white, Downs stresses the nation's obsession with color as the demarcation for insiders and outsiders. Writing simultaneously as a detached scholar and as a descendant of the slave girl, Downs complicates the insider-outsider dichotomy on multiple levels. David Davis blurs the insider-outsider duality further by studying a group that fits in both categories: namely, "southern white trash." His close reading of white trash autobiographies explores abjection and the aesthetics of waste. Like Downs, Davis enriches his analysis by presenting himself as both a detached scholar and an insider when he tells his own story of growing up white trash. Finally, Robert Jackson surveys the strange career of the "professional southerner," a character that appears in literature and criticism from the late nineteenth century through the twentieth. Jackson's essay produces not only a colorful canon of professional southerners but also a broad history of ideas and changing attitudes about the South by studying who has spoken for the region and how their messages have changed over time. Together these essays show how an author's position as a southern insider or outsider, whether consciously assumed or not, shapes the voice, authority, order, and readership of a text. In many cases insiders defend mastery while outsiders subvert it, but these essayists present more complicated dynamics between the author's vantage point and hegemony. In refreshing fashion, they reveal how their own work cannot avoid the effects of an insider or outsider designation.

Individually, these essays contribute a host of ideas and approaches that enrich southern studies; collectively, *Storytelling, History, and the Postmodern South* enhances southern studies in three ways. First, by studying southern mastery and storytelling within a postmodern context, these scholars showcase new ways of interpreting texts and crafting scholarship. Instead of wedding themselves to a particular postmodern theory or practice, the authors remain open to multiple approaches. They insist that eclecticism, not commonality, is the key to overcoming a monolithic South and its master narratives. Like their southern subjects, the contributors work with ambiguities and produce hybrid texts. In the process they transcend simple dichotomies and recommend multiple ways of addressing the challenges of postmodernism. In particular, the contributors showcase diverse methods of overcoming problems of narration, voice, perspective, and the binary world of fact and fiction without an overarching theoretical bias. Second, because storytelling has always been an important element of southern identity, exploring that phenomenon deepens our understanding of the South. So, while southern scholars can engage postmodernism, it is also true that postmodernism can elevate southern studies. The power of stories is more than a common thread in these essays, and it is more than a faddish, postmodern subject; it is at the heart of southern identities and power. *Storytelling, History, and the Postmodern South* enhances the sensibility scholars bring to this important subject. Third, our collection illustrates how interdisciplinary work can strengthen both history and literary studies. Working at this intellectual hub forces historians to face theory and acknowledge its existence within their discipline and within their own work. Conversely, it compels literary scholars to move beyond theory to consider the historical context of southern stories and storytelling. These lessons teach historians to read evidence more deeply and literary scholars to read stories more broadly. The results are closer readings and more compelling interpretations.

At first glance, the notion of a postmodern South may seem antithetical. According to stereotypes, postmodernism challenges modern meaning, order, and authority, while the South upholds them. Postmodernism is blatantly offensive, while the South is patently defensive. The former seems avant-garde, intellectual, and diverse; the latter appears orthodox, instinctive, and monolithic. One reputedly discards the past in favor of the present and future, while the other embraces the past at the expense of the present and future. But when we put stereotypes aside and take a deeper look at postmodernism and the South, we realize that both see history as a form of storytelling. Unlike most of their critics, postmodernists and southerners are quite comfortable at the intersection of history and literature. On the night Ellison called historians liars, C. Vann Woodward affirmed the kinship between historians and novelists. "We are in fact siblings," Woodward confessed. "The novel is the youngest of the literary forms—the only one the Greeks didn't invent. It was born only in the mid-Eighteenth Century, not long before professional historiography first saw the light of day in Germany. Both sprang from a common parentage of story tellers." Woodward attributed the genres' affinities and "sibling rivalry" to "the growing historical consciousness of western man" and competition to satisfy that thirst for knowledge. Professional historiography and the novel were also born when print culture started to eclipse traditional oral forms of storytelling. The essays in this volume demonstrate that southerners have approached history as a form of storytelling for centuries. In a time when academics prophesy an amalgamation of history and fiction, the scholars in this book point to a long tradition of cross-pollination in southern history and literature. Indeed, when we reflect on this history, it seems the South was postmodern *before* it was modern.[5]

In the spirit of Fred Hobson's work on southern writers, this book presents southern scholars in a postmodern world who explore subjects engendered by postmodernity without embracing and promoting specific postmodern theories. By discarding narrow analysis in favor of diverse, broader approaches, our work surpasses faddish applications of theory and speaks to both historians and literary scholars. As historian Peter Burke explains, "We are living in an age of blurred lines and open intellectual frontiers, an age which is at once exciting and confusing." Finding our way in this world requires an open mind and a critical eye. Blind devotions to old conventions and overzealous worship for the latest theory will get us lost in the postmodern South. We need to disenthrall ourselves from familiar dichotomies and chronologies that obscure as much as they reveal. The essays of *Storytelling, History, and the Postmodern South* illustrate many approaches that embed theory in historical analysis. By spanning four centuries of southern history, we show how the process of telling, receiving, and interpreting stories has affected mastery for historical participants and scholars ever since the South began. Combining history and literature, contextual and textual analysis, offers a more promising escape from hegemonies of the "South" and the academy. In recent years a willingness to see and explore southern worlds that exceed simple binaries of race, religion, gender, geography, and class has greatly enriched southern studies. The future of the field will brighten even more when it transcends another rigid dichotomy, modernism-postmodernism.[6]

*Storytelling, History, and the Postmodern South* suggests ways of unmooring the binary chronology of modernism and postmodernism to reveal deeper meanings and problems that have marked southern storytelling for ages. Clearly, the promise and peril of working between southern history and literature are not inherently postmodern issues. All three of Ellison's co-panelists in 1968 won Pulitzer Prizes for writing historical fiction or fictional history, and two of them endured controversies for their efforts. Minutes after Ellison accused historians of lying, the audience charged William Styron of falsifying history and denigrating Nat

Turner in his Pulitzer Prize–winning novel *The Confessions of Nat Turner* (1967). Fifteen years later, when C. Vann Woodward won a Pulitzer for *Mary Chesnut's Civil War*, he was accused of promoting a hoax as history because he defended Chesnut's writing as authentic even though she had rewritten her Civil War diary during and after Reconstruction. Both Styron and Woodward tried to rewrite master narratives of the Old South. Styron presented an alternative reading of the original *Confessions of Nat Turner*, written by Thomas Gray, a slave owner. Woodward stressed the liberal, antislavery sentiments in the wartime and postwar writings of a slave-owning mistress, Chesnut. Both imbroglios can be explained contextually. At a critical moment in the civil rights movement, Styron, a white southern man, challenged the popular image of a rebellious slave. At a perilous point in the feminist movement (when the Equal Rights Amendment finally failed), Woodward, a white southern man, challenged the popular image of a respected female author. Only Warren, a white southern male writing about another white southern male, Huey Long, *under a pseudonym*, won praise without fire.

Contexts may explain the heat each controversy generated, but the underlying problems posed by each work transcended contemporary issues. As the essays in this volume demonstrate, difficulties with objectivity, authenticity, and intentions have for centuries dogged writers who intersect history and literature. What a writer considers history or truth can be perceived as a hoax or lie by readers. Whether a writer chooses to pose as an insider or outsider shapes the possibilities of a text, but self-designations are always subject to the readers' judgment and can change over time. One more example of these quandaries shows how universal they are. No one could be less contemporary—less modern, postmodern, or southern—than the "Father of History," Herodotus, the ancient Greek whom Aristotle branded a "storyteller" and others called the "Father of Lies." Like Styron and Woodward, Herodotus considered history a form of truthful storytelling and viewed himself as an impassioned outsider who collected evidence and sought deeper meanings. His critics, like those who assailed Styron and Woodward, branded him an unscrupulous mixer of fact and fiction who masked the biases of an insider behind the false facade of an outsider. Ralph Ellison was not the first to call historians liars, and he will not be the last.[7]

1. An edited transcription of the panel discussion appears in James L. W. West III, ed., *Conversations with William Styron* (Jackson: University Press of Mississippi, 1985), 114–44. All quotations in this paragraph appear on 119–20.

2. Ibid., 124 (first and last quotations), 126 (second, third, fourth, and fifth quotations).

3. Nathan Irvin Huggins, "Integrating Afro-American History into American History," in *The State of Afro-American History: Past, Present, and Future*, ed. Darlene Clark Hine (Baton Rouge: Louisiana State University Press, 1986), 159–60; West, *Conversations with William Styron*, 142.

4. Anne Goodwyn Jones, "'The Tools of the Master': Southernists in Theoryland," in *Bridging Southern Cultures: An Interdisciplinary Approach*, ed. John Lowe (Baton Rouge: Louisiana State University Press, 2005), 174 (first quotation), 183 (second quotation), 192 (third quotation), 193 (fifth quotation); Timothy B. Tyson, "Robert F. Williams and the Promise of Southern Biography," *Southern Cultures* 8.3 (Fall 2002): 39. Also see Audre Lorde, "The Master's Tools Will Never Dismantle the Master's House," in *This Bridge Called My Back: Writings by Radical Women of Color*, ed. Cherríe Moraga and Gloria Anzaldúa (Waterton, Mass.: Persephone, 1981).

5. West, *Conversations with William Styron*, 114–15; Walter Benjamin, "The Storyteller: Reflections on the Works of Nikolai Leskov," in *Illuminations: Walter Benjamin Essays and Reflections*, ed. Hannah Arendt (New York: Harcourt Brace Jovanovich, 1968), 83–109.

6. Peter Burke, *History and Social Theory* (Ithaca: Cornell University Press, 1992), 21.

7. Arnaldo Momigliano, "The Place of Herodotus in the History of Historiography," reprinted in Walter Blanco and Jennifer Tolbert Roberts, eds., Herodotus, *The Histories* (New York: Norton, 1992), 361; J. A. S. Evans, "Father of History of Father of Lies: The Reputation of Herodotus," reprinted ibid., 369–77.

# Will Percy and *Lanterns on the Levee* Revisited

W illiam Alexander Percy's *Lanterns on the Levee: Recollections of a Planter's Son* (1941) remains a memorial to a long-vanished southern culture. In his preface to a paperback edition in 1973, Walker Percy begins a lively and sensitive introduction to the master-piece written by his "fabled relative."[1] His word for his "Uncle Will," as he called him, was appropriate. It applied not only to the author but to the actual character of his memoir as well. Both his life in the Missis-sippi Delta and other places and his most prominent literary work are the subjects of this essay. *Lanterns on the Levee* has remained in print since 1941. With his antiquated views, the long-dead author is likely to please neither the current gay community nor those involved in civil rights. Yet *Lanterns* holds our interest by the beauty of its style, the humor it gen-erates, and the profound sense of humanity Percy conveys. Because he was so complex a figure, the confusing nature of his character makes it almost impossible to separate the various threads of his identity. To call him a poet, memoirist, storyteller, bon vivant, world traveler, planter, attorney, civic leader, is only to touch upon his many sides. Furthermore, in 1932 he became a foster father responsible for the care of three young orphan sons of his first cousin LeRoy Pratt Percy, an attorney of Birming-ham, Alabama, and his wife, Martha Susan (Mattie Sue). Both had died tragically.

Inwardly, Will Percy suffered. Thus he remains a curious puzzle to readers as well as, perhaps, to himself. We prefer characters who are deemed either good or bad, but he defies simple categories. Instead, contradictions and ambivalences abound. He lacked a sturdy confidence in his own selfhood but managed to develop a lively social presence. His mother and father did not accord him the respect that a growing lad needs, yet he was a dutiful son who followed the dictates of the Fifth Commandment. He rejected the Christian creed but found in the Stoic tradition of Marcus Aurelius a stirring, warlike replacement. Indeed, for a man small in stature and somewhat womanly in manner, Percy loved war.[2] In battle Percy discovered an excitement that made ordinary living seem irrelevant, but the Aurelian principles that guided his war experiences could not adapt to the changing times. Still, they helped to elicit a yearning for a distant, mythical past significant in his thoughts. He had a joyous exuberance about him that was severely compromised by a deep sense of loneliness coupled with depression. Melancholia was a family curse. Despite its effects, Percy explored the creative aspect of his soul as a means to hold the shade of despondency at bay. So often, like other depressives, he found in humor a way to challenge those ill feelings.

In terms of racial matters, Percy was far more appreciative of the black race than he was of poor whites, especially the bloodthirsty racists among them. He offered much help to African Americans in trouble—without, however, ever thinking of them as equal to himself. As a wealthy Delta plantation owner, he adhered to the southern faith in white superiority, both in terms of morals and intelligence. While he had a respectable legal practice, he hated litigation. The strain tossed him into emotional turmoil. Percy's sexual leanings were toward other men. Yet, remaining closeted, he found in art and music a constant source of inspiration and an escape from the frowns of other Mississippians. In that day and that locale, nothing could have been quite so repellent to ordinary folk as homosexuality. It was a source of mortification in the South that persists in its stubborn prejudice to our own time.

How could all these selves, as it were, complement each other? Somehow they did. Therein lies the enigma of a man with some of the flaws of the human species but also the gifts of a literary artist.

In *Lanterns on the Levee* Will Percy, as he was known, created a grand southern fable. Throughout his short life he had to negotiate between the anti-intellectual proclivities and conventions of a rural, hierarchical, southern world and his own far more generous and accepting spirit and cosmopolitanism. Somehow he managed to belong in both these separate and seemingly unbridgeable spheres. One suspects that he seldom reflected with complete candor on the dilemma. He found relief by living part of his life far away from Mississippi. He would, though, return to his native land because another part of him found that duty, family honor, and a deep affection for his hometown, Greenville, and his friends there required his residence on Percy Street.

As half-memoir and half-myth, Will's meditation on the past reveals his complicated but charismatic personality in a way that constantly delights the reader. As quoted on the back cover of the 1973 edition, a critic for the *Saturday Review of Literature* had commented in 1941 that the author's "prose has dignity and vigor and style, and in every sentence he writes, his own character is manifest." In 2004 Benjamin Schwarz wrote in the *Atlantic Monthly*, "Few memoirs are as haunting as William Alexander Percy's *Lanterns on the Levee*."[3] No doubt Will, who had hitherto composed slim volumes of poetry, would have been pleased with the continued success of his famous prose work. But he might have been mystified too. Pessimistic about the future, nostalgic about the allegedly glorious southern past, he would have graciously, we imagine, accepted the laurels of literary acclaim but then dismissed them with a self-deprecating laugh and a fleeting smile.

As a member of a fast-dying order of gentleman planters, memories of whom he lovingly recalls in these pages, Will Percy, a romantic and old-fashioned thinker, tried to keep alive a South of plantation ease and perfect decorum that had never really existed. He did not make common cause with those literary contemporaries who would establish a fresh and vital southern literary awakening—William Faulkner, Robert Penn Warren, Allen Tate, Caroline Gordon, Lillian Smith, W. J. Cash, and many others. They boldly and often harshly challenged southern intellectual and social traditions and questioned the chivalric past that Will Percy celebrated. They reflected a modernistic psychological realism about the region they all loved. Even though Percy, too, lamented the South's vulgarity, intolerance, and materialism, these writers' visions were not his.

There should be no genuine mystery, though, about why *Lanterns on the Levee* continues to engage us—and even tempt readers into second and third readings. The first reason is Percy's sense of humor. Although literary historians have often stressed the pervasive melancholy of *Lanterns on the Levee*, its quick thrusts into levity are no less important to its continuing appeal. Percy provides throughout both joy and gloom in equal measure. At risk of spoiling a future reader's pleasure, only a few examples of his wit are given here. In his exquisitely realized chapter about his days at the University of the South, in Sewanee, Tennessee, he notes that the liberal arts college was not strong in science, economics, or sociology. Yet its humanities curriculum instruction was inspiring. Will attended the course on ethics under William Porcher DuBose, a renowned Episcopal theologian. "He was a tiny silver saint who lived elsewhere, being more conversant with the tongues of angels than of men. Sometimes sitting on the edge of his desk in his black gown, talking haltingly of Aristotle, he would suspend, rapt, in some mid air beyond our ken, murmuring: 'The starry heavens—' followed by indefinite silence."[4]

Percy's sense of the absurd could be infectious. The description he gave of a dinner party at Cambridge when he was a law student at Harvard presents another priceless moment of cheerful abandon. It concerned an accidentally wayward torpedolike dinner roll. His hosts were members of the Boston elite, accustomed to stylized decorum. In the midst of telling some fanciful story, the exuberant Percy flung his napkin, unaware that a dinner roll was lodged in the folds. It flew across the room and landed against a canary cage. "No one could pretend it hadn't happened. . . . The impact with the bird-cage sounded like a Stravinsky chord on an untuned harp." The feathery occupants announced their alarm with much screeching. "I couldn't decide whether I wanted to die or giggle. But my hosts never batted an eye." He admired the sangfroid of the guests, who said nothing of the incident. And then the soup arrived. But Will Percy remembered that at home someone would have shouted, "Good shot," or announced, "The last time Senator Omygosh did that he hit two canaries and killed the auk."[5]

A further illustration of Percy's humorous side drew from his enjoyment of the give-and-take of political campaigning on behalf of his father. By then he was a young lawyer in Greenville. Incumbent senator LeRoy Percy, Will's father, ran for the full term in 1911. The campaign was far more vicious even by the crude standards of that era in the South. Theodore Bilbo and James K. Vardaman, racist populists, whom Percy justly ridiculed in memorable scenes in *Lanterns,* were determined that the Percy grandee would be trounced at the hands of the hardscrabble white farmers. Will Percy told the story of how the senator's brothers tried to goad State Senator Theodore Bilbo into a lethal confrontation during breakfast at the local hotel. Bilbo was Vardaman's chief supporter when he sought to unseat Percy and the old and wealthy ruling class. Armed with a pistol, LeRoy's brother, attorney John Walker, shouted across the dining room a gross insult in the manner of a determined duelist. But "the object of his outburst," Percy wrote, "did not fall for the ruse, he made no motion to his hip or elsewhere; he kept on eating oatmeal." No shootout resulted. But in *Lanterns* he revealed a gloomy outlook. Senator Percy was so roundly defeated that Will, an aide in the campaign, felt the loss as keenly as his father. He expressed his bitterness in his memoir: "Thus at twenty-seven I became inured to defeat; I have never since expected victory."[6] A longtime Percy supporter mourned as well: "The Bilbo-Vardaman triumph is complete. It simply proves that the 'cattle' of Mississippi are incapable of intelligent self government. The only salvation of the state is to restore the ballot to the negroes. Things would be at least no worse."[7] But the African Americans of Mississippi had still years to wait before gaining access to the ballot box.

Another reason for admiring *Lanterns on the Levee* is Will Percy's sense of the dramatic—the pulse of recounted events that he makes seem momentous, whether he is writing of defeat or triumph. Sometimes he combined his joyousness of spirit and a deep unrelenting loneliness. An example emerges from memories of his participation in the Great War. In *Lanterns* he amusingly recounted his training for officer rank at a camp in Texas. His description captured the anxiety, absurdity, and poignancy of young civilians thrust into the mindless exigencies of army discipline. He belonged to the so-called Pee Wee Squad of Company D. They were smart but tiny. Unlike the hulks who mocked them, they did not faint when the hypodermic needle struck their behinds. Percy went on to serve as an infantry officer in France, and his account of the war does not reflect its full horror and cruelty. Yet, as a young man seeking to prove his worth, he discovered a kind of liberation from the humdrum constrictions of southern society. Nonetheless, he recalled in *Lanterns* the letdown that followed the armistice. "It's over, the only great thing you were ever part of. It's over, the only heroic thing we all did together. What can you do now? Nothing,

nothing." He mourned that he recalled everything "step by step—as if it moved *sub species aeternitatis*." He had hated the horrors of war, but that conflict had provided fulfillment, whereas "daily life hasn't; it was part of a common endeavor, and daily life is isolated and lonely."[8]

Helping to sustain his experience in the trenches was his adoption of the ancient ethic of honor, to which his memoir makes frequent reference. He knew the code had largely disappeared from public life, but its passing was for him a signal of a civilization in decay. "Politics used to be the study of men proud and jealous of America's honor, now it was a game played by self-seekers which no man need bother his head about; where there had been an accepted pattern of living, there was no pattern whatsoever." Elsewhere in *Lanterns* he declared, "Going mad for honor's sake presupposes honor. In our brave new world a man of honor is rather like the Negro—there's no place for him to go." The code to which he had pledged himself contributed to his depressive moods. Living up to the strict rubrics of honor, rooted in a warrior culture long since vanished, was nearly impossible. Failure to do so could bring on an agonizing sense of shame. Christian faith was no alternative, as "Uncle Will" saw it. Walker Percy, his adopted son, told an interviewer, "Will Percy was a lapsed Catholic who aesthetically admired the rich heritage of his Creole mother, but remained fatalistic."[9]

In fact, the *Meditations* of the philosophical Roman emperor was Will Percy's Bible. Marcus Aurelius Antoninus offered a refined ideal of honor that sought more than warrior valor and a glorious reputation, although both aims were important. The second-century emperor believed in the Stoic virtues of prudence, temperateness, fortitude, justice, and devotion to honorable duty. "There is left to each of us, no matter how far defeat pierces, the unassailable wintry kingdom of Marcus Aurelius, which some more gently call the Kingdom of Heaven," Percy mused in *Lanterns*. While a college student at Sewanee, he had left the Catholic faith of his mother. Rejecting formal Christian commitment, he found in the Stoic tradition another means to assuage doubt, depression, and solitude, and he shared it with his three wards.[10] The "broad-sword tradition," as Will summed up the Aurelian message, should guide the three young Percy brothers, Walker, LeRoy, and Phinizy, in their separate pursuits. In his chapter "For the Younger Generation," most particularly, Will Percy upheld the ancient Roman virtues that he found compelling. The realm of chivalry, Percy continued, lies "not outside, but within, and when all is lost, it stands fast."[11] Like Francis I of France after Charles V at Pavia defeated his army, he meant, "We have lost all, save honor." Percy mourned in *Lanterns* that "the Old South, the old ideals, the old strengths have vanished."[12] Thus, like Walker Percy in his literary work, he brought elements of despondency and honor together in the same scheme of things.

Another episode linked this concept of honor to public events in his way of thinking. The occasion was the memorable Percy-led victory over the Greenville Ku Klux Klan in 1922. Once again, Will Percy told the tale with great expressiveness and great wit. What he did not highlight, though, was just how important it was to LeRoy Percy and the family as a whole to keep a grip on the levers of power in the Delta. Without LeRoy's robust leadership and brave speeches against the Klan, the hooded order would have won control of the county offices. That victory would have spelled harassment and worse for local Catholics, Jews, Lebanese, African Americans, and members of other ethnic minorities in Greenville. After Senator Percy gave a rousing speech about the bigotry of the Klan and how it would affect the Catholics, Jews, and other minorities, he won a standing ovation. The Klan leaders slinked off, their candidates for local office defeated. A grand party at the Percy house followed. With four kegs of beer on hand, the fun began. "Father called to the crowd," Will recalled, "Come on in, boys," and they did. "Lucille and her band appeared." She was a hefty soul, "weighing twenty stone, airily pulled the grand piano into her lap, struck one tremendous chord—my Steinway's been swayback ever since—and the dancing began." This was a moment of joy for Will Percy and indeed for his often depressed father. For once, the governing class had overcome the local know-nothings. Good had triumphed, an honorable, Aurelian vindication for the Percys after the senator's humiliating election loss in 1911 at the hands of racist demagogues. The feeling was almost as uplifting and exciting as Will Percy's fight in France had been.[13]

After the triumph over the Klan, Percy and his father became more intimate than they had been before. The next crisis, though, again revealed the contradictions in Will's life and, in particular, the strains of being his father's son. The Great Flood of 1927 would have taxed the capabilities of more commanding natures than Will possessed. But, to a degree, his mix of success and failures indicated that, while competent in some respects, he was not the effective leader that Senator Percy was. He would have been the first to acknowledge his imperfections. The very title of Will's memoir speaks to us with special poignancy. *Lanterns* refers to the night patrollers who, with lanterns in hand, looked for signs of where the river might be working its way underneath the levees and abruptly dissolving them in a wild rush of churning waters. William Armstrong Percy III, a cousin of the memoirist, affirms that the title is "evocative of Uncle Will's lifelong sense that what remained of the Old South's aristocratic planter culture required vigilant defense, lest it too be swept away."[14]

During the harrowing ordeal of the 1927 flood, Will Percy served conscientiously as chairman of the county relief effort under the auspices of the Red Cross. Like the Katrina calamity of 2005, the disaster killed thousands. It produced over 700,000 half-starved refugees. The Mississippi River washed over twenty-seven thousand square miles, a wide and long expanse equivalent to the states of Connecticut, Massachusetts, New Hampshire, and Vermont combined. Most terrifying were the huge crests of waves, sometimes thirty feet high, bearing down on levees, farmlands, towns, and villages. Yet government plans and preparations—whether federal, state, or local—to deal with natural disasters were hardly more adequate in 1927 than were the programs to meet recent disasters. No doubt Will's months with Belgian relief under Herbert Hoover at the beginning of the Great War was a reason for his selection to direct the effort in Greenville. In 1915 he had shipped off to Europe partly to escape from his law practice, from parents, from Delta society, and from feelings of loneliness and uselessness. But his enlistment in Hoover's agency was also to meet his craving for "self sacrifice" and fulfillment of some heroic duty.[15] Nonetheless, in the 1927 crisis he was simply an ordinary citizen volunteer who had to deal with a mountain of difficulties as best he could.

The crisis of the Mississippi flood was a momentous episode in Will Percy's relatively short life. The chapter that he devoted to it dealt honestly and eloquently with those problems facing the Delta community. After the waters had subsided, Henry (Harry) Waring Ball, one of Will Percy's neighbors and friends, recalled how a "pandemonium of terror and confusion" had overtaken Greenville in April. The "whole population" fled to the town's levee, "many half-naked and shrieking in the midst of a chaos of terrified livestock. Even the most sensible people seemed to be either panic stricken or paralyzed."[16] Will's directions of affairs helped to calm fears and restore order. As he explained in *Lanterns*, one of his first public decisions was to request a contingent of the National Guard. The state governor quickly met the emergency. Will Percy's prompt and courageous response to the calamity was no surprise to family members. Phinizy Percy, youngest of the three Birmingham Percy brothers whom Will later was to adopt, recalled in 1980, "If he saw anything that approached a duty he would reach out and grab it."[17]

Nonetheless, Will Percy did not wholly master the situation. Yet he was not entirely to blame. As he himself reported in *Lanterns*, his father, the formidable Leroy Percy, was often most helpful. Yet the old man undercut Will's humanitarian effort to evacuate thousands of Greenville and Washington County African American residents from the beleaguered city and its surroundings. The whites had been removed first and in an orderly fashion. The black workers and their families were supposed to follow. From his experience of running vast plantation operations in the Delta, Senator Percy was all too aware, however, that many of the stranded sharecroppers and tenants would never willingly return. Once they had lost forever their ruined dwellings, they would start to settle in Chicago, St. Louis, or somewhere else.

This time the situation was even more perilous than it had been during the turmoil that the Klan had generated. Such a labor shortage on the rich alluvial soils of the Delta would desolate the plantation economy. Former senator Percy and his wealthy friends heartily agreed on that point. In conferring with his son Will, LeRoy Percy would only have had to hint about the family's reputation being in jeopardy, not to mention the loss of old friendships and power. It was far better, the Delta planter reasoned, to write off the idea of evacuation. His son earnestly disagreed. Will himself, though, stood in the greatest peril. Some townspeople considered him effeminate even though he had been a decorated hero in the Great War.[18] Meanwhile, the town fathers and large-scale planters loudly insisted that he should not permit any black laborer to leave the county. Outraged, Will Percy retorted that their wallets, not their consciences, were uppermost in their motives.

Unbeknownst to Will Percy until after his father's death in 1929, as he recalled in *Lanterns*, LeRoy Percy had already persuaded his son's colleagues on his committee to choose the safer policy. Over Will Percy's objections, they voted unanimously to scuttle the evacuation. After two hours resisting their vote, he finally capitulated and had to send the ship captains away. They hotly protested the wasted time when they had other rescue calls to answer. Much to his chagrin, Will Percy had to stand by his committee's decision. As a result, some thirteen thousand refugees, tentless, had to shiver on the cold, dark, and rain-soaked levee that stretched some eight miles downriver. They had no shelter, little food, and less warmth. Another five thousand huddled in Greenville warehouses and other locations still above water. It had made sense, however, as Will Percy pointed out in his memoir, to assemble as many flood victims in one place as possible in order to feed, house, and clothe them efficiently.

In *Rising Tide* and in appearances in the PBS television documentary *Fatal Flood*, the historian John Barry justifiably questions how well the forty-two-year-old attorney, working under the Red Cross, managed the Greenville calamity.[19] Percy proved to be an especially shortsighted leader in dealing with the black community. Rather than have African Americans choose their own staff to represent their interests, he had appointed a group subservient to the white elite. Had he done otherwise, though, he would have met strong white resistance. The planters would have been alarmed if an autonomous band of black leaders had risen up to challenge white hegemony. But the idea never even occurred to Will. When ordered to move Red Cross supplies, all but a handful in the black assemblage refused what they thought was an arrogant command. When one black worker outspokenly refused, a policeman fatally shot him. At a subsequent meeting with the restive community, Will Percy denounced the protestors' attitude—"their sinful laziness." But, instead, they followed the spiritual's message: "We Shall Not Be Moved."[20] Clearly, Percy's white prejudice and his deepening frustration had betrayed his cooler sense.

Unhappily, after overseeing some weeks of the crisis, LeRoy Percy went off to lobby for federal aid. But it is doubtful he could have prevented Will's outburst because he shared his feelings about the subordinate race. He was seeking large investments from Washington politicians and business leaders. Yet, in the absence of cautionary advice from his father, who knew the local situation far better than he, Will Percy made other mistakes. Although he vigorously protested, he could not prevent the abuse delivered on the backs of the black populace. Mrs. Percy McRaney, a black Greenvillian, recalled in a 1977 interview how poorly her people had been treated. For four months the poor had to live on the levee. The whites patrolling it treated them wretchedly: "Kicking them and beating them and knocking them around like dogs—hungry people, they wouldn't feed them sometimes."[21] Nor could Percy stop the price gouging, and, above all, the political squabbles that crippled efforts to obtain the relief funds that other Delta counties received. In any event, if federal bureaucracies, company executives, and others in power could have failed in so many respects in more recent times, it is hardly a wonder that someone like William Alexander Percy should have been overwhelmed at moments of grave need.

Showing a more generous side of his nature, the autobiographer in *Lanterns* suppressed his vexations and did not truculently answer the harsh criticisms leveled at him. The Stoic tradition requires a willingness to remain silent, albeit with dignity and honor. He did not totally succeed in living up to the creed. Most lustily, he denounced the Yankee press that had screamed about his prejudiced handling of the black community. He wrote in *Lanterns* that their accusations fed "the inflammable, uneducated whites whom the best part of our lives is spent in controlling and teaching" them further reasons for hating the governing class. His failure with the blacks and the flood committee over the evacuation issue preyed on his mind. Percy felt deeply humiliated and depressed. After the Mississippi River returned to its original banks, problems of rebuilding were not easy to resolve. Exhausted, Percy resigned and turned the duties over to Hazlewood Farish, who later became his law partner. Percy left town for a long vacation to Japan, which gradually restored his spirits. This pattern of escape to foreign parts suggests that he sometimes could not meet the challenges facing him head on. His wealth gave him the wherewithal to salve a bruised identity and find solace in exotic lands where no one knew him.

Yet, despite this failing, Percy's memories of the flood never sank into self-pity. Nor was there any finger-pointing at specific leaders. Quite the opposite. Upon returning from Japan, he reported that he discovered that he had not been indispensable. Farish had won wide commendation for his post-flood work. Percy, however, was not envious. He stated quite handsomely that he learned from the experience just how "hellish" and "divine" human beings can be when they suffer under enormous stress.[22] He meant himself as well as others. Yet his escape from Greenville to Kyoto was his way of handling humiliation and a sense of inadequacy. As a gay man, locally suspect, flight seemed the best course. The places he chose—Tahiti, Japan, Taormina, and Capri—were far more tolerant of homosexuals than his hometown.

Although good-hearted in less critical moments, Percy had no doubts that the races were unequal and should remain so. Even during the Depression years after the Flood, he retained his negative view of African American potentialities. Hortense Powdermaker was a Bronislaw Malinowski–trained anthropologist from Yale University. Will Percy befriended her in the mid-1930s. After long conversations with her host, she concluded that "any attempt at any kind of social equality [between blacks and whites] would result in some disaster so overwhelming that it is dangerous even to talk about it and so terrible that it cannot be thought of concretely but must remain vague." The northern researcher found that in the Delta a white planter would deplore such obvious transgressions as cheating tenants and lynching. Yet even these evils were "part of the *status quo* which it is in his interest to maintain. It is therefore to his interest to consider them inevitable." With the frozen attitudes of the planter class in mind, the brilliant anthropologist sarcastically observed, "Negroes" were thought to be "happy Pan-like beings living only in the present."[23]

Percy owned Trail Lake, an extensive plantation with a small army of African American tenants. He thought himself to be a benevolent patriarch. Although he had their houses painted, garden plots planted, and other amenities supplied, they had a different perspective of their proprietor. An example emerged from his visit to Trail Lake in a brand-new limousine sometime in the mid-1930s. When Ford Adkins, his black chauffeur, pulled up in front of the supply store, a tenant wanted to know whose car it was. Another bystander loudly declared, "Dat's *us* car." Percy felt gratified to think how happy the tenants were to take pleasure in his ownership, in which they could share. During the ride back to Greenville, he basked in the sunshine of his benevolence. Then he asked Ford Atkins for his opinion of the "funny" sentiment. "Funnier than you think," the chauffeur replied. How so, queried Percy. "He meant that's the car *you* has bought with *us* money." The Trail Lake tenants had read Percy's thoughts exactly. They also knew he had missed the sarcasm. "They wuz laughing to theyselves," Ford chuckled.[24]

Under such circumstances Percy's complacent and demeaning attitudes, as passages in *Lanterns* sadly attest, would be roundly and justly condemned in these racially more enlightened days. Like nearly all southern white people of that era, he shrank from the alleged horror of "amalgamation" of the races. Protesting that "Northern philanthropists" cheerfully approved the prospect of eventual racial mixing, Percy observed in *Lanterns*, "The trouble is that the white Southerner is stubbornly averse to playing the necessary role" in such a perverse integration. Oblivious to their own history, he charged that American blacks were "interested neither in the past nor in the future, this side of heaven. He neither remembers nor plans." Even before the memoir's publication, Percy's friends David L. Cohn, a southern author who shared most of Percy's political and social views, and Huger Wilkinson Jervey, dean of international studies at Columbia, begged him to omit all these and other aspersions against the race. On the other hand, Alfred Knopf, his publisher, was highly pleased with the manuscript. He advised him not to change a word. Unfortunately, he took the New Yorker's counsel.

Percy understood the Stoic principle of noblesse oblige, and he prided himself on his magnanimity. One example was his aid to a poor black man named Jim whom the sheriff had beaten in jail. Brought there on a stretcher by his friends, Jim wanted Percy to sue the sheriff, as he told his story of horrifying torture. Percy hired him as a house servant, but he also confronted the sheriff about the case. "The sheriff was furious, stormed, threatened, and became my bitter enemy. I recovered a few hundred dollars for Jim and, considering it inadequate, gave it to him without deducting a fee." Walker Percy recollected, "I can remember black people coming to the house who'd been imprisoned and beaten-up, and he would take them in and defend them and attack the sheriff's office or the chief of police, in public, and was branded as a nigger lover and such."[25]

Despite his adherence to the code of Jim Crow, perhaps at some level, because of his own sexual isolation, Will felt a sympathy for the members of a race excluded from the white social and moral realm. That possibility might seem to stretch a point. Yet it offers another example of his puzzling nature. Such a sense of empathy, however, did not extend to the poor who shared his own skin color. After all, they were the mean-spirited voters who had ousted Senator Percy and overthrown the old order of gentility in politics. Percy revealed his contempt in *Lanterns*. "The poor whites of the South: a nice study in heredity and environment."

"Who," he asked, "can do them justice? Not I." They lacked "mental attainments."[26] The poor whites were "the sort of people that lynch Negroes, that mistake hooliganism for wit, and cunning for intelligence, that attend revivals and fight and fornicate in the bushes afterwards. They were undiluted Anglo-Saxons."[27] Percy moaned once again that his father and other civic-minded gentlemen of Mississippi had fallen into powerlessness and disfavor. By his lights they had been the sole upholders of honest rule.

No doubt one reason for his revulsion against the lower orders was their blatant ridicule of "pansies," "fags," and other insults against him and others like him. That source of misery did not appear in *Lanterns*. Closely connected with his homosexuality was his ambivalence about a father and mother who did not accept him wholeheartedly. Almost from the very start of his conscious life, Will recognized that he did not meet his father's criterion of manliness and interest in those things that boys are supposed to love—hunting, fishing, sports, and guns. LeRoy thought him a "queer chicken," although he probably meant that as a mark of pity rather than a reflection on his son's sexual orientation.[28] Moreover, Camille Bourges Percy, from a once-rich New Orleans family, shared her husband's views of their son. She was a formidable matron of Gallic disposition. Percy remarked to his close friend and cousin Janet Dana Longcope: "She's one lovely & lovesome person. It's an awful pity I have such a wide queer streak in me—she would have enjoyed so a lot of normal children." That sort of self-mockery pervaded *Lanterns on the Levee.*[29] He seemed to love his grandmother Armstrong Percy—whom he called "Mur"—more than his mother. She was his "first chum," and his description of her undressing ritual was amusing. "She prepared herself for the night" in "a splendid ritual." The first act was to remove "her switch, a rather scrawny, gray affair, like a diminutive horse's tail, which, when on duty, enlarged the knot of hair at the nape of her neck. Then she combed it briskly until it fluffed out into a fascinating silver cone before she rested it for the night on the bureau." Despite her efforts to make him happy, however, he recalled a young sense of loneliness. As the philosopher William James remarked in 1890, "The great source of terror in infancy is solitude."[30] That was a hazard that Will had to deal with from childhood onward.[31]

Why he felt so is scarcely self-evident, but it had to be related in part to his sexual identity. Even the occasional allusions in *Lanterns* to his sexual interests tell little about what he did and only suggest what he thought. Book reviewers in 1941 and 1942 completely missed or chose to pass over in silence Will's homoerotic references. An example was his narrative about a trip through the Greek-influenced region of Turkey. His party came upon a sight that Percy clearly romanticized in the classic Victorian idolization of Greek male beauty. "A young man, white and naked, with a mop of gold hair," Percy recalled, "was swimming beneath us, and as he swam he sang. Oblivious of us, enraptured and alone, brimming with some hale antique happiness not ours to know, he clove the flashing water and sang into the sun."[32]

Despite all appearances, though, the Greenville attorney was not committed to complete secrecy, at least not upon leaving the South. He did not hide his friendships with gay men. Will's comrades were not like his father's chums—brothers in a fraternal order, duck blind, or poker club. Instead, his wide circles of friends shared his temperament and interests and also his thirst for knowledge and aesthetic engagement. All of them were intellectually gifted and dedicated, as he was, to art, literature, and fine music. Mostly they were men, but the famous New York sculptor Malvina Hoffman, a lesbian, was also one of Will's confederates. For a sum of twenty-five thousand dollars, Percy commissioned her in 1930 to design a bronze casting of Will's father, who had died in 1929. The senator is represented as a "brooding knight," Will rhapsodized in *Lanterns,* "sunshine flowing from his body" while standing "on the stone stele behind, and the river at his feet." Will Percy had the statue placed near his father's grave in the cemetery of St. James Episcopal Church in Greenville.[33]

In that era it was quite common for gentlemen to enjoy close personal but purely social ties with those of their own class and sex without arousing suspicions. Women suitable for respectable marriages seldom met a man's need for bonded companionship. It must be added, though, that sociable, talented women were easily drawn by Percy's wit and charm, particularly his older female acquaintances when he went to parties and teas at Sewanee. Will Percy did have a special tie to his cousin Janet. She was married to Warfield Longcope, a distinguished physician who became head of medicine at the Johns Hopkins University Medical School. Another favorite was Charlotte Gailor of Sewanee, an artist and serious botanist. She read his yet-unpublished memoir but worried about the title. "Recollections of a Planter's Son" would not catch the public eye, she advised. Instead, she thought he should add "Lanterns on the Levee," and wisely he did so.[34]

During World War I, Percy had worked in the army with Gerstle Mack, whom he greatly liked. Mack later became a noted architectural expert and author of well-received biographies of Paul Cézanne, Gustave Courbet, and Henri Toulouse-Lautrec.[35] Together after the war, Mack and Percy became acquainted in London with Siegfried Sassoon, the famous English war poet. Will Percy told a young cousin and artistic protégé, also gay, about the encounter with Sassoon. Will confessed to his cousin that Mack had been acutely "'fascinated at the man's intellect and physical beauty' and so was I, I suppose." Percy's cousin "explained to me that Sassoon was a British Army Officer, staggeringly handsome, sensitive, with great talent, a homosexual whose masculinity placed him beyond most gossip and innuendo." But on the latter point, he misspoke. The Englishman's sexual partialities were much more defiantly open than Will Percy's ever were.[36]

In addition to gaining much from his association with gay men of talent and substance, Percy also discovered in writing poems a welcome release. He wrote some of his best lines while away in distant parts. During his service in France in 1918, for instance, he penned these words:

> We are the sons of disaster,
> Deserted by gods that are named,
> Thrust in a world with no master,
> Our altars prepared but unclaimed;
> Wreathed with the blood-purple aster
> Victims, foredoomed, but untamed.[37]

Poetry, it seems, was a secure outlet for his inner and his sexual feelings. He declared, "What I wrote seemed to me more essentially myself than anything I did or said. . . . When you feel something intensely, you want to write it down—if anguish, to stanch the bleeding; if delight, to prolong the moment."[38] It could be said that his best poems were written as he gazed out of his hotel room window at Taormina, which nestled beneath Mount Etna. That Sicilian village had become a favorite sanctuary for gay Europeans and Englishmen. They were likely to visit the photograph gallery of Baron Wilhelm von Gloeden. The North German aristocrat displayed pictures of young Italian male adolescents, totally nude, presented in chaste poses next to Grecian vases or broken stone columns. Some of the Taormina vacationers, whom Percy knew well, belonged, like the homosexual Siegfried Sassoon, to the English upper classes. (The playwright Tennessee Williams, also from Mississippi, and the bisexual novelist Graham Greene were sometime residents there.)[39]

In Florence and Capri, Percy was drawn to the charismatic Norman Douglas, a best-selling novelist. His Villa Daphne on Castiglione Hill, "the fairest spot on Capri," was a popular gathering place for gay society. His satirical novel *South Wind* extolled ancient pagan ways on "Nepenthe" (Capri) and mocked Victorian prudery. It is now largely forgotten. According to an artistic cousin whom Will Percy had befriended, the Scottish novelist "had never been very reticent about his preference for the companionship of young men." Will was more circumspect, at the same time enjoying the Douglas group. The novelist was sometimes in trouble with the Fascist police for imposing himself on teenage boys. Although a married man, Douglas boasted about his "jovial immoderation" and "frolicsome perversity." That was far from Will Percy's style. Nevertheless, like others who knew Douglas, Percy did find the Scotsman most amusing and intelligent.[40] The novelist had Percy produce a foreword to his rather precious *Birds and Beasts of the Greek Anthology.*[41] Douglas died a suicide from an overdose of drugs in 1952.

In New York, after returning from France, Percy often joined up with his fellow bachelor friends. They were men of considerable achievement and stature. Huger Jervey, later a dean at Columbia University, had been one of Percy's favorite instructors at Sewanee. In 1925 the pair had bought a sandstone house, Brinkwood, for summer vacations. It perched over a beautiful valley called Lost Cove, a few miles from Sewanee proper. Another companion was the poet Lindley Williams Hubbell, who then worked at the New York Public Library. His work was first published in 1927 under Will Percy's editorship of the Yale Series of Younger Poets. The Manhattan band of bachelors used to venture uptown for an evening's entertainment in such places as the Sugar Cane Club. There Louis Armstrong, Duke Ellington, Bessie Smith, Ethel Waters, and other African American performers held the spotlight. William Armstrong Percy III writes, "Like Carl Van Vechten [a novelist and *New York Times* music critic], Will haunted Harlem nightspots." He ran across and soon took up a friendship with Langston Hughes. The African American poet was also gay.[42] Hughes must have shocked his listeners, unaccustomed as they were to hearing words of black protest and charges against white discrimination. Walker Percy observed about his adoptive father: "My uncle was absolutely fearless. He wasn't afraid of anybody." Nor was Hughes. Perhaps their shared sexual orientation somehow gave them the courage to defy convention in other respects.[43] In this regard Will Percy lived before his times, whereas he is remembered for his fashioning a very outworn perspective about the past.

Will Percy's degree of worldly sophistication—and social valiance—was remarkable not only for a white Mississippian but for almost anyone else in 1920s and 1930s America. According to Benjamin Wise, the author of Will Percy's recent biography, his closest companion on his earlier trips to Europe had been another New Yorker, Harold Bruff. They had been classmates at the Harvard Law School and had gone to France together in 1908.[44] Yet Percy could not break with the people of the Delta and their conventions. It was his ambivalence and pathos that help to shape the memoir and deepen its dramatic tension. When a young cousin had him read his fledgling novel about the author's love for another male, Will claimed to admire what was really an immature work. Yet he warned the aspiring writer that "due to the subject treated, and to the subsequent repercussion upon your family (in a small community), it is just not for today. Perhaps some years hence all the inhibited things will become less so and the world will develop a policy of live and let live (although I doubt this, and don't count on it)." On another occasion Percy praised the would-be novelist for "keeping quiet" about such unmentionable matters. In his own autobiographical work Percy's unhopeful outlook, like his doubts of a future liberality, assumed a more universal character. Yet the strain was always manifest between his love of family and region and his alienation from both. Under his father's tutelage the unmarried attorney dutifully practiced law—and detested it. He served on local boards and took part in the civic routines expected of him, even after his parents' deaths in 1929. That approach made it possible for him to survive in the Delta. As one of his friends wrote, "Throughout his life innuendos were inevitable, [but] facts [were] never to surface."[45]

Will Percy's loneliness was not an uncommon reaction to the inhibitions that closeting compels upon homosexuals, but there was an additional component to his sadness. Percy recognized that his family, past and present, and not he alone, was subject to the relentless tides of melancholy. In five generations of this branch of American Percys, there was at least one descendant who suffered from chronic depression. A genetic factor in such a medical history seems most likely. Charles Percy (or "Don Carlos," as the memoirist prefers) was the family's founder. A Spanish magistrate and indigo planter when Spain ruled Louisiana in the late eighteenth century, this Percy was the first of several male suicides in direct line. Leroy Pope Percy, one of Charles Percy's great-grandsons and Will's bachelor great-uncle, took an overdose of laudanum in 1882. In 1917 John Walker Percy, who was Will's uncle and also Walker Percy's grandfather, a Birmingham, Alabama, attorney, shot himself in the chest with a hunting rifle. He had been the attorney for the Tennessee Coal and Iron Company. Twelve years later his son LeRoy Pratt Percy, another Birmingham attorney and Walker Percy's father, did likewise in an almost perfect replication of his father's means to end life. Walker himself, though never suicidal, suffered acutely from the genetic complaint.[46] "OK, I wrote for the last 15 years, did what I wanted to do, succeeded—so what? There doesn't seem to be a great deal of point," the novelist wrote his daughter, Ann, on one occasion. "Middle-age depression no doubt, plus a Percyean disposition toward melancholia."[47]

*Lanterns on the Levee* mentions but does not spotlight these familial difficulties. Nor does the work disclose that several Percy women, while never suicidal, also inherited the malady. Some had to be hospitalized.[48] Clearly, the author knew that the family faced a mysterious curse. To handle the disorder as best the Percys could, they developed an extraordinary, creative proficiency—in acquiring wealth, power, and literary achievement. After reading the hundred or so letters that Gerstle Mack had sent to Will Percy, Walker wrote to his oldest and dearest friend, Shelby Foote, who also wrote novels, about his guardian's poor health and low spirits after the boys and their widowed mother had arrived from her hometown, Athens, Georgia. She had tragically died in 1932. Walker Percy reflected that it "makes you see how much fell on him in such a short time, death of parents in 1929, the Depression, [my] mother's death, having to lawyer, bad health (do you remember how often he got the 'flu' and took to his bed for days?)."[49]

Percy's moral prescriptions set the goal of human perfectionism not only before himself but before the three sons he had adopted. Yet it was an emotional burden that he well knew he could not wholly master. How was it possible to reconcile these old virtues—the conventions of the Old Cavalier South—with its modernizing twentieth-century character? Only a Faulkner or an O'Connor or, indeed, a Walker Percy could grasp the region's complexities. At the same time, along with his Aurelian faith, Will found an outlet from melancholy in warfare. That engagement combined for him Stoic honor with martial daring. A fascination with war demonstrated his manhood most clearly. This was more baffling than it might seem at first. In his day, military courage and homosexual inclinations were not thought possible in one man. When he had signed up for enlistment, Percy was so slight of frame, as he noted in another memorable chapter of *Lanterns,* that he barely managed entry into the army during the Great War. By drinking water and eating more than his tiny frame could handle, he barely met the minimum weight requirement for admission to officers' training school at Fort Logan H. Roots. He graduated after enduring the ordeal of being a member of what was derisively called the "Pee Wee Squad of Company D." In fact, despite his war record, proven gallantry, and steely willpower, Will Percy was regarded as "rather effeminate, but not extremely so," recalled Leon Koury, the Greenville sculptor whom he had assisted financially. "Some people were very unkind," Koury remembered, but "those who knew him well loved him dearly for all his great qualities of mind and soul." The abrasive tension between his own mode of manner and the southern male style that he was supposed to emulate must have dismayed him almost daily. Walker Percy recollected that "Uncle Will" had been elated over the prospect of going to war against Adolf Hitler, as if military glory meant more to him than he liked to admit. "The only time he was happy," Walker reported, "was in the Argonne Forest in 1918 when he was shooting at Germans." But when war broke out in 1941, Will Percy "became miserable when he learned that he was too old" for military service.[50]

Perhaps in compensation for his own limitations, Will Percy in his memoir goes to some lengths of distortion in the hope that mythmaking might be accepted as a restoration of a lost southern world. He did so almost as if to hide from himself the discrepancy between his intellectuality in a community where mind took second place to manly backslapping pursuits. He followed a strong southern tradition of storytelling that was most evident in the widespread adoration of Robert E. Lee, "Stonewall," and other great war heroes. In *Lanterns* Uncle Will did not dwell so much on the Confederate "Lost Cause," with its inartistic statues of veterans and "sentiment driveling into sentimentality, poverty, and, I fear, lack of taste."[51] He made little mention of graceful antebellum ladies in hooped silks, cheerful slaves, and benign, julep-sipping gentlemen planters. Instead, he turned to family history to provide color, drama, entertainment, and sardonic comment to his account, all done with a certain military flavor.

The first example of his gentle critique of southernness was his satirical treatment of the Percy family's founder, Charles Percy. With delightful embroidery, the memoirist renders the progenitor as a figure of fun and enigma. After all, he had abandoned a wife and two children in England, lived for a time with another woman on the island of Bermuda, and had established a new family on a plantation in what years later became Wilkinson County, Mississippi. Percy embellished family stories that strongly suggested noble warrior blood from the earls of Northumberland—Harry Hotspur and others—coursing through Charles's veins. Perhaps a bigamist—or even "trigamist"—Don Carlos had carefully hidden his true identity even as he pretentiously titled his modest dwelling on a Mississippi River tributary "Northumberland House." That was the name of the Northumberland dukes' immense London residence. Its gardens once ran from the Strand just east of Trafalgar Square to the banks of the Thames. He claimed to have been an officer in the Royal Army during the Seven Years' War. According to the investigations of a London law firm in 1894, a Charles Percy turned up but not on a list of officers after all. That name, with an *I* by it to signify "Irish," belonged to a foot soldier in the short-lived Irish Eighty-Third Regiment of Foot. As far as the lawyers could ascertain, he was the only Irishman so named in the entire country. The future "Don Carlos" adroitly marched and countermarched with his mates over the Portuguese countryside while serving under "Gentleman Johnny" Burgoyne. (He was noted for his later role at the American Battle of Saratoga.) The campaign of the British-Portuguese allies against the Spanish invasion in 1762 was successful. There were few casualties, and it was mercifully brief. Percy's unit was quickly mustered out upon returning to Dublin. However well the foot soldier had performed in the army, in the London lawyers' review of the records, he had not been promoted to a higher rank. Thus, it happened that the founder of the American Percy lineage was neither an officer nor a member of a distinguished unit nor even respectably English or Scottish by birth.[52]

Jane Percy Sargent Duncan, an enormously wealthy New York descendant, had hired the London attorneys. She had once speculated that he was a Scotsman with a medical degree. But, in addition to the unpleasant details that her solicitors had discovered, she was horrified to learn that her ancestor could have been—dare one say it—shanty Irish. For a Fifth Avenue dowager who had sold her Long Island mansion to J. P. Morgan, that information was too much to bear. She spirited the damning evidence into a trunk and never mentioned the matter to her daughter, Janet Dana Longcope, Will's close friend. Nor did she confess to anyone else in the Percy clan. (The relevant documents remained hidden in a western Massachusetts attic until years later, when this writer was allowed to see them.)[53] Jane Duncan, however, could well have overreacted. Charles Percy's handful of surviving letters were written in a respectable hand. Their literacy suggests a gentleman's upbringing. Also, he was known to have collected a number of literary works in his crude backwater plantation of West Florida. He was no ordinary rake, but was he kin to the Northumberland nobility? That is another matter. While composing his memoir, Will had no means to obtain the facts that Jane Duncan had uncovered. Instead, the autobiographer conjectured that the "old bird" might have fought under the black flag of a pirate ship or possibly was a distant heir to the immense Northumberland holdings in England. Wisely, though, he concluded, "Playing Tarzan in the family tree is hazardous business; there are too many rotten branches."[54]

More was involved here than merely an effort to lampoon a southern pastime of genealogical obsessions. Musings about the possible aristocratic and soldierly elements in the family's history constituted part of the larger vision of how Percys were to present themselves to the world. Colonel William Alexander Percy of Alcorn's Brigade, Army of Mississippi, for whom the poet was named, won a high reputation for battle ardor. He was called the "Gray Eagle of the Delta" for his military daring. Even he seemed less significant in the memoirist's mind, though, than the first Percy in the United States and the first to die at his own hand. As I have written elsewhere, to Will Percy "ancestor Charles represented the transitory nature of life, rank, and pretension, the rise and fall of families and nations—ideas thoroughly typical of the Southern conservative mentality."[55]

Another example of these seemingly disparate elements appears in Will's depiction of his father's political cronies. General Thomas L. Catchings, General Samuel Wragg Ferguson, and Captain John Seymour Mc-Neilly were heavy drinkers and partygoers. They spent evenings with LeRoy Percy at Sarah Compton's shady professional catering house. (Camille, Will's mother, usually left early, if she came at all.) There was wild dancing, gambling, and other activities upstairs in the bedrooms. LeRoy Percy was "Ching" Compton's attorney and kept the mulatto hostess away from legal snags. General Ferguson, treasurer for the Levee Board, overspent at the Compton establishment and elsewhere. To pay off debts, he embezzled funds from the board. He had to flee the country for a time. In *Lanterns* Will recounted his sudden, bedraggled appearance years later when a dinner party at the senator's house was under way. Otherwise, Will Percy mentioned not a word of this seamier side of Greenville high society. Instead, he placed his father's chums "on the west portal of Chartres with those strong ancients, severe and formidable and full of grace, who guard the holy entrance."[56] The image is stately and grand. No doubt Percy was subtly referring to Henry Adams, whose *Mont-Saint-Michel and Chartres* celebrated the great cathedral's statuary, stained glass, and soaring Gothic architecture.

Absurdity, however, could give way to a more profound angle of vision. Adams's closing words to his magisterial work seem so appropriate to Percy's reference to Chartres and to his fantasizing. The Yankee historian wondered how a structure such as Chartres Cathedral seemingly defied the laws of nature in its stubborn fixedness through the ages—for instance, the improbable "leap downwards of the flying buttress." "Faith alone supports it," Adams insisted, and a "danger" of the edifice collapsing "lurks in every stone." The author concluded: "The delight of its aspirations is flung up to the sky. The pathos of its self-distrust and anguish of doubt is buried in the earth of its last secret."[57]

The disparity separating the weight of fact and genuine history and the relative insubstantiality of imagination and artfulness was so much a part of Will Percy's reminiscence. One suspects an intellectual indebtedness to this melancholy author of another, more famous memoir. But that tension also grew out of his ambivalent relationship to his father and his values in contrast to the way Will Percy felt about himself. The appeal to warfare and the attraction to what those knights at Chartres represented might indicate, too, that the fighting in France had been much more unsettling than Percy cared to admit—despite his stress on warfare, medieval or modern. In reference to his bland letters home from the front, he confessed that soldiers seldom describe the appalling chaos they witnessed, the stench they endured, the bloody grimness of the struggle. His account of the war in *Lanterns* left out these dreadful experiences.

On returning home, Percy declared, "I have never before or since felt so incapable of emotion, so dead inside."[58] Indeed, Will Percy "faced a world in which meaning had been lost, but he soldiered on," suggests the historian Anne Rose. His faith in the old Stoic values that inspired his Gothic analogy could well have been a way to hide a quite different mood. It was one shared by the disillusioned poets and writers Wilfred Owens, Erich Maria Remarque, Jean-Paul Sartre, and Siegfried Sassoon. Percy does argue that German aggression and the Allied response had destroyed the happy world he had loved. Rose has speculated that, beneath the sometimes optimistic surface of his memoir, Percy could have been conversant with the "defiant emotional pose of existentialism." He could have been uncovering a universe devoid of meaning, especially in relation to the simpler and less modernistic era, about whose loss he so deeply sorrowed.[59]

The reader of *Lanterns on the Levee* will discover a most remarkable but complex personality as well as a gifted writer. For instance, Will Percy's house was filled with such distinguished guests as psychiatrist Harry Stack Sullivan, historian and poet Carl Sandburg, poets Stephen Vincent Benét and Vachel Lindsay, and many others. Phinizy remembered that the house "always seemed to be full of people, all the time. You never knew who was going to be at dinner. It was almost like living in a hotel." Another writer, David L. Cohn, came for a weekend and stayed a year to complete his Delta memoir, *God Shakes Creation*. The North Carolina journalist Jonathan Daniels was particularly impressed with Percy's character and interesting lineage. He called a chapter of a book on the contemporary South "Hotspur's House," to celebrate an unforgettable visit in Will Percy's mansion with its many guests. Hard on their neighbors' foibles, they were a witty band, Daniels reminisced, and lit "with anger and humor a darkness like despair" and shared "an unloving knowledge of the people on the land which they loved."[60]

Here was a singular bachelor serving as father to three boys, the eldest of whom, Walker, was just entering his teens. Selfless and concerned for the boys' well-being, he did everything necessary to assure them a normal and secure upbringing. For instance, young Phinizy had accompanied his mother in the car outside Greenville. When the automobile in which they were riding plunged over a railless bridge into a deepwater creek, he managed to escape through a window. As a result, though, he suffered from night terrors. "Frequently I would wake up sometimes screaming from a nightmare, and he [Uncle Will] would come in and we would go in his sitting room and he would try to talk to me about what the nightmare was about, and then he would read to me, Greek mythology or something. You know it might have been a night when he had been throwing up for the fear of a trial. . . . His only thought was comforting me and getting me to go to sleep."[61] All three Percy brothers married, fared outstandingly well in their careers, had children, and proved no less caring and affectionate in their rearing of offspring than Will Percy had been.

At the same time, Uncle Will did offer advice but never dictated how the brothers should find their careers. In *Lanterns*, he explained, "Now, I am admonished, a child's personality is as fragile as precious and if you try anything stronger on him than sweet reasonableness you will warp his psyche, foster complexes, and probably end up with a paranoiac or a Jack the Ripper on your hands." "I don't know how I'd have managed," he continued in *Lanterns*, "if the boys had not saved me the trouble by deciding to be good and infinitely considerate." Once grown, he recalled how they found themselves. "Pressure" to take up medicine, Walker's first vocation, "didn't come from [Uncle Will]," the novelist reported.[62]

Walker reflected that his adoptive father "had this extraordinary capacity for communicating enthusiasm for beauty. He had this great love which I'd never seen before, which was unusual and is even now, to see somebody who actually gets a high delight, great joy," from listening to music or reading great works of art. Will's own artistic bent for prose was very late in development. A visit from Alfred Knopf to Greenville set the wheels in motion for the writing of his autobiography. Knopf had published his *Selected Poems* in 1930 and wanted him to compose a memoir of a small-town attorney. "Damned if I'll write about the law!" was Percy's reaction. In the summer of 1936, however, Percy sailed to Tahiti from Los Angeles. According to his journalist friend Ben Wasson, on the way back he began a study of the island people, an effort in prose that inspired further experimentation. David Cohn urged him to try his hand at reminiscence, and Percy began in earnest. Considering Percy too poetically inclined to write prose, Janet Dana Longcope and others, however, had doubts of his success. So, for a time he put the manuscript aside. On a hot summer day while seated in the Percy library, Cohn found some loose pages stuffed behind the cushions on a sofa. Scooping them up, he went out to the gallery and read them with growing interest. Excitedly, he told Will that he had no choice but to resume work on a very promising autobiography that was marked by a tone of reflective nostalgia and deep insight into the human condition.[63]

With its rich sense of humanity, *Lanterns on the Levee* reaches the distinction of a classic. A fellow Mississippian, friend and literary critic Roark Bradford, wrote in 1942 that "Will Percy plucked his own lyre and sang his own songs to the stars and to the wind and to the dawn." In poetry and in prose he was always true to himself. The scholar Fred Hobson called *Lanterns* one of the most "brilliantly conceived and controlled works of art" in southern literature.[64] That judgment is true because the writer and his creativity were so intimately joined together. The memoir belongs in the American literary galaxy along with the more famous writings of the Southern Renaissance. It is a memoir that speaks the truth as Will Percy wished it to be.

Of course, we cannot accept his mixture of realism and pleasant and often handsomely framed fabrications as historical fact. Nor can we share his sense of white mastery and black subordination. Although living into the beginnings of social and racial change, he stubbornly clung to the past. He belonged to that long-departed era that rejoiced in the overthrow of Republican Reconstruction and the suppression of freedpeople's civil and voting rights. Yet, with his expansive spirit of beauty and of grief, William Alexander Percy will live on for many years to come in the unforgettable pages of *Lanterns on the Levee*. Shelby Foote once wrote Walker: "What a thing it would be to try really to recapture him as he was in life. . . .

All we can do is take pieces of him and distribute them here and there through our books, and all of them together don't add up to more than a fraction of what he was." So the mystery lies in how he managed to hold the contradictions together to pursue a creative life. Perhaps it is beyond any full understanding. This we do know in Aristotle's language: he was a *megalopsikoi*—"a great-souled man."[65]

NOTES

1. Walker Percy, introduction to William Alexander Percy, *Lanterns on the Levee: Recollections of a Planter's Son* (1941; repr., Baton Rouge: Louisiana State University Press, 1973), vii. Hereafter, William Alexander Percy is identified as "WAP" in the notes. Walker Percy, *The Moviegoer* (New York: Knopf, 1961). Walker Percy won the National Book Award in 1962 for his first novel. I wish to acknowledge the careful readings of David Hackett Fischer, Lawrence Friedman, Susan Marbury, Anne Wyatt-Brown, and Ruth Zollinger.

2. WAP, *Lanterns,* 169–83; LeRoy Percy (Greenville) to LeRoy Percy (Birmingham), September 21, 1917, Percy Family Papers, Mississippi State Department of Archives and History, Jackson, Miss. (hereafter cited as MDAH).

3. Benjamin Schwarz, "The South in Black and White," *Atlantic* (November 2004): 131.

4. WAP, *Lanterns,* 93.

5. Ibid., 118.

6. Ibid., 151.

7. Henry Waring Ball Diary, entry for August 4, 1911, WAP Memorial Library, Greenville, Miss.

8. WAP, *Lanterns,* 223.

9. Ibid., 72, 312; William Delaney, "A Southern Novelist Whose CB Crackles with Kierkegaard," *Washington Star,* March 20, 1977, in *Conversations with Walker Percy,* ed. Lewis A. Lawson and Victor A. Kramer (Jackson: University Press of Mississippi, 1985), 152.

10. Quoted in Billips Phinizy Spalding, "William Alexander Percy: His Philosophy of Life as Reflected in History" (Master's thesis, University of Georgia, 1957), 108. It is worth mentioning that the *Meditations of Marcus Aurelius Antoninus* was also treasured by the mid-nineteenth-century novelist Sarah Dorsey, a member of the Percy lineage (see Wyatt-Brown, *The House of Percy: Honor, Melancholy, and Imagination in a Southern Family* [New York: Oxford University Press, 1994], 132.) In other words, the Stoic tradition was part of the family's history.

11. WAP, *Lanterns,* 313.

12. Ibid., 313.

13. Ibid., 138, 238–39. Will was himself quite partial toward the small but intellectually gifted group of Jewish and Middle Eastern families in Greenville, all of whom the Klan had threatened. He had most admired a Miss Carrie Stern, a teacher without a husband but only a very penurious invalid father to care for. "She was not my favorite Jew," he wrote. "I

had dozens of favorites. To no people am I under greater obligation." In spite of the denial, she was indeed his favorite Jew and was his most beloved mentor.

14. William Armstrong Percy, review of John Barry, *Rising Tide* (see n. 28), www.williamapercy.com/wiki/images/Rising_tide_the_great_mississippi_flood.pdf.

15. Wyatt-Brown, *House of Percy*, 209; Lewis Baker, *The Percys of Mississippi: Politics and Literature in the New South* (Baton Rouge: Louisiana State University Press, 1983), 76–78.

16. Harry Ball Diary, entry for July 27, 1927, WAP Memorial Library.

17. "Phinizy Percy Interview with John Jones, conducted in New Orleans on Coliseum Street, 4–17–80," 8, MDAH.

18. Hodding Carter, *Where Main Street Meets the River* (New York: Rinehart & Co., 1953), 70.

19. John M. Barry. *Rising Tide: The Great Mississippi Flood of 1927 and How It Changed America* (New York: Simon & Schuster, 1997).

20. Wyatt-Brown, *House of Percy*, 244.

21. Barry, *Rising Tide*, 331; Mrs. Leonia Collins Dorsey, interview of Mrs. Percy McRaney, March 25, 1977, WAP Memorial Library.

22. WAP, *Lanterns*, 269.

23. Hortense Powdermaker, *After Freedom: A Cultural Study in the Deep South* (1939; repr., New York: Russell & Russell, 1968), 23, 301–2; WAP, *Lanterns*, 27, 94, 49, 298; Hortense Powdermaker, *Stranger and Friend* (New York: Norton, 1966), 191–93.

24. WAP, *Lanterns*, 291.

25. "An Interview with Dr. Walker Percy, April 17, 1980," interviewed by John Griffin Jones, MDAH; WAP, *Lanterns*, 304.

26. WAP, *Lanterns*, 19, 22–23.

27. Ibid., 149.

28. See "Will Percy's Book," review of *Lanterns on the Levee*, *Jackson (Miss.) Clarion*, March 23, 1941, clipping, Percy Papers, MDAH.

29. WAP to Janet Dana, October 2, 1915, Janet Dana Longcope Papers, Louisiana State University Library, Baton Rouge.

30. WAP, *Lanterns*, 27–28. William James quoted by John Bowlby, *Separation: Anxiety and Anger* (New York: Harper, 1973), 31; see also John Bowlby, *Attachment and Loss*, vol. 1: *Attachment* (New York: Basic Books, 1969), 30; Charles A. Sarnoff, "The Father's Role in Latency," in *Father and Child: Developmental and Clinical Perspectives*, ed. Stanley H. Cath, Albert R. Gurwit, and John Munder Ross (New York: Basil Blackwell, 1982), 253–63.

31. Walker Percy's introduction movingly addresses this aspect of his cousin Will Percy's makeup. Walker, LeRoy, and Phinizy all called Will "uncle" because he took on that role with them after became orphans, but he was actually their second cousin. Will was the son of Walker's uncle. In other words, Walker's grandfather was the brother of senator LeRoy Percy, who was Will's father.

32. WAP, *Lanterns*, 26, 340–41.

33. Carol Malone, "William Alexander Percy: Knight to His People, Ishmael to Himself, and Poet to the World" (Master's thesis, University of Mississippi, 1964), 19; Wyatt-Brown, *House of Percy*, 258–59; WAP, *Lanterns*, 345.

34. Phone conversation with Nancy Gailor of New York, February 21, 2006. The letter from which she drew this information is in the Gailor Family Papers, Archives, DuPont Library, University of the South, Sewanee, Tenn.

35. Obituary, "Gerstle Mack, 88, Author; Biographer and Historian," *New York Times*, February 17, 1983; Gerstle Mack and Thomas Gibson, *Architectural Details of Southern Spain: One Hundred Measured Drawings, One Hundred and Thirteen Photographs* (New York: W. Heilburn, 1928); Gerstle Mack, *Toulouse-Lautrec* (New York: Knopf, 1938); Gerstle Mack, *Paul Cezanne* (New York: Knopf, 1936); Gerstle Mack, *Gustave Courbet: A Biography* (New York: Da Capo, 1986).

36. WAP, quoted in the late John Seymour Erwin's memoir "A Harp Tuned for Mourning," 8A, MS in my possession. See Max Egremont, *Siegfried Sassoon: A Life* (New York: Farrar, Straus & Giroux, 2005).

37. WAP, "The Soldier Generation," *Collected Poems of William Alexander Percy* (New York: Knopf, 1950), 192.

38. WAP, quoted in Roark Bradford, foreword to WAP, *Collected Poems*, 3.

39. WAP, *Collected Poems;* WAP, *Sappho in Levkas and Other Poems* (New Haven: Yale University Press, 1915). See Jean-Claude Lemagny, ed., *Taormina, Début de Siècle: Photographies du Baron de Gloeden* (Paris: Chêne, 1975), 5–11; Timothy d'Arch Smith, *Love in Earnest: Some Notes on the Lives and Writings of English "Uranian" Poets from 1889 to 1939* (London: Routledge & Kegan Paul, 1970), 62–63; Michael Sheldon, *Graham Greene: The Man Within* (London: Heineman, 1994), 78–84.

40. Lewis Leary, *Norman Douglas* (New York: Columbia University Press, 1968), 10.

41. Ralph D. Linderman, *Norman Douglas* (New York: Twayne, 1965), 61–62; WAP, foreword to Norman Douglas, *Beasts and Birds of the Greek Anthology* (New York: Jonathan Cape and Harrison Smith, 1929), ix–xv; Leary, *Douglas,* 22; Erwin, "Harp Tuned for Mourning," 8A.

42. See Cary D. Wintz, *Black Culture and the Harlem Renaissance* (Houston: Rice University Press, 1988), 92–99. In 1953 Hubbell taught at Doshisha University, Kyoto, renounced his American citizenship, and adopted the Japanese name of Hayashi Shuseki. Japan was also a country where Will Percy found temporary peace, natural beauty, and freedom from sexual cant.

43. Wyatt-Brown, *House of Percy,* 277; John Griffin Jones, "Walker Percy," 1980 interview in Covington, La., MDAH; also in Lawson and Kramer, *Conversations with Walker Percy,* 261; "B[illups] Phinizy Percy Interview with John Jones," MDAH. Only his cousin William Armstrong Percy mentions that when Hughes first entered "Will's Mississippi home," he came through "the front door much to the astonishment of local blacks."

44. Benjamin E. Wise, *William Alexander Percy: The Curious Life of a Mississippi Planter and Sexual Freethinker* (Chapel Hill: University of North Carolina Press, 2012).

45. Erwin, "Harp Tuned for Mourning," 19.

46. Wyatt-Brown, *House of Percy,* 175–77, 248–49, 326.

47. Walker Percy, quoted in Jay Tolson, *Pilgrim in the Ruins: A Life of Walker Percy* (New York: Simon & Schuster, 1992), 390.

48. Sarah Percy Ellis Ware, "Don Carlos" Percy's daughter; Mary Jane LaRoche, Sarah Ware's daughter; and Lady Percy McKinney, Will Percy's aunt, were all medically treated for insanity, the first two in Philadelphia and the latter in Knoxville, Tennessee. Bipolar depression also apparently runs in the other branch of the mysterious Charles Percy's descendants. For further information, see Wyatt-Brown, *House of Percy*, 40–42, 56–58, 101–2, 111, 308, 335–37, 377n; and Wyatt-Brown, *The Literary Percys: Family History, Gender, and Legend* (Athens: University of Georgia Press, 1994).

49. Percy to Foote, September 3, 1980, Walker Percy files, Southern Historical Collection, Wilson Library, University of North Carolina, Chapel Hill; also in Jay Tolson, ed., *The Correspondence of Shelby Foote and Walker Percy* (New York: Norton, 1997), 235. Unfortunately, Walker Percy once told me that he had no knowledge at all about any letters from Gerstle Mack to his guardian. They have indeed vanished.

50. Conversation with Leon S. Koury, September 29, 1992, at his Greenville residence; Walker Percy, *The Message in the Bottle: How Queer Man Is, How Queer Language Is, and What One Has to Do with the Other* (New York: Farrar, Straus & Giroux, 1975), 4. Moreover, his health was very precarious. In fact, Will Percy died of multiple small strokes on January 21, 1942.

51. WAP, *Lanterns*, 11.

52. See Wyatt-Brown, *House of Percy*, 343–48.

53. Ibid., 341–55.

54. WAP, *Lanterns*, 40.

55. Robert K. Krick, ed. and comp., *Lee's Colonels: A Biographical Register of the Field Officers of the Army of Northern Virginia*, 4th ed., rev. (Dayton, Ohio: Morningside House, 1992), 471. I thank Professor Michael Chesson for this citation.

56. WAP, *Lanterns*, 74. LeRoy Percy to Sarah Compton, January 27, 1909, Compton File, Percy Papers, MDAH. The Ferguson scandal is narrated in Wyatt-Brown, *Literary Percys*, 44–54.

57. This insight about the influence of Henry Adams must be gratefully attributed to William Armstrong Percy III, in a conversation by phone on February 20, 2006. Anne Rose must also be equally acknowledged. I quote from her e-mail message, March 4, 2005. Henry Adams, *Mont-Saint-Michel and Chartres* (1913; repr., Garden City, N.Y.: Doubleday Anchor, 1953), 422.

58. WAP, *Lanterns*, 223.

59. Anne Rose to author, e-mail, March 4, 2006.

60. Jonathan Daniels, *A Southerner Discovers the South* (New York: Macmillan, 1938), 177; John Griffin Jones, interview, 1983, in Lawson and Kramer, *Conversations with Walker Percy*, 256.

61. "B[illups] Phinizy Percy Interview with John Jones," 10, MDAH.

62. WAP, *Lanterns*, 311; Philip D. Carter, "Oh, You Know Uncle Walker," in Lawson and Kramer, *Conversations with Walker Percy*, 38.

63. Quotation, WAP, *Lanterns*, 135. See WAP to Charlotte Gailor, May 27, 1936, University Archives, Jessie Ball DuPont Library, Sewanee, Tenn.; interviews with LeRoy Pratt

Percy and Ben Wasson, in Malone, "William Alexander Percy," 128; David L. Cohn, "The Eighteenth-Century Chevalier," *Virginia Quarterly Review* 31 (Fall 1955): 575.

64. Bradford, in WAP, *Collected Poems*, 7; Fred Hobson, *Tell About the South: The Southern Rage to Explain* (Baton Rouge: Louisiana State University Press, 1983), 245.

65. Anthony Kenny, *Aristotle on the Perfect Life* (Oxford, Eng.: Clarendon Press, 1992), 93.

# Rewriting American Borders
*The Southern Gothic, Religion, and U.S. Historical Narrative*

FARRELL O'GORMAN

I n approaching our common concern, I want to address what many believe to be the most potentially fruitful recent development in scholarship on the U.S. South: its turn to New World or Hemispheric American studies. Scholars working in this area are, I believe, quite right to have us looking south of the South in order to better understand the region's history and literature alike. Nonetheless, in doing so we should pay more consistent heed to Caroline Levander and Robert Levine's too-brief caveat that interest in developing an expanded "North-South" perspective in the American hemisphere should not blind us to vital "East-West" perspectives (14). In our enthusiasm for new geographical configurations, that is, we should never forget the fundamental relationship that the South and Latin America alike have historically borne—for better or worse—to Europe in particular. Furthermore, we must learn to pay closer attention to just how profoundly New World cultures and narratives of nationhood have been shaped in relation to religion.[1] We must more insistently remember that the U.S. South and the Americas as we know them came into being in an era marked not only by conflicts between the colonial powers of Spain, France, and England but also by what Chris Baldick and Robert Mighall have rightly deemed "the most enduring and formative ideological conflict of modern European history," that between Catholicism and Protestantism (216).

Baldick and Mighall make this characterization in order to remind literary scholars of the necessity of maintaining a proper historical perspective in approaching the genre I want to focus on here: Gothic fiction (that is, the fiction of horror, generally marked by supernatural or seemingly supernatural phenomena, originally featuring medieval trappings such as the monastery or castle and later the haunted mansion or simply the haunted family). In their authoritative overview of twentieth-century criticism of Gothic literature, Baldick and Mighall contend that too many scholars have tended to display a "de-historicising bias" in their analyses of the Gothic, favoring supposedly universal psychoanalytical readings or, more recently, readings particularly attentive to depictions of race and gender, all the while maintaining "an embarrassed silence upon the matter of early Gothic fiction's anti-Catholicism" (216). Baldick and Mighall are primarily concerned with this critical error in regard to analyses of the British Gothic, which clearly highlighted national anxieties regarding religion in seminal classics such as Horace Walpole's *The Castle of Otranto* (1764), Anne Radcliffe's *The Mysteries of Udolpho* (1794), and Matthew Lewis's *The Monk* (1796)—all novels written by Protestant authors living in an ascendant imperial Britain (the Anglo-Saxon North), all set in a horrifically imagined and decadent Catholic Mediterranean world (the Latin South).

I want to first examine this British literary tradition and how it was initially translated into Anglo-American form by Poe, Hawthorne, and particularly Melville; I will then explore how their antebellum texts were in turn responded to in major novels by William Faulkner, Walker Percy, and Cormac McCarthy. In doing so, one of my goals is to apply a broad historical awareness of religion's complex role in American cultures in order to reconfigure our reading of these specific fictions and paradigms of the "southern" Gothic generally. But I also want to explore how these fictions are fundamentally concerned with historiography—as much significant Gothic fiction has been, originating as it did in an age marked by a perceived crisis of authority. Specifically, I will demonstrate how the Gothic and therefore profoundly ambiguous histories imagined in *Absalom, Absalom!* (1936), *Lancelot* (1977), and *Blood Meridian* (1985) play on long-standing Anglo-American fears regarding Catholicism, a Catholicism which along the southern borders of the overwhelmingly Protestant South is seen as threatening to break down apparently rigid cultural borders between innocence and guilt, white and black, mind and body, male and female, Anglo-American "purity" and Latin "impurity," present and past. Ultimately, these Gothic texts write the confrontation with Catholicism in such a way as to deconstruct myths of Anglo-American exceptionalism which feature the South and the larger United States as somehow purifying or righteously escaping the tainted past. And while many historians might be inclined to prefer more obviously realistic forms of fiction than the Gothic, I would contend that these seemingly fantastical fictions should perhaps be required reading for U.S. historians precisely because they so profoundly undermine popular Anglo-American cultural assumptions: they not only challenge a narrative of history as inevitably progressive but also demonstrate the ultimate inability of the autonomous individual intellect—generally figured in these fictions as belonging to the putatively self-reliant Anglo-American frontiersman—to author an accurate history.

## The Anglo-American Gothic: Crossing the Atlantic

First, it is crucial that we understand the origins of Anglo-American Gothic fiction—both its historical context and its essential concern with history, as exemplified in what is universally acknowledged as the first Gothic novel. *The Castle of Otranto* was written by the son of Sir Robert Walpole, the de facto first prime minister of Great Britain. A zealous Whig, Walpole was a member of that ascendant party which at mid-eighteenth century wished to erase even the memory of the two centuries of religious strife which had ended only a generation previous with the succession of William and Mary. But the question remained: what in fact legitimated Britain's increasingly parliamentary government, along with the accompanying rise of the mercantile class and of capitalism generally? Walpole and his Whig colleagues attempted to ground their burgeoning rule—including its entrenched anti-Catholic laws—in the myth of a piecemeal native constitution (sometimes deemed a "Saxon" or "Gothic" constitution) which reached back to the Magna Carta and was perceived as a "bulwark" of the democratic and therefore fundamentally "Protestant freedoms" which had finally prevailed for good in the Glorious Revolution (Miles, "Gothic and Ideology" 61). But in *The Castle of Otranto* Robert Walpole's son Horace wrote a novel marked by the suspicion that history was not necessarily such a neat narrative of inevitable moral progress—that it perhaps remained a crude power struggle marked as much by might as right and that present prosperity was inevitably built on past wrongs.

Walpole's novel about a powerful family's hidden history "dwells obsessively," as Robert Miles has put it, "on illegitimacy and usurpation, on gaps and ruptures" in that history. Hence, *The Castle of Otranto*, though set in medieval Italy, can ultimately be read as a critique of eighteenth-century Whig rule: while in public Horace Walpole upheld his father's "political image," in his fiction "he dons the garb of the family's ancestral [Catholic] enemies and turns assassin" by effectively calling all political authority into question. And he does so in a very complex manner. "It's not just that [in the novel the ruling patriarch's] attitude toward divorce unhappily recalls Henry VIII and the Reformation or that the plot concerns usurpation," Miles writes; in fact, "the theme of illegitimate possession pervades all aspects" of the novel, including the way the narrative not only turns upon the discovery of a falsified will but also insistently points to the likelihood of its own "textual fakery" (61). For Walpole initially published *The Castle of Otranto* under a pseudonym, masquerading as the translator of the work of a supposed Counter-Reformation Italian priest who is in turn presented as the likely forger of the primary narrative, a tale set at the time of the Crusades. This priest's tale is so offensive to the modern mind, the faux-translator warns his readers in a lengthy preface, that it was likely intended to confirm its original and supposedly Italian readers in their Catholic superstitions, as "[its] principal incidents are such as were believed in the darkest ages of Christianity" (5). In its self-questioning framing device, then, as well as in Walpole's preface to the second edition—which forthrightly defends what Miles deems the text's apparent "generic miscegenation"—this eighteenth-century fiction is strikingly postmodern in form.[2] Yet its "postmodern" elements take definitive root in those questions regarding the nature of authority—that is, textual authorship and interpretation as well as political legitimacy—which were so central to that most foundational of early modern events, the Reformation.

This fact is highlighted again at the novel's conclusion, when the deposed patriarch and his wife, stripped of their worldly power, are effectively forced to "take on the habit of religion" and disappear into monastic communities adjoining their former realm (114). Read in historical context, then, the major cultural question raised by *The Castle of Otranto* and its violent tale of usurpation becomes: what is the proper basis of ultimate authority? If not the Roman Catholic Church or the divine right of kings, can parliamentary representation be trusted to be much better— particularly when it seems to replace older Christian traditions only with imperialistic nationalism and when rule of the nation-state appears to be grounded only in the calculating wills of self-interested individuals (at this time, of propertied white males)? Diane Long Hoeveler foregrounds these concerns as she characterizes the early British Gothic, in the wake of *Otranto*, as both reflecting broad developments in intellectual history and seeking, in effect, to exorcise the religious past: "The killing of Catholicism in England took more than two hundred years, and the gothic charts that murder in all its convoluted moves. Killing the king becomes in the gothic the killing of a corrupt duke or monk, while the rationality so highly prized by Protestant individualism and Enlightenment ideology moves to center stage, creating a new cultural ideal that chastised idolatry, superstition, hierarchy, and popery in all its forms" (12–13). Early British Gothic fiction, in short, "charts the death of the old world of Catholicism, communalism, [and] feudalism, and the rise in its place of the Protestant subject, individual, modern, secular," and "capitalist." This representative Protestant subject—"the new social and cultural divinity"—is further figured as "middle class, white, male, heterosexual," and essentially bodiless, representing "Enlightenment beliefs in the self as unitary, reasonable, and located somewhere above and beyond the body" (6–7, 9).[3]

Such, in any case, was the dominant Enlightenment construct which informed the nascent Gothic. Yet Hoeveler rightly maintains that it would be a mistake to deem the Gothic an "Enlightenment genre." Indeed, multiple critics have observed how Gothic fiction essentially plays on the fear that neat rational dichotomies—between mind and body, male and female, white and black, good and evil, living and dead, present and past— might somehow break down. In the early Gothic, "Protestant" (that is, modern) generally corresponds to the first and putatively positive of these opposed categories (mind, male, white, living, present), "Catholic" to the second and putatively negative ones (body, female, black, dead, past). But in this cultural milieu Catholicism, like the Gothic itself, is also associated with the complete breakdown of such dichotomies, with a horrifying intermingling between seemingly opposed states of being, and, accordingly, with ambiguity—including, as seen in *Otranto,* a narrative ambiguity which implicitly critiques the monolithic mythmaking upon which nationalism inevitably depends.[4]

But how did these patterns manifest themselves in an American context? Gothic fiction was a popular import in the early-nineteenth-century United States and emerged as a domestic product most famously in the work of Poe, who at times sought to cash in on long-standing Anglo-American fears of the European and Catholic past—for example, in "The Pit and the Pendulum" (1842), an imagined captivity narrative set during the Spanish Inquisition, and "The Masque of the Red Death" (1842), a tale of moral and bodily corruption featuring decadent aristocrats in a "castellated abbey" in Europe. He did so more sporadically in fictions such as "The Black Cat" (1843), wherein the narrator kills his wife and walls her corpse up, he reports, "much as the monks of the Middle Ages are recorded to have walled up their victims" (354). Yet Poe is not merely catering to the prejudices of his audience. For "The Black Cat" and stories such as "William Wilson" (1839) and "The Tell-Tale Heart" (1843) finally offer less reason to fear medieval or European authorities than the quintessentially modern and willfully autonomous individuals—democrats? Americans?—who serve as the criminal and significantly unreliable narrators of these tales. Furthermore, Poe finally tends to associate not only Catholicism but also the feminine with a limiting embodiment which such modern individuals seek to deny and escape—the hypersensitive intellectual Roderick Usher being a prime exemplar as he buries his cataleptic twin sister alive in "The Fall of the House of Usher" (1839).

Poe's contemporary Hawthorne links gender to religion explicitly in *The Scarlet Letter* (1850), wherein Hester Prynne, clutching her illegitimate daughter as she ascends a public scaffold, is introduced as follows: "Had there been a Papist among the crowd of Puritans, he might have seen in this beautiful woman . . . with the infant at her bosom, an object to remind him of the image of Divine Maternity" (42). Hester Prynne, then—whose scarlet *A* might as well stand for *Ambiguity*—initially appears as a dark Madonna. She is also oddly nun-like at points in the novel and is in effect held captive in Protestant New England, which in *The Scarlet Letter* is hardly characterized by the bright typological narrative the Puritan fathers wished to write for it. Hawthorne more obviously than Poe, then, shifts to insistently *American* Gothic settings even while beginning to write what Jenny Franchot has deemed a "doctrinally ambivalent" fiction which increasingly focused on American Protestantism's most intimate other, Catholicism. While Hawthorne clearly saw Europe and Catholicism as flawed, he was finally more concerned with exploring the flaws in his own Anglo-American culture, including—as John Gatta has contended—its tendency to devalue the feminine and particularly the "divine feminine" represented by Mary.[5]

In different ways and to different degrees, Poe and Hawthorne engage what Allan Lloyd-Smith has identified as the four distinguishing factors informing early U.S. formulations of the Gothic: the Puritan legacy, the frontier, slavery, and the new nation's utopian visions and accompanying dystopian fears. I would argue that religion is in fact worthy of far broader consideration than Lloyd-Smith gives it here, as is made manifest in at least one primary source which Teresa Goddu has identified as exemplifying the early U.S. Gothic: Crèvecoeur's *Letters from an American Farmer* (1782). Crèvecoeur initially praises the general religious "indifference" of Americans in the Middle Colonies, yet he then proceeds to paint horrific pictures both of a coastal South where Protestant ministers yield moral authority to the slave owners who pay their salaries and of a southern frontier where unchurched and radically individualistic settlers become "little better than carnivorous animals."[6] Nonetheless, Lloyd-Smith's fixation on the Puritan legacy in particular is appropriate in light of his general claim that all four factors informed a tendency toward "Manichean formulations of good and evil" in U.S. culture. Such dualistic formulations neatly correspond with the Enlightenment dichotomies discussed by Hoeveler (as is also made evident in what Lloyd-Smith identifies as early U.S. Gothic fiction's tendency to associate masculinity with virtuous self-control and manifest an accompanying "fear of the feminine").[7]

More than any other major antebellum author, it is Melville who most fully and concisely exemplifies these larger patterns in their connection not only to the British Gothic but also to the South and its borders.[8] He does so in a number of his shorter fictions of the 1850s—but I want to focus on his 1855 novella *Benito Cereno*. Here Melville overtly rewrites not only Poe but also Lewis, Radcliffe, and Walpole (all of whom he had read) in a Gothic narrative set aboard a seemingly haunted Spanish slave ship off the coast of Latin America, a ship which strangely resembles both a seductive Peruvian woman and "a monastery in the Pyrenees."[9] Here Melville's U.S. sea captain, who boards the apparently disabled Spanish ship in a gesture of seeming goodwill, perfectly exemplifies Hoeveler's "Protestant subject": consistently identified as the "American," this character is insistently white (in opposition to the African slaves); insistently male (his ship is named the *Bachelor's Delight*); insistently rational (in opposition to the apparently superstitious Spanish captain Cereno); and essentially secular, indulging in occasional hopeful sentiments that there is "someone above" who watches over him but essentially trusting in his own abilities.[10] He is insistently self-reliant both in this sense and in that he is a proud democrat, a self-made man who on this maritime frontier has earned his captain's rank—unlike Cereno, who presumably inherited it.

Indeed, the Spaniard, while not as obviously alien as the Africans, gothically differs from the American captain in every respect: he is neither black nor white but suspiciously off-white, with "yellow" hands and a "dark" countenance; he is male but effeminate, wearing an empty scabbard rather than a sword; he and his crew are seemingly superstitious and submissively religious, mouthing prayers of supplication to the Blessed Virgin.[11] Furthermore, Cereno—in contrast to the American captain, whose body (like his technology) seems to serve him primarily as an effective weapon—is intriguingly embodied: his "cadaverous" appearance throughout the narrative suggests that he is a kind of zombie, at once living and dead. This aspect of the Spaniard's appearance not only stresses his embodiment as a form of limiting enclosure but also befits his ultimate sense that the past is always present—both of which concerns are fully developed in the narrative's final image of Cereno's death inside a Peruvian monastery, where he has retreated in the incipient knowledge of his own guilt in supporting the slave trade. By contrast, the American captain—who has ultimately, violently, put down a slave rebellion aboard the Spaniard's ship—walks away blithely convinced of his own innocence and, furthermore, that "the past is passed; why moralize upon it?" (257).

*Benito Cereno*, then, is a Gothic fiction not only in its horrific action and quasi-medieval setting (the slaves themselves initially seem to resemble "black monks," for example, and the perennial specter of the Inquisition haunts the American captain's mind) but also in its forthright concern with ambiguous histories. The American's faith in a vaguely imagined "providence"—which nonetheless definitively protects him—and his accompanying blindness to the complexities of history, moral and otherwise, make him unable to read his own present properly. The slaves have in fact taken over the ship before he even boards it, forcing the Spanish captain to act out a role that is designed to lead the American to his doom, but the American cannot see this because of his aforementioned characteristics—more specifically manifested here both in his racial biases and in his tendency to believe in the goodness of human nature (which together have blinded him to the fact that the institution of slavery is evil). After the main action is complete and the American's crew has captured the slaves by force, excerpts from the "official Spanish documents" ultimately written to condemn the rebellious slaves are inserted into the text, though only to be subtly called into question by the omniscient narrator (Melville)—just as the American's self-righteous sense of his role in maintaining legitimate authority in the New World here is undermined in his final conversation with the Spanish captain. For while the thoroughly defeated Cereno has become incipiently aware that the New World history his own Catholic nation has tried to write is lacking, the triumphant American captain has no sense whatsoever that he and his nation are flawed—and, accordingly, he himself finally emerges as the chief horror in this Gothic tale.

If we pay attention to various textual details as well as the fact that *Benito Cereno* was published at the height of the slavery crisis yet set in the late eighteenth century, the text's larger significance is clear: here Melville breaks down national borders as he takes on the entire history of New World slavery, alluding to specific events ranging from its origins in Hispaniola and first major defeat in Haiti to the *Amistad* incident and the U.S. passage of the Fugitive Slave Law. Given that by 1855 slavery had been outlawed in almost all of Latin America and that Toussaint Louverture was widely known to be a devout Catholic, Melville might be read here as in part critiquing his nation's assumption that its principles—generally seen as embodying the best of the Reformation and the Enlightenment alike—provided the best basis for a universal moral and political order, or at least that it was putting those principles into practice.[12] The text's repeated monastic imagery and its specific allusions to Bartolomé de Las Casas—the Dominican friar credited both with first advocating the importation of African slaves to the New World and with later becoming the first outspoken opponent of slavery in the Americas—do not, of course, simplistically suggest that the Latin Catholic South has been morally superior to the Anglo-American North. Rather, *Benito Cereno* as a whole suggests that the United States needs to recognize its own morally ambiguous history, its kinship with Latin America, rather than trumpeting its exceptionalism. Most relevant to our concerns in this regard is the novella's implicit commentary on both slaveholding in the U.S. South and the legacy of the Mexican-American War. The former is perhaps obvious enough: from the beginning many critics have read the decadent aristocratic "Spaniard" as in part a stand-in for southern planters and "the American" as a northerner complicit in capturing fugitive slaves. More interesting, however, is Allan Moore Emery's reading of *Benito Cereno* as critically responding to the mid-nineteenth-century Anglo-American desire to control a seemingly disorderly Latin America, to impose willful "democratic" authority on a region that—seemingly retrograde in its politics as well as its religion—was lacking the full benefits of Reformation-cum-Enlightenment values which ensured individual autonomy, material prosperity, and the separation of peoples into clearly dichotomized categories such as elect or damned, progressive or regressive, white or black.[13] That desire was sufficiently widespread throughout the United States to have fostered adequate popular support for the Mexican-American War and the general notion of Manifest Destiny. But it was particularly prominent among southern leaders because of their region's proximity to Latin America and made clear in the activity of southern filibusters.

*Benito Cereno,* then, is a Gothic fiction directly indebted to its British precursors in its religious imagery and concern with historiography, but in its subtle commentary on Manifest Destiny and the U.S. South, it also prefigures Smith and Cohn's reading of the region as "a space of degrees of overlap *between* . . . the Yankee and the plantation," a "simultaneous embodiment" of *both* a progressive, Anglo-dominated capitalist (Protestant) North and a multiracial Latin (Catholic) South that has never fully escaped its colonial past (8). And by profoundly complicating both that dichotomy and the moral history that citizens of the United States have generally wanted to write for themselves, it sets the mold for the southern Gothic fictions I want to discuss next. In those fictions the character whom Melville figures as the "American"—the self-reliant and only apparently innocent frontiersman—becomes quintessentially southern and, to varying degrees, a more obvious figure of horror himself.

## Writing Gothic Americas: Beyond Southern Borders

Melville's representative American is drawn from a variety of sources. He is, for one thing, an ironic variation on the American Adam figure—an Adam, crucially, without an Eve—famously identified by R. W. B. Lewis as central to much of nineteenth-century U.S. literature. But one useful *historical* analogue and likely inspiration for Melville's American—figured even more darkly in *Moby-Dick*'s Ahab (1851) and *The Confidence Man*'s "Indian-hater," Colonel John Moredock (1857)—is Andrew Jackson. Melville came of age during the presidency of this common man turned seeming tyrant, this southern frontiersman and largely unchurched (though professedly Presbyterian) slaveholder whose career included not only unrelenting warfare against Native Americans but also seizing Florida from the Spanish on the premise that the disorderly region provided a refuge for runaway U.S. slaves.[14] As witness to the age of Jacksonian democracy, Melville necessarily saw the South as playing a central role in the U.S. national narrative, as opposed to the peripheral, merely oppositional, or contrapuntally regressive one that many Americans (southerners included) saw it playing for a century after the Civil War.

In that regard the southern Gothic novels I am about to discuss pick up where Melville left off. *Absalom, Absalom!*, *Lancelot*, and *Blood Meridian* all enter into dialogue with the U.S. myth of the self-made man (the American version of Hoeveler's "Protestant subject") which Jackson might obviously be seen as representing—though also with a native southern myth in which the likes of Jackson had no place at all. I mean the myth of a Cavalier South rightfully and placidly dominated by a genteel planter aristocracy which supposedly embodied the best of early modern Europe. This myth is most memorably articulated in Reconstruction-era fictions such as Thomas Nelson Page's "Marse Chan" (1884), wherein a former slave narrates his service as faithful retainer to a chivalrous Virginia gentleman—an Episcopalian like Page himself, we must assume—who seems to have stepped out of the pages of a novel by Sir Walter Scott. The

South is, of course, the only region of the United States which has ever seemed fertile soil for this sort of positive medievalism (or positive faux-medievalism, as Walker Percy, for one, would insist), which was openly mocked by Mark Twain and more subtly critiqued by figures as diverse as W. J. Cash, Charles Chesnutt, and Allen Tate—all of whom finally saw the Old South's system of chattel slavery for what it was, not a feudal idyll but a modern horror, and saw the region's identity as more profoundly characterized by the self-made frontiersman than the Cavalier. And I think the Gothic fictions I am about to discuss are among the richest the South has produced because, like *Benito Cereno*, they strangely emphasize the violence of the frontier even as they place the United States in juxtaposition with a Latin Catholic culture which threatens to undermine dominant Anglo-Protestant narratives of personal, regional, and national identity.[15] Each novel is explicitly concerned with historiography, and each ultimately depicts a Gothic encounter with a Latin Catholic South and concordant experience of racial, gender, and moral ambiguity which deconstructs both the southern Cavalier myth and, ultimately, the myth of the self-reliant and in some sense "innocent" Anglo-Protestant frontiersman.

Faulkner, who greatly admired Melville, does so most profoundly in *Absalom, Absalom!*, a clearly Gothic and clearly historiographical novel in which—to put it only a little too simply—nineteenth-century Mississippi planter Thomas Sutpen plays the role of *Benito Cereno*'s "innocent" American and Charles Bon his Latin Catholic foil. But before developing this claim, I should say a few words about the historical context which informs this novel. Like Melville, Faulkner was not a Catholic himself, but he was a person of cosmopolitan sensibilities who began writing in a provincial culture during a period of intense anti-Catholic nativism (the 1920s being perhaps the most intense such period in the United States after the 1850s), and, like Melville, he was profoundly interested in exploring the flaws and lacunae in our dominant national narratives. So Faulkner is interested in Catholicism or its image insofar as it might prove useful in critiquing his own culture, with its Anglo-Protestant notions of American exceptionalism and purity and its modern emphasis on practicality and individual autonomy. He was interested in Catholicism, that is, insofar as it suggests cosmopolitanism, decadence, aesthetic indulgence, and perhaps a fundamentally premodern Christian-pagan syncretism. In this regard it is worth quoting an enthusiastic postcard which Faulkner sent home to Oxford from the Piazza del Duomo in Milan in August 1925, during his first visit to Europe: "This Cathedral!" he exclaimed. "Can you imagine stone lace? Or frozen music? All covered with gargoyles like dogs, and mitred cardinals and mailed knights and saints pierced with arrows and beautiful naked Greek figures that have no religious significance whatever."[16]

There is much more that could be said about the interest that Faulkner's fellow literary modernists—American and otherwise—expressed in such elements of European Catholic culture. But Faulkner experienced such urbane Catholic contrasts with the plain-folk Protestantism of north Mississippi during not only his time in Europe but also his sojourns in New Orleans, an American Catholic city marked by its distinctively non-Anglo history and popular associations with open ethnic and racial mixing.[17] In any case, in Faulkner's early fiction Catholic imagery is linked to the persons of non-Anglo "others" such as the young Italian girl Quentin Compson glimpses in Boston in *The Sound and the Fury* (1929) and, much more extensively, Joe Christmas, the central and obviously somewhat Christlike figure in *Light in August* (1931), who is feared as being part Negro, identified with Italians and Mexicans and described as looking like a "monk" and "choir boy" before being ritually murdered in a work that explicitly invokes the legacy of the Mexican-American War and tensions between Calvinist insiders and Catholic outsiders in U.S. history.[18]

*Absalom, Absalom!* is both the culmination of this first major period of Faulkner's career and his most explicitly historiographical fiction. The novel depicts the failed struggle of displaced southerner Quentin Compson to piece together a coherent narrative of the apparently haunted Sutpen family and their doomed house. He attempts to do so with his Canadian roommate in a Harvard dorm room that is oddly Gothic, a "snug monastic" space where one young man from the South and another from Alberta find themselves "born half a continent apart yet joined, connected after a fashion in a sort of geographical transubstantiation by that Continental Trough, that [Mississippi] River," which Faulkner imagines as draining the whole of North America into the Gulf of Mexico (208). Appropriately so, for *Absalom, Absalom!* concerns the South, the United States as a whole, and the Americas at large. It devastatingly critiques the southern Cavalier myth as it stresses that the nominally aristocratic Sutpen clan, with their grotesquely large white manor house and plantation in north Mississippi, is in fact less than a generation removed from the poverty and violence of the frontier. Patriarch Thomas Sutpen has established his family here in order to escape not only his own humble western Virginia origins but also the perceived taint of blackness his name stood to acquire when he fathered an apparently mixed-race son during his brief marriage to a supposedly Spanish or Creole woman in the Caribbean. Upon doing so, Sutpen—obsessed with maintaining what Quentin Compson's father calls his "innocence"—immediately fled back to the United States, to the "peculiarly Anglo-Saxon" and "puritan" culture of northern Mississippi (Mr. Compson's words), in order to escape a Latin world which in *Absalom, Absalom!* is forthrightly associated with the breakdown of racial dichotomies (86).[19] Nonetheless (as best Quentin and his roommate can piece together at least), Sutpen's mulatto and effeminate son Charles Bon—identified as "a Catholic of sorts"—emerges in New Orleans, that northernmost outpost of the Latin South, and travels into north Mississippi to threaten and finally destroy Sutpen's bid to achieve his abstract design of purity (75).[20] In Faulkner's New World Gothic tale, then, like Melville's, regional and national obsessions with purity (moral and racial alike) are haunted by fears of Latin Catholic impurity—though in Faulkner's text that impurity is connected even more explicitly to uncontrolled fertility, for example, to miscegenation.

Other differences are noteworthy as well. Sutpen, as Faulkner's representative American, manages to be both more clearly deserving of moral censure and more ultimately pitiable than Melville's in *Benito Cereno* (Sutpen perhaps more resembles Ahab in this regard). And Faulkner's concern with historiography is much more explicit. *Absalom, Absalom!* is as much a story of Sutpen's potential biographer, Quentin, as of Sutpen himself. When confronted with the proliferating narrative perspectives that stem from reflection on Sutpen's relationship with Bon in particular, that biographer is in effect overwhelmed and subsequently driven to suicide by his fruitless desire to find authority or meaning in a "traditional" southern and U.S. narrative dominated by seemingly self-made and therefore godlike father figures. Sutpen, as many commentators have noted, has in fact naively tried to rival Jehovah himself—but his body, not only in its mere mortality but also in its entangling encounters with women and the Latin world which spawns Charles Bon, dooms him. And when confronted with such facts or seeming facts, the budding moralistic historian Quentin, like the nominally self-reliant Sutpen himself, finds that he cannot make sense of them, cannot write the master providential narrative which would give Sutpen—and the larger culture he reflects—purpose or meaning or order.

It is appropriate to begin with Faulkner because both Percy and McCarthy are directly indebted not only to the broader American Gothic tradition but to *Absalom, Absalom!* in particular. Percy's *Lancelot* (1977)—his sole Gothic novel—obviously follows Faulkner and Poe alike in that it is the narrative of the fall of a house. Here narrator Lance Lamar, heir to an aristocratic Louisiana family, has disintegrated into criminal madness (which is at first subtle) after discovering both his wife's infidelity and the apparent erotic excesses of the entire United States in the decade immediately following the sexual revolution. From his hospital room Lance tells us—or, rather, tells his priest friend Percival, a Catholic convert like Percy himself—his story, which he openly struggles to remember. Lance ultimately reveals that he has killed his wife's lover and, inadvertently, her, along with some sexually unruly houseguests—and so, despite his protests against the morally depraved world around him, Lance himself clearly emerges as the chief horror in the novel. Its Gothic elements are partly reflected in the confessional narrative form, which—given its potential unreliability here—reflects the influence of Poe as much as it does Percy's Catholicism, and the novel becomes broadly historiographical in that Lance's attempt to tell the story of his own hidden violence inevitably involves recovering and interrogating his southern ancestors' attempts to tell their history.

In certain respects Lance initially seems a stock early Gothic villain: he is heir to a mansion which, to visiting midwestern tourists, looks "as foreign . . . as Castel Gandolfo," the pope's summer residence (25); that mansion is in overwhelmingly Catholic south Louisiana; and Lance has certain medieval obsessions, notably with his own perverse notion of chivalry. In its overt Arthurian allusions the novel takes the romantic medievalism of Scott and gives it a dark Gothic face, yet it does so in a manner that, as with Poe, ultimately focuses on a modern rather than a medieval horror.[21] For one thing Lance is insistently post-Christian, though he is notably descended from "Tory English colonials" who, as his father told it, arrived in "corrupt" colonial Louisiana to build their own "chaste and incorrupt little Anglican chapels," despite being surrounded on all sides by "savage Indians" and "superstitious Romans" alike (14, 116). Lance's father's formulation of the Lamar family history therefore resembles the captivity narratives of early New England settlers, who routinely conflated Native Americans and Catholics.[22] It also subtly supports Lance's current belief that he is a representative of moral purity misplaced in a decadent setting. And, finally, it prepares us to delve more deeply into the Lamar family history: for, as the novel progresses, Lance begins persistently to recall not his gentle romantic father but his violent great-great-grandfather, who "carved" a man "limb from limb" in a duel on a Mississippi River sandbar, using not a broadsword but a bowie knife—the same knife which Lance himself ultimately uses to kill his wife's lover.

Despite his obsession with the Cavalier myth, then, Lance himself is finally neither displaced medieval knight nor Tory gentleman; and while in his researches regarding his wife's infidelity he aptly identifies himself as a kind of scientist or detective (another nod to Poe), these two modern identities merge finally and most crucially with his American identity as a self-reliant frontiersman who willfully and violently inflicts his abstract designs on nature—here on human bodies. In this regard Lance, like his great-great-grandfather, clearly resembles Sutpen, whose influence may also be felt in Lance's desire to leave an overly complicated and historically burdened south Louisiana for the Shenandoah Valley, imagined by Lance as a frontier less violent than Edenic—much as Sutpen's boyhood home in a nearly all-white western Virginia is initially imagined in *Absalom, Absalom!*

*Lancelot* as a whole does not turn directly on the concerns with race so central to Faulkner's novel (though Lance's great-great-grandfather's duel did stem from a charge that his "very white" Creole mother had an affair with a black man and that he himself was, accordingly, of mixed race). But it does, as we have seen, foreground the Catholic-Protestant divide that has historically marked the southern Louisiana-Mississippi border region. As a post-Protestant himself, Lance initially expresses some distant admiration for the Catholic Creoles, despite their apparent moral laxity, because—unlike his own family—they seem to have found the "secret of leading ordinary lives well" (24). But, as the novel progresses, Lance, like Sutpen, becomes a nightmare figure of a self-reliant rationality which is both strangely puritanical and narrowly dichotomizing; he becomes increasingly angry not just with women—he is clearly concerned with maintaining gender dichotomies—but also with Catholicism, post–Vatican II Catholicism in particular, for what he sees as its failure to establish and enforce clear moral dichotomies. Again, the bulk of the narrative is a monologue directed at the priest Percival—delivered, Poe-like, in a mental hospital room which doubles as a potential confessional booth, much as Quentin's "monastic" Harvard dorm room does. Lance expresses to Percival his anger at the gentle priest's own apparent moral ambiguity: "With you," he tells Percival—a celibate whose own stance in the novel has been explicated as "feminine" in some respects— "everything seems to get dissolved in a kind of sorrowful solution. Poor weak mankind! The trouble is that in your old tolerant Catholic world-weariness, you lose all distinctions. Love everything" (130–31).[23] "Damn you and your God," he rails later. "Between the two of you, you should have got it straight and had it one way or the other. Either it [sex or any other action] is good or it's bad, but whichever it is, goddamn say so. Only you don't. You fuck off somewhere in between. You want to have it both ways: good, but—bad only if—and so forth" (176).

Lance here is, like Sutpen, an "innocent" in his own way and equally representative of a Manichaean preference for seeing the world in black and white: hence, his anger at a Catholic Church which, at least as Percy's coreligionist Flannery O'Connor once put it, understands itself as being composed not of "good people"—the Creoles with their lax mores make this obvious to Lance—but "of those who accept what she teaches, whether they are good or bad, and there is a constant struggle through the help of the sacraments to be good" (346). The sacraments are themselves crucial to fully understanding Percy's revision of the Gothic—but that is another story.[24] What is relevant here is how Lance emerges as a U.S. southern frontiersman like his antebellum ancestor whose insistence on self-reliant masculinity and moral Manichaeanism hinders his attempt to author his own history accurately—and makes him a figure of horror.

Cormac McCarthy's *Blood Meridian* owes much more to Melville than to Poe but, like *Lancelot*, also pays homage to Faulkner. Like Sutpen, McCarthy's antebellum protagonist—identified here simply as the "kid," with eyes "oddly innocent"—leaves the Appalachian East in his early teens and makes his way south and west to an antebellum frontier where, it seems, he is finally "divested of all that he has been. His origins are become remote as is his destiny and not again in all the world's turning will there be terrains so wild and barbarous to try whether the stuff of creation may be shaped to man's will or whether his own heart is not another kind of clay" (4–5). And, like Sutpen, the kid ultimately finds that he is not a self-reliant master of creation. Here the Mexican-American border, rather than the Latin Caribbean, is the setting of his undoing, and his antagonist, the seemingly superhuman Judge, proves in many ways a horrific example of what Sutpen would have had to become in order to author his own history successfully. *Blood Meridian*, which is directly concerned with the genocide of Native Americans and the legacy of the Mexican-American War, becomes a historiographical novel in that it depicts the Judge deliberately obliterating the unwritten histories of "others" in writing his (and the nation's) history. Often those others—including, ultimately, the kid—are illiterate, while the Judge is both supremely literate and, despite a few seemingly "gentlemanly" qualities, a triumphant example of the self-reliant Anglo-American frontiersman. While primarily an Enlightenment man, even a mad scientist of sorts, the not-just-white but albino Judge draws on the Puritan legacy when convenient—he refers, for example, to Mexicans as "mongrels" (pseudo-scientific language) but to Native Americans as the "heathen" (religious language). These two aspects of his character converge in the fact that he is not only a modernizing military leader who effectively employs new technologies but also an iconoclast, one whose success in "purifying" the frontier in preparation for the new order broadly resembles that of Oliver Cromwell: he seeks to destroy not only other human beings but also their traditions, their material histories, including any works of art that others have produced—even in his act of obsessively cataloging them.[25]

The novel's historiographical concerns both converge with and revise Anglo-American Gothic associations of Catholicism with horror. As the kid approaches the Texas-Mexico border in the wake of the Mexican War, he discovers the ruins of a Catholic church: "an array of saints in their niches . . . shot up by American troops trying their rifles, the figures shorn of ears and noses. . . . The huge carved and paneled doors hung awap on their hinges and a carved stone Virgin held a headless child," and an actual dead child lies in the sacristy (26). Soon thereafter, the kid encounters in another Catholic church the "partly eaten bodies of some forty souls . . . pooled in their communal blood [alongside] a dead Christ in a glass bier [which] lay broken on the chancel floor" (60). The landscape of Mexico itself seems "a great stained altarstone," red with "the blood of a thousand Christs" (102).[26] And, in a crucial episode near the novel's beginning, a group of American filibusters seeking to realize their self-interested version of Manifest Destiny enter Mexico only to be fallen upon by Comanches and scalped, left "tonsured to the bone now . . . like maimed and naked monks" (54).

The monastic images are just one way of suggesting how *Blood Meridian* openly invites an intertextual reading with Melville's fiction—*Moby-Dick* and *The Confidence Man*, in fairly obvious ways, but also *Benito Cereno*. Much as the sea crew turned opportunistic bounty-seeking slave hunters are in effect introduced by a seemingly benevolent American captain in *Benito Cereno*, the nominally civilized yet demonstrably savage frontiersmen turned scalp hunters (predominantly southerners) who dominate *Blood Meridian* are introduced by a less obviously savage American adventurer. McCarthy's Captain White (U.S. Army), leader of the filibusters, is simply a more openly aggressive version of Melville's American sea captain, who in the wake of the Mexican War justifies his own land-grabbing invasion of Mexico using the rhetoric of Manifest Destiny—here used to condemn Mexicans in racial, moral, and religious terms. Mexicans are, White says, "a bunch of barbarians that even the most biased in their favor will admit have no least notion in God's earth of honor or justice or the meaning of republican government. . . . A race of degenerates. A mongrel race, little better than niggers. And maybe no better. There is no government in Mexico. Hell, there's no God in Mexico. Never will be" (33–34).

While White's racial comments here might seem Eurocentric, his soon-stated fear that Mexico will one day fly a "European flag" is perhaps connected to his implicit disdain for its Old World faith, already suggested in the actions of the U.S. troops who have defaced the Catholic churches. White is perhaps quasi-puritanical in this regard. Yet McCarthy (writing in the Reagan era) is, like Melville, interested in exploring how the language of Protestant Christianity seems to have merged too easily with the language of capitalism—the language of self-interest and self-making. Hence, the kid first learns of White via a crude emissary who identifies himself as simply "white and christian" and urges the seemingly lost kid to join White's filibusters—because he himself was lost and then found by the captain, raised up by him "like Lazarus. [White] set my feet on the path of righteousness. . . . He seen something in me worth savin and I see it in you." Therefore, the emissary preaches, the kid should join White's gang as they continue to "whip up on the Mexicans" and gain their own property in doing so: "It's a chance for ye to raise yourself in the world. You best make a move someway or another before ye go plumb in under" (28–30).

Yet this pseudoreligious narrative of righteous and successful American self-advancement, with its undertones of social Darwinism, does not hold. Beginning with the majority of the filibusters being "tonsured to the bone" and left to die "like maimed and naked monks" in the desert, the Americans in *Blood Meridian* cross the Mexican border only to encounter an ancient Catholic world of bodily suffering, moral ambiguity, and literal or figurative miscegenation where their own previous certitudes are dispelled in a maelstrom of Gothic violence. Despite their efforts at self-reliant masculinity, they are struck down so as to writhe with "a lurid female motion" (162) or castrated and left as corpses "with strange menstrual wounds" (153). And perhaps the novel's greatest horror comes in the penultimate chapter as the kid—who has begun to "speak with a strange urgency" of his previous bloody deeds, perhaps even desiring to confess them—comes upon a party of slaughtered Catholic penitents in the southwestern desert (305). Though he has fled from women his entire life, he makes his way through the corpses toward a woman who kneels statuesquely "in a small niche in the rocks," a Marian figure who resembles the Virgin of Guadalupe in particular, as her shawl is marked with "stars and quartermoons and other insignia of a provenance unknown to him." In this novel of unremitting violence the kid is suddenly overcome with the urge to do her some kindness, and perhaps thereby to redeem himself—but upon speaking to her he realizes that "she had been dead in that place for years" (315).[27] Immediately prior to this scene it has been suggested that the kid has the potential to become a historian, a "witness" of some sort, even a prophetic one (312). But still inarticulate and unlettered—he carries a Bible, "no word of which he could read"— and left to his own devices after his failed encounter with the woman, the kid can only fall prey to the Judge. In the final chapter the Judge's rhetoric and power finally overwhelm him as he is in effect swallowed up into the narrative (presumably raped and killed). The cryptic epilogue offers some meager hope that a larger story is still to be written. But the primary narrative of *Blood Meridian* ends with the triumph of the Judge, who appears here as a nightmare figure of the triumphantly self-reliant Anglo frontiersman and the only successfully autonomous individual in the novel, one who has written a history which McCarthy clearly reveals to be horrific.

The kid's encounter with the woman happens in the spring of his "twenty-eighth year": the spring of 1861. Only careful readers who recall that the kid was born in 1833 realize this. But in doing so, we become aware that McCarthy has not highlighted so much as obscured the beginning of that event which has traditionally been placed at the center of southern history. And simultaneously he, like Faulkner and Percy and Melville before him, has placed the South at the center of a larger U.S. history. He has told us a Gothic tale of the Americas at large, one dense with allusions to the religious and cultural differences which mark the southern borders of the South and one that should give us pause as we consider not only what the South is but also what our assumptions are in writing of it.

1. Recent scholarship which does address the religious concerns I highlight here includes Richardson; Goldschmidt and McAlister; and McConville.

2. Such "postmodern" features of *The Castle of Otranto* stand out all the more clearly when the novel is compared with the work of Walpole's most prominent near-contemporary, Jane Austen—a quintessential social realist whose third-person narrative voice is indubitably reliable.

3. By contrast, Hoeveler notes, in this milieu "women, people of color and the lower classes" were figured as "embodied" and therefore lacking full "agency" (9)—which generally parallels Miles's observation that the bodies of women, blacks, and "Catholic revenants" often become sites of "possible supernaturalization" in the early British Gothic ("Gothic and Ideology" 65).

4. Miles asserts that the Gothic calls all ideologies into question—not only those of the generally discredited past but also those of the generally divinized present and future. Accordingly, Hoeveler's overarching assertion that most early British Gothic fiction ultimately depicts the triumph of the Protestant subject even while subtly and subversively mourning the Catholic past is finally in concert with Miles's characterization of the Gothic as "arising

out of" a "nascent modernity without taking [clear] positions on it" ("Gothic and Ideology" 58). Also see Miles, "Abjection, Nationalism, and the Gothic," which demonstrates how the British Gothic incorporated horrific images of Catholicism not only as Latin other but also as past British other, that is, the "superstitious feudal subject" or Jacobite: such images in effect suggested to British readers that ambiguously, frighteningly, the other is also us—if we should relapse (58).

5. Franchot considers Hawthorne, Melville, and Poe along these lines at great length. Gatta essentially agrees with her as he contends that the many images of the "divine woman" in Hawthorne's fiction in part represent a direct challenge to the "masculine symbol system" which the author "inherited from the theology of his Puritan-Unitarian forebears" (32).

6. From letter 3, "What Is an American?": "The back-settlers of both the Carolinas, Virginia, and many other parts, have been long a set of lawless people; it has been even dangerous to travel among them." Indeed, "they are often in a perfect state of war; that of man against man, sometimes decided by blows, sometimes by means of the law; that of man against every wild inhabitant of these venerable woods, of which they are come to dispossess them. There men appear to be no better than carnivorous animals of a superior rank" (72).

7. Lloyd-Smith 109–11, 119–20. My point here is that Manichaeanism can well be seen as compatible with Puritan theology in particular. DeGuzman discusses Manichaean dualism in connection with habits of racial categorization, specifically demonstrating how the threat of the "Spaniard" who does not fit into Anglo-Americans' preferred black-white dichotomy informs *Benito Cereno* (1–3, 48–50).

8. See Boyagoda for a reading of Melville as prefiguring Faulkner in his juxtaposition of the U.S. South and the southern Americas at large.

9. For Melville's reading of the British Gothic, see Sealts 105, 154, 225; and Newton 33–48.

10. I follow Fessenden in the observation that even the dominant form of "secularism" in the United States is in some sense "Protestant": *Culture and Redemption* contends that British "Protestantism's emancipation from Catholicism both provides the blueprint for, and sets the limits of, secularism's emancipation from 'religion' itself" in the United States (4). Fessenden demonstrates that Americans have tended to see immersion in a definitively Protestant culture of reading, writing, and spiritual interiority as the key to "redemption" from a limiting premodern past—a past first conceived of as Catholic and then as simply "religious" in any form deemed "irrational, regressive, or inscrutable" and therefore "foreign to democracy" (2).

11. On Anglo-American associations of Spain with miscegenation in *Benito Cereno* and elsewhere, see DeGuzman, esp. 47–67.

12. See Beecher on Melville's interest in Toussaint Louverture in regard to *Benito Cereno*.

13. Relevant readings of *Benito Cereno* include both those stressing the novella's condemnation of the Catholic Church's role in the slave trade and those stressing its condemnation of a United States which wrongly deems itself morally superior to Catholic Latin America: see, respectively, Gloria Horsley-Meacham, "The Monastic Slaver: Images and Meaning in 'Benito Cereno,'" in Burkholder 94–98; and Eric J. Sundquist, "*Benito Cereno* and New

World Slavery," in the same volume, which is akin to Emery in its assertion that the novella plays on antebellum "American paranoia about Spanish, Catholic, slaveholding despotism" even as it undermines beliefs that the supposedly "Puritan, Anglo-Saxon spirit of liberty and religious freedom" has been perfectly manifested in the United States (156). Robert Levine notes how the American captain's mistaken perception of African rebels as monks "exemplifies the way in which fears of Catholic immigrants and blacks permeated one another in the mid-1850s" (*Conspiracy and Romance*, 225).

14. Early in *Moby-Dick* the narrator, Ishmael, employs religious language as he cites Jackson as the handpicked champion of America's God: "Bear me out in it, thou great democratic God! . . . Thou who didst pick up Andrew Jackson from the pebbles; who didst hurl him upon a war-horse; who didst thunder him higher than a throne! Thou who, in all Thy mighty, earthly marchings, ever cullest Thy selectest champions from the kingly commons; bear me out in it, O God!" (103–4).

15. My goal here is not to argue that all southern Gothic fictions might somehow be connected to Catholicism (Latin or otherwise) or fears of it. But a significant number are, including work by not only Poe and other authors addressed here but also Kate Chopin, Flannery O'Connor, Katherine Anne Porter, and Tennessee Williams. See Haddox for more on Catholicism generally as a source of fear in southern literature.

16. Quoted in Parini 86.

17. See, for example, Haddox, chap. 1, on Louisiana and Creole "Catholic miscegenations" in literature.

18. See Agiro on Faulkner's portrayal of Italians generally; Lind on religious tensions in *Light in August*; and Hays on race and religion in *Light in August*. Faulkner's interest in Willa Cather's novel *Death Comes for the Archbishop* (1927), which dramatizes Catholic life in the Southwest following the Mexican-American War, is also relevant here.

19. Faulkner's use of the term *puritan* in this period is a subject in and of itself. Bleikasten has perhaps explored it most extensively, particularly with regard to race in *Light in August*. The implicit association of "puritanism" and capitalism in *Absalom, Absalom!* may reflect the prominence of Max Weber's *Protestant Ethic and the Spirit of Capitalism* (1904–5) in early-twentieth-century intellectual circles.

20. The Gothic contrast between the two worlds is concisely highlighted in Mr. Compson's description of Sutpen's younger and legitimate son, Henry, as he enters a "foreign and paradoxical" New Orleans: "this grim humorless yokel out of a granite heritage where even the houses, let alone the clothing and conduct, are built in the image of a jealous and sadistic Jehovah, put suddenly down in a place whose citizens had created their All-Powerful and His supporting hierarchy-chorus of beautiful saints and handsome angels in the image of their houses and personal ornaments and voluptuous lives" (86). Charles Bon gradually exposes Henry to the city with its architecture "a little curious, a little femininely flamboyant and therefore to Henry opulent, sensuous, sinful," before finally introducing him to his own octoroon mistress—who lives behind "a curiously monastic doorway in a neighborhood a little decadent, even a little sinister" (88). For more on Bon as "cultural shibboleth," see Campbell, and especially Crowell, who convincingly analyzes Bon's aesthetic decadence and identity as an "androgynous pseudoaristocrat" as indebted to Oscar Wilde. Crowell fails

to note Wilde's lifelong association with Catholicism, but she thoroughly links *Absalom, Absalom!* to Wilde's "modern gothic tale" *The Picture of Dorian Gray* and even highlights the author's perceived racial ambiguity as an Irishman in a nineteenth-century milieu in which the Irish were frequently linked to Africans.

21. Allen Tate's reading of many of Poe's narrators as Cartesian male intellects who simultaneously objectify and fear (female) bodies undoubtedly influenced Percy's reading of Poe.

22. Franchot asserts that "Puritan and later Protestant captivity narratives" strangely resembled Gothic texts as they posited a "demonic" kinship between "the Catholic European and the American Indian" (88–89). Percy is also in some sense reflecting in the novel on his own family heritage, his own transition from being a young "post-Protestant" in Alabama and Mississippi to an adult Catholic convert in Louisiana. For more on Percy's extended family history, "Gothic" in its own right, see Wyatt-Brown.

23. See Hebert on Lance, Percival, and gender.

24. From Percy's own perspective, what is finally horrifying is not Percival's Catholicism, which via the sacraments stresses the union of body and soul; what is horrifying is Lance's own tendency to deny and distrust the body, to divide body and soul—or more precisely body and mind—in two. Late in the novel he openly expresses his anger at a God or at least a nature which his narrowly "scientific" perspective has convinced him has designed men to be rapists and women to submit to rape. To Lance human biology itself finally seems a trap, a limiting enclosure, and he expresses this conviction in ways that recall the earlier Gothic association of the body with a confining Catholicism. Most extended is the late scene, in which he secretly approaches Margot and her lover together in bed. The bed itself, he says, looks "like a cathedral, a Gothic bed, posts as thick as trees, carved and fluted and tapering to spires and gargoyles above the canopy. The headboard was as massive and complex as an altar screen. Panels of openwork braced posts and rails like flying buttresses" (237). Lance kneels behind one of these "buttresses," listening to his wife and her lover—who seem to be one body—and posing himself as "an unconsecrated priest hearing an impenitent confession." This is in fact Lance and Margot's own marriage bed and therefore an apt symbol of how Lance has come to see marriage and sex itself: not as potentially saving sacrament but as Gothic enclosure.

25. Cromwell would be of particular interest to McCarthy given his Irish Catholic upbringing (note the central presence of the Irish Tobin, a kind of counterpart to the kid, in *Blood Meridian*). British and later Anglo-American colonial activity in the New World bears at least a broad resemblance to British colonial activity in Ireland, where Anglo-Protestant settlers pushed the native Irish Catholic culture farther and farther into the west (see Brickman and Potts on McCarthy's interest in Irish identity). Also relevant to the character of the Judge: Fessenden traces the intrinsic connection of literacy and Anglo-Protestant dominance in the emergent United States from the colonial period up until the Civil War. Citing a number of primary documents, Fessenden demonstrates how Puritans wrote natives out of American history not only by "likening Indians to beasts and colonists to biblical personae" but also by representing the native "idolaters" as bereft of interiority, as actual "embodiments . . . of the Second Commandment's violation," and—accordingly—

as appropriate objects of iconoclastic violence resembling that exercised by Puritans upon medieval Christian artifacts in the British Isles (21, 23).

26. There is no haunted house in *Blood Meridian*, but the image of the Mexican landscape as stained altarstone, among others, suggests how the natural world itself is ultimately figured as a haunted enclosure in the novel—much as it is in some of Melville's Gothic fiction, most obviously "The Encantadas" (see my essays "Melville's Monkish Fables" and "Violence, Nature, and Prophecy in Flannery O'Connor and Cormac McCarthy"). For different but finally complementary perspectives on religious imagery in *Blood Meridian*, see also Spurgeon; and my essay "Joyce and Contesting Priesthoods in *Suttree* and *Blood Meridian*."

27. Given his impending doom, the kid and the dead woman here mirror the image of the Virgin and decapitated child in the desecrated church at the novel's beginning. For a reading of Catholic iconography and the feminine in McCarthy's *Suttree*—his last novel before *Blood Meridian*—see Woodson.

WORKS CITED

Argiro, Thomas. "'As though we were kin': Faulkner's Black-Italian Chiasmus." *MELUS* 28.3 (Fall 2003): 111–32.

Baldick, Chris, and Robert Mighall. "Gothic Criticism." In *A Companion to the Gothic*, ed. David Punter, 209–28. Oxford: Blackwell, 2000.

Beecher, Jonathan. "Echoes of Toussaint Louverture and the Haitian Revolution in Melville's 'Benito Cereno.'" *Leviathan: A Journal of Melville Studies* 9.2 (June 2007): 43–58.

Bleikasten, Andre. *The Ink of Melancholy.* Bloomington: Indiana University Press, 1990.

Boyagoda, Randy. "Just Where and What Is 'the (comparatively speaking) South'? Caribbean Writers on Melville and Faulkner." *Mississippi Quarterly* 57.1 (Winter 2003–4): 65–73.

Brickman, Barbara. "Imposition and Resistance in *The Orchard Keeper*." In *Myth, Legend, Dust: Critical Responses to Cormac McCarthy*, ed. Rick Wallach, 55–67. Manchester, Eng.: Manchester University Press, 2000.

Burkholder, Robert E., ed. *Critical Essays on Herman Melville's "Benito Cereno."* New York: G. K. Hall & Co., 1992.

Campbell, Erin E. "'The nigger that's going to sleep with your sister': Charles Bon as Cultural Shibboleth in *Absalom, Absalom!*" In *Songs of the Reconstructing South: Building Literary Louisiana, 1865–1945*, ed. Suzanne Disheroon-Green and Lisa Abney. Westport, Conn.: Greenwood Press, 2002.

Crèvecoeur, J. Hector St. John de. *Letters from an American Farmer.* New York: Penguin, 1981.

Crowell, Ellen. "The Picture of Charles Bon: Oscar Wilde's Trip through Faulkner's Yoknapatawpha." *Modern Fiction Studies* 50.3 (Fall 2004): 595–631.

DeGuzman, Maria. *Spain's Long Shadow: The Black Legend, Off-Whiteness, and Anglo-American Empire.* Minneapolis: University of Minnesota Press, 2005.

Emery, Allan Moore. "'Benito Cereno' and Manifest Destiny." In Burkholder 99–115.

Faulkner, William. *Absalom, Absalom!* New York: Vintage, 1986.

Fessenden, Tracy. *Culture and Redemption: Religion, the Secular, and American Literature.* Princeton: Princeton University Press, 2007.

Franchot, Jenny. *Roads to Rome: The Antebellum Protestant Encounter with Catholicism.* Berkeley: University of California Press, 1994.

Gatta, John. *American Madonna: Images of the Divine Woman in Literary Culture.* New York: Oxford University Press, 1997.

Goddu, Teresa A. *Gothic America.* New York: Columbia University Press, 1997.

Goldschmidt, Henry, and Elizabeth McAlister. *Race, Nation, and Religion in the Americas.* New York: Oxford University Press, 2004.

Haddox, Thomas. *Fears and Fascinations: Representing Catholicism in the American South.* New York: Fordham University Press, 2005.

Hawthorne, Nathaniel. *The Scarlet Letter and Other Writings.* New York: Norton, 2005.

Hays, Peter L. "Racial Predestination in *Light in August*: The Elect and the Damned." *English Language Notes* 33.2 (December 1995): 62–69.

Hebert, Maria. "Between Men: Homosocial Desire in Walker Percy's *Lancelot.*" *Mississippi Quarterly* 56.1 (Winter 2002–3): 125–45.

Hoeveler, Diane Long. "Inventing the Gothic Subject: Revolution, Secularization, and the Discourse of Suffering." In *Inventing the Individual: Romanticism and the Idea of Individualism*, ed. Larry H. Peer, 5–16. Provo, Utah: International Conference on Romanticism, 2002.

Levander, Caroline, and Robert Levine, eds. *Hemispheric American Studies.* New Brunswick: Rutgers University Press, 2008.

Levine, Robert. *Conspiracy and Romance: Studies in Brockden Brown, Cooper, Hawthorne, and Melville.* Cambridge: Cambridge University Press, 1989.

Lewis, R.W.B. *The American Adam.* Chicago: University of Chicago Press, 1959.

Lind, Ilse Dusoir. "The Calvinistic Burden of *Light in August.*" *New England Quarterly* 30.3 (September 1957): 307–29.

Lloyd-Smith, Allan. "Nineteenth-Century American Gothic." In *A Companion to the Gothic*, ed. David Punter, 109–21. Oxford: Blackwell, 2001.

McCarthy, Cormac. *Blood Meridian.* New York: Vintage, 1992.

McConville, Brendan. *The King's Three Faces: The Rise and Fall of Royal America, 1689–1776.* Chapel Hill: University of North Carolina Press, 2006.

Melville, Herman. *Billy Budd and Other Tales*. New York: Penguin, 1986.

———. *Moby-Dick*. New York: Norton, 2002.

Miles, Robert. "Abjection, Nationalism, and the Gothic." In *The Gothic*, ed. Fred Botting, 47–70. Cambridge: Brewer, 2001.

———. "The Gothic and Ideology." In *Approaches to Teaching Gothic Fiction*, ed. Diane Long Hoeveler and Tamar Heller, 58–65. New York: MLA, 2003.

Newton, Arvin. "Melville and the Gothic Novel." *New England Quarterly* 22.1 (March 1949): 33–48.

O'Connor, Flannery. *The Habit of Being*. New York: Farrar, Straus and Giroux, 1988.

O'Gorman, Farrell. "Joyce and Contesting Priesthoods in *Suttree* and *Blood Meridian*." *Cormac McCarthy Journal* 5.1 (2005): 100–117.

———. "Melville's 'Monkish Fables' of the 1850s: Catholic Bodies Haunting the New World." MS.

———. "Violence, Nature, and Prophecy in Flannery O'Connor and Cormac McCarthy." In *Flannery O'Connor and the Age of Terrorism*, ed. Robert Donahoo and Avis Hewitt. Knoxville: University of Tennessee Press, 2010.

Parini, Jay. *One Matchless Time: A Life of William Faulkner*. New York: Harper Collins, 2005.

Percy, Walker. *Lancelot*. New York: Picador, 1999.

Poe, Edgar Allan. *The Selected Writings of Edgar Allan Poe*. New York: Norton, 2004.

Potts, James. "McCarthy, Mac Airt, and Mythology: *Suttree* and the Irish High King." *Mississippi Quarterly* 58.12 (Winter 2004–Spring 2005): 25–39.

Richardson, Miles. *Being-in-Christ and Putting Death in Its Place: An Anthropologist's Account of Christian Performance in Spanish America and the American South*. Baton Rouge: Louisiana State University Press, 2003.

Sealts, Merton M., Jr. *Melville's Reading*. Columbia: University of South Carolina Press, 1988.

Smith, Jon, and Deborah Cohn, eds. *Look Away! The U.S. South in New World Studies*. Durham, N.C.: Duke University Press, 2004.

Spurgeon, Sara. "The Sacred Hunter and the Eucharist of the Wilderness: Mythic Reconstructions in *Blood Meridian*." In *Cormac McCarthy: New Directions*, ed. James Lilley, 75–101. Albuquerque: University of New Mexico Press, 2002.

Walpole, Horace. *The Castle of Otranto*. New York: Oxford University Press, 1996.

Woodson, Linda. "Visual Rhetoric and Cognitive Identity in *Suttree*." *Cormac McCarthy Journal* 5.1 (2005): 171–83.

Wyatt-Brown, Bertram. *The House of Percy*. New York: Oxford University Press, 1994.

# The Jack Burden of Southern History
*Robert Penn Warren, C. Vann Woodward, and Historical Practice*

ANNE MARSHALL

I n November 1968 historian C. Vann Woodward and novelist Robert
Penn Warren appeared together at a symposium at the annual meeting of the Southern Historical Association in New Orleans. Their
panel was entitled "The Uses of History in Fiction" and included southern writers Ralph Ellison and William Styron, whose controversial new
book, *The Confessions of Nat Turner,* provided the genesis for the gathering.
The star-studded cadre of writers aimed to probe the boundaries of history and fiction, facts and truths, and the boundaries of each. The session was a contentious one. There were some extremely tense exchanges
between the author and audience members during the question-and-
answer period as several attendees voiced their disapproval of Styron's
portrayal of Nat Turner as a rage-filled, would-be rapist of white women.
In a year that saw Martin Luther King Jr.'s assassination, Detroit go up in
flames, and police release tear gas at the Democratic National Convention, the atmosphere that night at the Jung Hotel merely reflected the
tensions of the times. But none in attendance could have missed the
point that examining the southern past, whether in historical scholarship
or fiction, was fraught with peril and pain.[1]

Despite the session's focus on Styron's fictionalized version of a historical figure, Woodward, as the moderator of the panel, focused much attention and praise on his good friend Robert Penn Warren. At one juncture

in the conversation, he lauded Warren's early books for "constitut[ing] a moral history of the South," and at another he turned the discussion to Warren's famous protagonist, Jack Burden, from his novel *All the King's Men* (1946). In front of the room full of southern historians, Woodward recalled, "Jack Burden, incidentally, was an historian, a seeker of a Ph.D., as some of us have been." He probed his friend and Yale colleague to make the distinction between Burden's ability to collect "facts" in his research and his quest for historical truth within the plotline of Warren's Pulitzer Prize–winning novel, saying, "I think it's to the nub of our discussion, perhaps." Warren concurred that Burden's investigative journey, which was marked by an incomplete dissertation and ended with the suicide of the man he discovered to be his own father, was indeed a parable about the difference between "fact" and "truth" and his protagonist's inability to face up to moral dilemmas, both past and present.[2]

While this high-profile panel probably constituted the most famous discussion Warren and Woodward shared on the subject, it was only a small portion of the extended professional conversation that they had with one another in print and in person about the confluence of literature and history and the value of fiction to historians. One of the themes that becomes implicit and explicit in their work, both scholarly and fictional, is the ability of southern literature to reveal the pain in southern history and involved in writing about that past. Following these connections between Woodward, Warren, and Warren's character Jack Burden reveals insights into the historian's task of shouldering the "burden of southern history."

I first encountered C. Vann Woodward, Robert Penn Warren, and Jack Burden nearly thirty years after the Southern Historical Association panel discussion. I was a college senior taking a course entitled "Southern Literary Renaissance" for elective credit, and at the time I had no context for their relationship to one another. By the time I took the class, I was in the midst of applying to graduate programs. I was a history major who wanted to pursue a Ph.D. degree, but I was not sure which area or time period of history I wanted to study. The literature I encountered in that course led me to decide that I would become a scholar of southern history, and two books in particular, Woodward's 1960 collection of essays entitled *The Burden of Southern History,* and Warren's *All the King's Men,* inspired me to do so.[3]

I am certainly not the first historian whom the Renaissance writers have led to the well of southern history. Working in the 1920s and 1930s, they produced an extraordinary body of fiction that established the South as a place with a separate, distinct identity—one that was based on a history that deviated from that of the rest of the United States. They created what Allen Tate called "a literature conscious of the past in the present" and a distinctive identity for the South. They did so, however, by stripping away "Lost Cause" mythology and taking an unsentimental look at the region's past in a manner that has since beckoned generations of historians to take a harder, less apologetic look at southern history.[4]

Reading *The Burden of Southern History* and *All the King's Men* in tandem introduced me to both the gravitational pull of southern history and its problematic nature. It was historian Woodward who, for the first time, posited that such darkness was the cornerstone of southern distinctiveness in his collection of essays, *The Burden of Southern History*. In this slim volume, which has become a foundational treatise on southern exceptionalism, Woodward posited that the features that made the South distinctive were not elements of honor, gentility, tradition, and grace. The marrow of southern history was, instead, dark and complicated. This was an intriguing revelation to me. But I was just as captivated by Robert Penn Warren's protagonist in *All the King's Men,* Jack Burden. He was the tortured, erstwhile history graduate student who provided me my first glimpse of both the attractions and the pitfalls of studying southern history. Beyond the fact that one was real and the other fictional, these two historians were pretty different from one another. Woodward was the staid, pipe-smoking, elbow patch–wearing ordained dean of southern history who provided me with my historical bearings. Jack Burden, on the other hand, was southern history's alienated youth.

I am struck each time I think of Woodward, Warren, and Burden as points of origin on my scholarly journey by how interconnected they were in both their sectional outlook and by their personal and professional camaraderie. It was, after all, from Robert Penn Warren's admonition (as spoken by Jack Burden) that people needed to "accept the past and its burden" that Woodward drew the title for his collection. Beyond this, however, both Warren's and Woodward's work speak to what was at the time they wrote a new awareness of the dark and troublesome nature of the southern past itself as well as to the responsibility borne by those who would research, interpret, and write that history.[5]

In his seminal 1958 essay, "The Search for Southern Identity," which later became part of *The Burden of Southern History,* Woodward articulated the concept that the South was an exception from American exceptionalism and that the region's distinctiveness was to be found in its past. Writing before the Vietnam War, Woodward asserted that, unlike the nation's past as a whole, southern history "includes large components of frustration, failure, and defeat." With their messy history of poverty, Civil War loss, and persistent racism, southerners had been left out of both the reality and the pervasive mythology of American prosperity, military success, and national innocence.[6]

As Woodward shifted the paradigm of southern history, he suggested that it was an entirely different discipline—literature—to which southerners could look for the survival of their unique heritage. Woodward contended that, in the face of modern development and the homogenizing cultural forces (including desegregation) which had, by the late 1950s, started to make the South look more like the rest of the country, it would not be the continuance of these historical trends that would maintain southern distinctiveness. Rather, it was through the fictional work of William Faulkner, Eudora Welty, Robert Penn Warren, and Thomas Wolfe—and within what Allen Tate called "the peculiar historical consciousness of the Southern writer"—that southern identity would endure. As Woodward explained: "The themes which inspired the major writers have not been the flattering myths nor the romantic dreams of the South's past. Disdaining the polemics of defense and justification, they have turned instead to the somber realities of hardship and defeat and evil and [as Faulkner once described] 'the problems of the human heart in conflict with itself.'"[7]

Woodward continued to emphasize the role of southern writers in giving "history meaning and value and significance" in yet another essay in *Burden* entitled "The Historical Dimension." He highlighted the debt historians owed to the region's novelists and what he called the "vital relations between the crafts" of history and literature. He gave special praise to Renaissance authors for being the first to lay bare the region's problems: "The best of the southern novelists have never set out to defend the values or the prejudices or the errors of any particular age or section," he contended. With implicit criticism of those in his own profession for taking an apologetic and romantic approach to writing about the southern past, he said of southern novelists: "It is true that their books are often filled with tales of horror and lust and betrayal and degradation. But they have not paused to reckon their popularity in attacking the values of their own age or any other. They have not set up as defenders of a cause, either one lost or one still sought. They have proved themselves able to confront the chaos and irony of history with the admission that they can fit them into no neat pattern and explain them by no pat theory."[8]

Woodward no doubt had the work of Robert Penn Warren in mind when he referenced the "chaos and irony of history." In *The Burden of Southern History* Woodward, who greatly admired Warren's use of history in his fictional writings, credited him with being "the southern novelist who comes nearest approaching an historical subject after the manner of an historian" and dedicated the entire volume to him. He would later write that "the dedication and the title could only begin to suggest the influence of the man and his work and my sense of indebtedness to him." Decades later, in his memoir *Thinking Back,* Woodward remembered that it was Warren and his fellow authors who revealed to him the possibilities of southern history: they "wrote about the obscure, the provincial, the eccentric, the tormented, and the humble—the uncelebrated," and "if obscurity and provinciality of subject matter prove not obstacle to literature, why should they prove so to history?" He particularly celebrated "the appeal of Warren's complex attitudes toward history, the art with which he used history in his poetry and fiction, and his scorn of using it as 'a private alibi-factory' for losers or as a 'treasury of virtue' for winners."[9]

While Woodward admired Warren's ability to embrace the complexity of southern history, he certainly realized that the novelist was himself an example of the contradictions within it. Despite his ability to portray the harsh realities of the southern past, Warren's most famous early writing was marked by a sense of wistful affection for the very rural institutions that Woodward became so famous for demythologizing. The Guthrie, Kentucky, native and future Rhodes Scholar became friends with Fugitive writers Donald Davidson, John Crowe Ransom, and Allen Tate during his college days at Vanderbilt University. In 1930 he contributed an essay to their seminal collection *I'll Take My Stand,* a manifesto that raged against the industrialization of the South and lamented its perceived corrosive effects on southern culture.

The fact that Woodward was exhilarated by Warren's approach to history did not stop him from criticizing the nostalgia for a preindustrial southern past intrinsic to the Agrarians' work. In 1939 he published a review of a book by Herman Clarence Nixon, a contributor to *I'll Take My Stand*, in the *Southern Review*, the literary magazine that Warren had cofounded. In it he criticized agrarianism as an "ideological witch." Warren struck back, complaining to his friend Frank Owsley that the review was "damned silly," and accused Woodward of mischaracterizing the Agrarian movement with "the usual clichés about agrarianism—plantation system, magnolias, and that bilge." Although he referred to him as "the fellow who did what I considered a pretty good biography of Tom Watson," Warren commissioned a rebuttal of Woodward's Nixon review for the next issue of the *Southern Review*.[10]

In time, however, the admiration between Warren and Woodward became mutual. They became friends and, in 1961, colleagues at Yale. Woodward credited Warren with helping Yale woo him away from his job at Johns Hopkins by holding a party in his honor at which "were assembled fellow Southerners to assure me that I would not feel too lonely in Yankeedom." Indeed, Woodward wrote on more than one occasion that he and Warren's status as "exiles in alien territory" and "exiles from the South" bound them even closer. They came to refer to one another by their familiar nicknames, "Red" (because of Warren's hair color) and "Vann," and often read and critiqued each other's in-progress writings. Late in his life Warren would write Woodward of the kinship he felt with him, saying, "Our early lives were almost parallel in various ways. In one way or another, allowing for differences, our situations were remarkably similar. . . . The relation, that is, to the worlds in which we grew up . . . and my (late) passion, that's the word, for reading American history." Warren, by his own admission, never measured up to Woodward's talents as a historian. When asked by an interviewer once whether he would ever be interested in writing archivally based history, he replied, "No, no. I wouldn't have any interest in doing that. Besides, I'm not qualified. I'm not Vann Woodward. I'm terribly interested in history, but writing it is not for me. . . . If you're going to be a good historian, it's a very demanding profession."[11]

Despite Warren's modesty, writers and historians have consistently and ardently championed Warren's use of the historical discipline. Literary scholars have long acclaimed Warren's historical consciousness and the keen eye for historical detail he displayed in his carefully constructed backdrops, whether they be antebellum New Orleans, Kentucky's early-twentieth-century Black Patch Tobacco War, or Depression-era Louisiana. Warren even ventured to try what few novelists would, writing a handful of historical works on subjects such as John Brown and the Alamo. For him the boundaries of historical and fictional writing were fluid. He knew they were for everyday Americans too. One of his hallmarks was the particular attention he paid to the role of mythology in history. Long before examining historical memory became a major historiographical trend in the late twentieth century, in works such as *The Legacy of the Civil War* Warren was exploring the ramifications of what Americans remember and what they choose to forget. Perhaps even more important, Warren recognized, well before the rise of postmodern theory, the acute weakness of historians—the futility that is the task of piecing together a reliable portrait of the past. In his novel *World Enough and Time*, for example, Warren's narrator explains the task of a historian this way: "Puzzling over what is left, we are like the scientist fumbling with a tooth and thigh bone to reconstruct for a museum some great, stupid beast extinct with the ice age."[12]

It is not surprising, then, that Warren could construct such a convincing student of history as Jack Burden and that he would place him and his historical craft at the center of what would become his most important novel. It is also not so unpredictable that this character would seem so compelling to an aspiring graduate student like me. Looking back on it, though, it does seem a bit odd that I would see in Burden a sort of role model. He is, after all, what no graduate student wants to be—someone who never finishes his or her dissertation. I think what intrigued me so much about Jack was that he provided a cautionary tale not merely because of his inability to finish his work but also because of the manner in which he so candidly identifies the cause of his own failure. His downfall, he admits, comes because he has "tried to discover the truth and not the facts" of history. "Then when the truth was not to be discovered, or discovered could not be understood by me," he continues, "I could not bear to live with the cold-eyed reproach of the facts."[13]

The facts and the truth that Jack Burden tries to discover revolve around the subject of his dissertation, a man named Cass Mastern. Mastern, whom Jack presumes to be his great-uncle, is a man of humble Georgia red-dirt farming origins, who, with the help of his older brother Gilbert, becomes a rather successful Mississippi cotton planter. He later joins the Confederate army and dies wounded in 1864 in an Atlanta hospital. The trajectory of Mastern's life is, on the face of it, not so extraordinary and only comes to Jack's attention when he inherits Mastern's personal relics. These private archives, which Warren inventories in careful detail, include "a large packet of letters, eight tattered black-bound account books tied together with faded red tape, a photograph, about five by eight inches, mounted on cardboard and stained in its lower half by water, and a plain gold ring, man-sized, with some engraving in it, on a loop of string." Upon a professor's suggestion, Jack sets out to write a biography of Mastern and a social history of his time.[14]

Jack gets more than he bargained for when he begins investigating what his nineteenth-century kinsman describes as his time of "darkness and trouble." This sordid portion of Cass's life begins when his brother Gilbert dispatches him from Mississippi to Lexington, Kentucky, to Transylvania College to obtain a proper gentleman's education. There Cass proves a quick study not only in Latin and Greek but in the pleasures of gambling, drinking, and horse racing. It is also in Lexington that he embarks on a forbidden love affair with his best friend's wife. Cass's brazenly indiscreet relationship with his married love continues for a year and a half, until her husband, Cass's friend, dies after shooting himself (apparently accidentally) while cleaning his pistol.

In the wake of the tragedy Cass learns from his lover that his friend had learned of their affair and had staged his suicide to look like an accident. The only other person to discover this truth is his lover's slave, Phebe. Unable to face the chance that Phebe will reveal her horrible secret, and unable to face the judgment she would forever see in her face, Cass's widowed lover secrets her bondswoman off to western Kentucky. There she sells her to some traders, who intend to install the light-skinned Phebe in a New Orleans brothel. When Cass learns of their plan, he begins to drown in reverberations from his actions: "I suddenly felt that the world outside me was shifting and the substance of things," he writes in his journal, "and that the process had only begun of a general disintegration of which I was the center."[15]

Unable to cope with the idea that his romantic indiscretion led not only to the death of his friend but to the sale of Phebe away from her home and husband into sexual slavery, Cass feels "as though the vibration set up in the whole fabric of the world by my act had spread infinitely and with ever increasing power and no man could know the end." He endeavors to atone for his sins by trying to track down Phebe in order to purchase her from the trader. Unsuccessful, he returns to his Mississippi plantation and, after a period of contemplation, decides to free his own slaves— "to relieve my spirit of a burden, the burden of their misery and their eyes upon me." When the Civil War begins, Cass marches into battle for a cause in which he does not believe, wearing his betrayed friend's wedding ring on a string tucked inside his butternut coat and bearing a death wish that is eventually fulfilled in a crowded, stinking military hospital.[16]

Warren constructs the Mastern episode with the sensibilities of a historian. His descriptions of Jack's historical detective work and his explanations of how, as a historian, he pieces together the details of Mastern's story are central to the narrative. For example, Cass Mastern never pens the name of his lover or his wronged friend. We only know their names were Annabelle and Duncan Trice because Warren tells us that Jack discovers their identity in an obituary in some Lexington newspaper files from the 1850s. He informs us that Jack travels to Lexington to visit the physical setting of Mastern's story, including the former Trice residence, where the secret tryst took place. In a similar fashion Warren takes care to define the provenance of each bit of knowledge that Mastern leaves and that Burden collects. He does so in a way that, as one scholar has written, makes the reader "aware of the closeness of history." Together, the sparse and despairing relics left by Cass Mastern and the corroborating evidence that Burden unearths combine to create the tragic tale.[17]

Despite this surfeit of primary evidence that grows into a stack of three-by-five-inch index cards, Warren tells us that "the day came when Jack Burden sat down [to write his dissertation] and realized that he did not know Cass Mastern. He did not have to know Cass Mastern to get the degree; he only had to know the facts about Cass Mastern's world. But without knowing Cass Mastern, he could not put down the facts about Cass Mastern's world." Rather, Jack sits night after night, staring at Mastern's photograph and writing nothing. After a period of inert depression he calls the "Great Sleep," Jack walks away from it all. He leaves graduate school with no dissertation, no degree in hand, to become a journalist and then, of course, Willie Stark's all-purpose minion, in which capacity he puts his research skills to good use digging up dirt on his boss's political opponents.[18]

Two decades later Warren elaborated on the source of Jack's paralysis at the 1968 Southern Historical Association symposium. When pushed by Woodward to make a distinction between fact and truth in relation to Burden's inability to complete his dissertation, Warren replied: "The question about his peculiar researches, as I look back on them, is simply this. Being a very badly disorganized fellow, he didn't really want the Ph.D. anyway." After investigating Cass Mastern, a man who ends up taking improbable actions in order to "find a moral position for himself," Burden, who is "without any moral orientation for himself . . . (he's an old-fashioned lost boy, not the new kind—there have always been these lost boys)," "couldn't face the fact that in his own blood, there was a man who *had* faced up to a moral problem in a deep way. He couldn't follow it through, could not bear to face the comparison to the other young man." Warren also admitted under Woodward's questioning that Burden's investigative journey was a parable about the difference between "fact" and "truth." While truths may seem to be more elusive and menacing than empirical and indifferent facts, Warren noted that the latter could be dangerous too. "Well, the facts Jack Burden gets are deadly things. Facts may kill. For one thing, they can kill myths," he said.[19]

Within the framework of *All the King's Men* the Cass Mastern episode occupies only a single chapter set in the middle of the book. Despite its brief appearance, literary scholars have consistently underscored the installment's importance as central to Warren's narrative structure. Jack's scholarly investigation of Mastern mirrors the detective work that he does later for Willie Stark in looking into what he calls the "case of the upright Judge." Even in his contemporary historical research, Jack realizes the power of history. He wields it to jar his physician friend Adam Stanton, who is a man of science, out of his "All tidy. All neat" world of predictable behavior by giving him what he calls a "history lesson." Using information he has exhumed in the course of his investigation, he informs Stanton that, as governor, his father had engaged in corrupt dealings, thereby disabusing Adam of his own proud, dignified past. This knowledge eventually causes Adam to assassinate Willie Stark, an act for which he is then shot and killed. These turn of events cause Jack to experience firsthand what Cass Mastern had learned: that "life is all of one piece . . . an enormous spider web and if you touch it, however lightly, at any point, the vibration ripples to the remotest perimeter and the drowsy spider feels the tingle and is drowsy no more but springs out to . . . inject the black, numbing poison under your hide." Despite the parallel structure of Mastern's and Burden's stories, however, this chapter of the book was omitted from the first British edition of the novel as well as from both the 1949 and the 2006 film versions.[20]

Yet for many historically minded people, the Cass Mastern episode is the heart of *All the King's Men*. As a history graduate student, I reread the novel several times and on each occasion found new aspects of this portion of the book to admire. Key among them was Warren's unflinching portrayal of the most sinister aspects of slavery at a time when most influential historians still considered the "peculiar institution" a benign relic of the southern past. In his effort to drive home the viciousness of human bondage, Warren turns to thick historical description and a supporting cast of real historical characters, including the odious Lewis Robards, a major Lexington slave trader infamous for running a kidnapping ring in which he captured and sold legally free African Americans. In one scene Cass Mastern visits Robards's barracoon, where he finds a New Orleans slave buyer physically examining and sexually objectifying a mulatto woman who is, like Phebe, bound for a life in a New Orleans brothel. Warren also recounts an instance of cruelty in the tale of another real-life infamous Lexington resident, Caroline Turner. Turner was a native Bostonian turned slave owner who, in a fit of rage, threw one her slave boys out of a second-story window, crippling him for life. She was eventually killed some years later by another of her slaves, who strangled her as she was beating him.

As an undergraduate, I had found these vivid and unsparing representations of the peculiar institution to be disconcerting but not surprising. It was only as a graduate student that I realized that, at the time Warren wrote these scenes, U. B. Phillips's argument that slavery had been a civilizing agent for African Americans still remained the historiographical standard. It would be another ten years after the publication of *All the*

*King's Men* before historians such as Stanley Elkins and Kenneth Stampp began to alter the state of the field by arguing that slavery was indeed brutal and exploitive. As historian James C. Cobb has noted, it was authors such as Warren who, "in the absence of a critical historical tradition," in the early twentieth century were the ones who began to question the historical narrative implicit in the Lost Cause version of history. For southern writers in the 1930s and 1940s the burden was not just the history itself but how to cut through the lies that southern historians, plantation school writers, and everyday citizens had told themselves and the outside world about their past. No one felt this more keenly than C. Vann Woodward, who, invigorated by the interpretational spirit of the Renaissance writers, arrived to pursue his Ph.D. degree at the University of North Carolina barely a decade before *All the King's Men* appeared. In his memoirs he described his disappointment at finding a southern historical establishment averse to any interpretation that might counter the "regional consensus" that southern history was about continuity between Old South and New, white solidarity and black inferiority. "What a striking contrast, what a letdown, what a falling off!" he remembered, "No renaissance here, no surge of innovation and creativity, no rebirth of energy, no compelling new vision."[21]

Warren himself, and not only his characters, knew something about grappling with the burden of southern history. Over the course of his career, his own ability to face up to the evil legacy of slavery and the southern past clearly evolved. In his contribution to *I'll Take My Stand,* an essay entitled "The Briar Patch," which he penned in 1930, Warren considered the situation of African Americans in the South since the Civil War. He essentially endorsed the segregated status quo and maintained that black southerners' best hope was to seek self-sufficiency through vocational education and by continuing to work at agrarian pursuits. Warren offered a very circumscribed vision of racial progress, writing with detached sterility: "The rural life provides the most satisfactory relationship of the two races which can be found at present, or which can be clearly imagined if all aspects of the situation are, without prejudice, taken into account." As his friend Ralph Ellison later remarked, he appeared in this essay to be "orthodox and unreconstructed."[22]

Warren later came to view these conclusions with painful regret. By 1964 he had written two volumes that called for desegregation and racial equality: *Segregation: The Inner Conflict of the South* in 1956 and *Who Speaks for the Negro?* in 1964, two introspective works that looked at his own complicated relationship with the subject. Years before he recanted his "Briar Patch" doctrine in these books, however, Warren had displayed a much more conflicted, unsparing view of the South's racial woes in his novels. Moreover, Warren credited the form of fiction for forcing him to confront the ills of slavery and Jim Crow segregation. He remembered that, while writing "The Briar Patch," he felt the "jangle and wrangle of writing the essay and some kind of discomfort in it, some sense of evasion. . . . In a little while I realized I simply couldn't have written that essay again. I guess trying to write fiction made me realize that. If you are seriously trying to write fiction, you can't allow yourself as much evasion as in trying to write essays." In a later interview he repeated this assertion and elaborated: "Fiction involves, simply, your reseeing in your imagination a world, and this brings the problem of your immediate response, your immediate feeling about what you are seeing, without justification, without intellectualization." Here Warren seems to be providing one reason for why some southern novelists were able to assess the southern past so honestly long before the region's historians could.[23]

The Cass Mastern episode showcases how completely Warren's ability to wrestle with the sins of the southern past in fiction evolved. More than underscoring the corruptive evils of slavery, the Mastern episode points to the peculiar institution and all that it reveals about the weakness of human nature as nothing less than the basis of the burden of southern history. While Cass Mastern's transgressions begin with adultery, betrayal, and the subsequent death of his friend Duncan Trice, it is not for these sins that Cass Mastern tries to atone. Instead, Warren uses the sale of Phebe and sordid scenes portraying the worst acts of racial bondage to implicate the collective sin of antebellum white southerners. Despite the gripping personal intrigue that lies within the fourth chapter of *All the King's Men*, the Mastern narrative is, in the end, not so much a story of personal evil as a story that personifies the shared culpability of an entire region.

This is why Jack Burden finds it impossible to make sense of his subject's life. He muses that "perhaps he laid aside the journal of Cass Mastern not because he could not understand, but because he was afraid to understand for what might be understood there was a reproach to him."

Significantly, however, it is not simply Cass's adultery or betrayal with which Jack cannot come to terms. Certainly by the end of what he refers to as his "second excursion into the past"—his detective efforts on Willie Stark's behalf—he, like Cass, must deal with the unforeseen consequences of individual actions and uncovered truths. But those are lessons he would learn later. At the time he is wrestling with his dissertation, Jack, the southern historian, struggles to comprehend both the humanity and the profound inhumanity that he finds in Cass Mastern and, more fundamentally, in the southern past. As he explains later: "What we students of history always learn is that the human being is a very complicated contraption and that they are not good or bad but are good and bad and the good comes out of the bad and the bad comes out of the good, and the devil take the hindmost." While Jack may understand this truth, he finds himself incapable of making sense of it.[24]

In writing about a southern historian conflicted by his subject, Warren was, again, pushing historiographical boundaries. While Jack Burden was paralyzed by the reproach of southern history, professional historians were still dedicated to presenting the region's past as idyllic and righteous. The southern tragedy embodied in the Mastern episode was of a wholly different nature than the one invoked by the "Tragic era" interpretation of Reconstruction that was still in vogue at the time. And Cass Mastern, who is personally demoralized and guilt-ridden by his slave-owning paternalism, who dons his gray uniform "in anguish of spirit and hope of expiation," and for whom his musket is "but a meaningless burden," represents none of the esprit de corps touted by the Lost Cause interpretation of the Civil War. Within the Mastern narrative, then, Warren truly subverts the orthodox narrative of southern history of his time.[25]

But if I was admiring of Warren's willingness to punch large holes in regional paradigms, I was less sure of what to make of Jack Burden's inability to finish this historical project. Certainly, my perceptions of Jack's dissertorial efforts were shaped and altered on each subsequent reading by my own evolving graduate education. Poor Jack, I thought more than once. If only he had studied history after postmodernist theory took hold. Every second-year graduate student now knows there is no such thing as absolute historical objectivity, let alone a singular truth—historical, moral, or otherwise. A good dose of Jacques Derrida, Michel Foucault, or even Hayden White might have freed him from his hang-ups and enabled him to finish his task. But I was also learning that, at the same time historians deny objectivity, they also insist on having some distance from their subject. What responsible dissertation advisor would today endorse his or her student to write a biography of a family member, I thought? As historian Jill Lepore has written, "Finding out and writing about people, living or dead, is tricky work. It is necessary to balance intimacy with distance while at the same time being inquisitive to the point of invasiveness. Getting too close to your subject is a major danger, but not getting to know her well enough is just as likely." Given all these factors, it seems Jack was doomed from the start.[26]

In one sense it is ironic that Jack Burden finds those three-by-five index cards containing the life of a dead man he never knew impossible to surmount while he is later able to push forward finding the dirty past of people to whom he has much closer personal connections. But if he understands the southern past as one big reproach to human nature, he is in good company. The idea of southern history as burdensome has been something of a constant theme among historians and writers. Think, for example, of southern literary critic Louis D. Rubin's reference to the "impossible load of the past" or Woodward's assertion that his own dissertation on Tom Watson was a story that "plunged [him] into all the dark, neglected, and forbidden corners of Southern life" or the insistence of modern southern songwriters, the Drive-By Truckers, that examining southern life means exhuming the "dirt underneath." And who could forget how the darkness of Dixie, along with the nihilism and futility of the southern past, creep into Quentin Compson's chilly Harvard dorm room as he recalls Shreve McCannon's entreaty: "Tell about the South. . . . Why do they live there? Why do they live at all?"[27]

Certainly, southern history does not hold a monopoly on depression, as scholars of subjects such as conquest or genocide can attest. But, as C. Vann Woodward laid out in *The Burden of Southern History,* the "experience of evil and the experience of tragedy" are integral parts "of the Southern heritage" and the cornerstone of what made the region and its history distinctive. Perhaps it is not so much that the South has endured such a particularly awful history but that, starting with Woodward's and Warren's generation, southern historians and writers have had to emphasize that evil in an effort to, as Woodward said, shed the "glasses of sentimentality" regarding that past.[28]

But how do we account for the contrary ways this task affected these two historians, the real Woodward and the fictional Burden? If Woodward was dismayed as a graduate student with what he called the "uniquely broad consensus that papered over the breaks and fissures and conflicts in Southern history with myths of solidarity and continuity," then Jack Burden found "breaks, fissures, and conflicts" big enough to swallow him. If Woodward's career embodied the call to shoulder the burden of peeling back the paper and exposing the fractured and often ugly past, Jack Burden showed the emotional toll that such a task can take on historians. For all of Jack's paralytic cynicism and his brazen declarations that "a student of history does not care what he digs out of the ash pile, the midden, the sublunary dung heap, which is the human past," we know that he does, and we do. Though we are trained to keep the history we study from becoming as personal as it does for him, it is impossible for it not to affect us in our very core. At some point all historians of the American South are in danger of being engulfed and overwhelmed by the sadness of their subject, by the weight of the past they investigate. The themes that Burden encounters in writing the life of Cass Mastern are the very ones with which we still come into contact on a daily basis in our work: people's willingness to enslave, abuse, and dehumanize one another in a systematic way and to deny them basic human rights over the course of generations and centuries. Then there are the outright lies that people told themselves and the rest of the world to justify their actions and, perhaps worse, the damaging assertions that in the post–civil rights era all of these problems and their reverberations are now resolved and quieted.[29]

Yet it is the burden of southern history that for many of us makes it worth studying. As much as I have wished for Jack Burden less investment in his subject, I have come to terms with the fact that it is impossible for us as historians to keep complete emotional distance from our subjects. The idea that Jack, or any of us who have studied historiography in the age of postmodernist theory, could have been shielded from the pain of the past by our ideas of relativity and the dismissal of objectivity is foolish and naive. The best we can hope for ourselves as historians is that we may bear up to the reproach that the events of the past hold for us all.

By the end of *All the King's Men* Jack's notion of his own history unravels. His detective work results in the deaths of three people for whom he cares deeply. He discovers he is not the son of Ellis Burden but, rather, of Judge Irwin, whose dark secrets he has uncovered. In the final pages of the novel he decides to finish his work on Cass Mastern but tells us he is only able to do so because he has been forced to confront his own fallibility and his own painful historical truth. He has finally learned, as he tells Anne Stanton, to "accept the past and its burden" and that if you do not "there is no future." There is a lot of wisdom to be gained from Robert Penn Warren and Jack Burden and their journeys with history for the rest of us who follow in their stead. They remind us in the final sentence of the novel that there are a lot of messy historical realities that keep us, as they kept them, going "into the convulsion of the world, out of history into history and the awful responsibility of time."[30]

NOTES

1. "The Uses of History in Fiction," in *Conversations with William Styron*, ed. James L. W. West III (Jackson: University Press of Mississippi, 1985), 114–44.

2. Ibid., 116, 133–34.

3. This course was a perennial favorite among Centre College students and for good reason. Every day Dr. Lucas would bring in a dog-eared copy of whatever treasure we were reading and an almost empty bottle of W. L. Weller with a candle sticking out of its mouth. He would light the candle in an effort to summon the spirit of Faulkner, as he explained on the first day of class. Whether or not Faulkner ever dropped in, it certainly added a nice touch of ambience to the 1970s-era classroom building in which we sat three days a week.

4. Allen Tate, quoted in James Cobb, *Away Down South: A History of Southern Identity* (New York: Oxford University Press, 2007), 130.

5. C. Vann Woodward, *Thinking Back: The Perils of Writing History* (Baton Rouge: Louisiana State University Press, 1987), 109; the quote "accept the past and its burden" is from Robert Penn Warren, *All the King's Men* (1946; repr., New York: Harcourt Brace Jovanovich, 1982), 435.

6. C. Vann Woodward, *The Burden of Southern History*, rev. ed. (New York: Mentor Books, 1969), 27.

7. Ibid., 30–31.

8. Ibid., 39, 32, 39.

9. Woodward, *Thinking Back*, 109–10. Woodward was quoting from Robert Penn Warren, *The Legacy of the Civil War: Meditations on the Centennial* (New York: Random House, 1961), 53–54.

10. The book that Woodward reviewed was Herman Clarence Nixon, *Forty Acres and Steel Mules* (Chapel Hill: University of North Carolina Press, 1938). *Southern Review* 4 (Spring 1939): 679; William Bedford Clark, ed., *Selected Letters of Robert Penn Warren* (Baton Rouge: Louisiana State University Press, 2001), 2:192–93.

11. C. Vann Woodward, "Exile at Yale," in *The Legacy of Robert Penn Warren*, ed. David Madden (Baton Rouge: Louisiana State University Press, 2000), 28–29; Woodward, *Thinking Back*, 109; Floyd C. Watkins, John T. Hiers, and Mary Louise Weaks, eds., *Talking with Robert Penn Warren* (Athens: University of Georgia Press, 1990), 264.

12. Ibid., 37; Warren, *Legacy of the Civil War*; Robert Penn Warren, *World Enough and Time: A Romantic Novel* (New York: Random House, 1950), 3–4. For examples of literary scholars' examination of Warren's uses of history, see Jonathan S. Cullick, *Making History: The Biographical Narratives of Robert Penn Warren* (Baton Rouge: Louisiana State University Press, 2000); L. Hugh Moore Jr., *Robert Penn Warren and History: The Big Myth We Live* (The Hague: Mouton & Co., 1970); James A. Perkins, ed., *The Cass Mastern Material: The Core of Robert Penn Warren's "All the King's Men,"* (Baton Rouge: Louisiana State University Press, 2005); and Hugh Ruppersburg, *Robert Penn Warren and the American Imagination* (Athens: University of Georgia Press, 1990).

13. Warren, *All the King's Men*, 157.

14. Ibid., 160, 163.

15. Ibid., 177.

16. Ibid., 183.

17. Moore, *Robert Penn Warren and History*, 45.

18. Warren, *All the King's Men*, 188.

19. West, *Conversations with William Styron*, 133–34.

20. Ibid., 248, 188–89.

21. Peter Novick writes that "no alternative [to Phillips's] overall synthetic treatment of slavery appeared during the interwar years, and many works dealing with the South written by authors out of sympathy with Phillips either skipped over slavery or treated it summarily." *That Noble Dream: The "Objectivity Question," and the American Historical Profession* (Cambridge: Cambridge University Press, 1988), 229; Cobb, *Away Down South*, 130; Woodward, *Thinking Back*, 23.

22. Robert Penn Warren, "The Briar Patch," in *I'll Take My Stand: The South and the Agrarian Tradition*, ed. Donald Davidson et al. (Baton Rouge: Louisiana State University Press, 1977), 262–63; Watkins, Hiers, and Weaks, *Talking with Robert Penn Warren*, 32–33.

23. Watkins, Hiers, and Weaks, *Talking with Robert Penn Warren*, 33, 158–59. For an insightful treatment of Warren's evolution in racial thinking, see David A. Davis, "Climbing Out of the Briar Patch," *Southern Quarterly* 40.1 (Fall 2001): 109–20.

24. Ibid., 189, 248.

25. Ibid., 187, 186.

26. Jill Lepore, "Historians Who Love Too Much: Reflections on Microhistory and Biography," *Journal of American History* 88.1 (June 2001): 129.

27. Rubin, quoted in Cobb, *Away Down South*, 130; Woodward, *Thinking Back*, 30; Drive-By Truckers, "Bulldozers and Dirt," *Pizza Deliverance* (Soul Dump Records, 1999); Faulkner, *Absalom, Absalom!* (New York: Vintage International, 1990).

28. Woodward, *Burden of Southern History*, 39, 28.

29. Woodward, *Thinking Back*, 27; Warren, *All the King's Men*, 157.

30. Warren, *All the King's Men*, 435, 438.

# Marse Chan, New Southerner

*Or, Taking Thomas Nelson Page Seriously*

K. STEPHEN PRINCE

The years have not been kind to Thomas Nelson Page. During the last two decades of the nineteenth century and the first decade of the twentieth, Page was a darling of the American literary world. He published a string of successful novels, placed his short stories in every major literary magazine in the country, and won praise from northerners and southerners alike for his fictional depictions of a genteel and harmonious Old South. Enthusiastic accolades abounded: reviewers called Page "the literary pride of the South," and a "complete master of the negro dialect of the old days."[1] No less an authority than *Uncle Remus* author Joel Chandler Harris once said of two of Page's stories, "Marse Chan" and "Unc' Edinburg's Drowndin'": "I would rather have written these two sketches than everything that has appeared since the war, or before the war, for that matter."[2]

The last two decades of the twentieth century and the first decade of the twenty-first, however, have been a different story. If his contemporaries cast Page as a master, historians have depicted him as something of a historical curiosity—a would-be southern aristocrat born fifty years too late, a talentless scribbler whose ridiculous and predictable fantasies struck a chord with a reading public afraid of modernity and desperate for an escape. When historians grapple with Page, they tend to follow a predictable formula. First, Page and his work are introduced, generally with reference to the "Old South," "faithful slaves," "dialect tales," or "moonlight and magnolias." At this point the historian may briefly editorialize on the artistic merit (or, more often, the lack thereof) of Page's fiction. Quickly, however, the lens shifts from Page himself to his readership, as the historian discusses the wild popularity of Page's stories and their role in fostering sectional reunion.[3] While this vision of the plantation tales as harbingers of reconciliation is undoubtedly on point, the exclusive focus on Page's writing thrusts a sort of intellectual passivity upon the man himself. By focusing solely on public responses to Page's work, historians strip him of any historical agency. Page is rendered invisible; his stories achieve critical success and historical significance, but they do so almost in spite of him. Most of all, the historiography leaves us with the impression that there was no theory—intellectual, artistic, political, or cultural—underlying the production of Page's works, beyond a firm conviction that "even the moonlight was richer and mellower 'before the war' than it is now."[4]

In the process of taking Thomas Nelson Page seriously, therefore, I mean to bring Page out of the shadows cast by his own work and to consider the proposition that Page may have been a thinker as well as a writer. Between 1884 and 1910—the peak years of Page's literary production— he published dozens of essays and delivered hundreds of speeches on southern history and storytelling.[5] Although he admitted in his unpublished memoir that his initial move into writing was rooted in simple "vanity" and a "desire to see myself in print," Page quickly styled himself a leading expert on southern literature.[6] In the process Page developed and perfected an intricate reading of the southern past and the sectional conflict, a distinctly modern take on the power of culture and public opinion, and an alternative conceptualization of the New South rooted in literature and storytelling.

At its heart Page's literary and historical philosophy rested on three central premises. First, he believed that the way that the public understood the South—as a location, a people, and a civilization—carried great social, cultural, and political weight. Second, he argued that, for the vast majority of U.S. history, northerners had exercised almost exclusive control over the images of the South at play in American culture. Third, Page insisted that the white South must learn to tell its own story to the nation in the post-Reconstruction era. The end of Reconstruction marked an important turning point in southern history, the moment at which the "Southern people"—a class, it should be noted, that Page limited to "the landowning or better class of whites, as contra-distinguished not only from the negroes, but also from the lower class of whites"—would come to control their own destiny, cultural as well as political.[7] Rather than allowing outsiders to define the South for the nation, white southerners would learn to do this work themselves. Thomas Nelson Page was not just writing stories. He was intentionally rewriting the past, present, and future of his beloved South so that the region could reclaim its place at the forefront of American life.

"Marse Chan: A Tale of Old Virginia" (1884), Page's first published story, opens with an unnamed white traveler's unexpected meeting with Sam, an elderly former slave, on a horse path in Virginia. While Sam looks for his old master's dog, the visitor questions him about their surroundings, prompting a lengthy recitation of the history of the plantation on which they stand, beginning with the birth of Master Channing—"Marse Chan"—and ending with his death on a Civil War battlefield. The story-within-a-story, written in dialect, is, of course, the essence of the tale.[8] As historian Grace Hale has noted, the use of dialect allowed white southerners to perform a sort of "literary blackface," naturalizing racial inequality while they sanitized and glorified the southern past.[9] Although the racial divide between Sam and the white traveler looms large in Page's story, we should not allow this fact to overshadow another relationship that exists between the two characters—that of the storyteller and his audience. Sam, the faithful slave, narrates. The white traveler (along with Page's readership) listens intently. This interaction is stable and comfortably predictable, a relationship defined by the fact that information travels in only one direction.

"Unc' Edinburg's Drowndin': A Plantation Echo" (1886) and "Meh Lady: A Story of the War" (1886), the next two stories Page published, are structured in the same fashion. In each case a white interloper enters into a former slave's sphere of influence, where he is regaled with stories of the past. Page's literary universe, therefore, might be divided into two groups: insiders and outsiders. Those who have intimate knowledge of a place are empowered to tell its story. Those who lack this knowledge would do well to listen. Page found this ordering of things to be natural and logical, a relationship too automatic to require explicit comment. Such relationships—between insider and outsider, between storyteller and audience—appear again and again in Page's writing and provide a central explanatory metaphor for his views of southern history and literature.

When Page turned his attention to the history of the United States, he was struck by the manner in which the sectional relationship strayed from this natural ordering of things. Page's views on the beauty and grace of southern society before the war are fairly well known. The Old South, he wrote, was a "civilization so pure, so noble, that the world to-day holds nothing equal to it."[10] Marked by a "singular sweetness and freedom from vice," it was a land of purity, honor, and wonderment, peopled by dashing gentlemen, blushing ladies, and faithful slaves.[11] Every day was marked by a fishing expedition for the children, a fox hunt for the gentlemen, and, judging by the frequency with which the holiday occurs in Page's writing, a Christmas celebration for all. "Whatever assaults may be made on that civilization," Page wrote, "its final defence is this. The men were honorable and the women pure."[12]

It would not, however, be the glories of the Old South, but its short-comings, that would have the greatest effect on the literary career of Thomas Nelson Page. For Page the central theme of American history, from settlement to the end of Reconstruction, was the consistent failure of the South to tell its own story. Studiously ignoring a well-developed tradition of antebellum southern apologia—a "rage to explain" whose practitioners ranged from James Henry Hammond and Alexander H. Stephens to William Gilmore Simms and J. D. B. DeBow—Page insisted upon the region's historical aversion to self-explication.[13] The "Old Southerner," Page wrote, "was eminently self-contained, and his own self-respect satisfied, he cared not for the world's applause. He was content to live according to his own will" and found "no human tribunal to which he wished to submit his acts."[14] Secure in his place in the world, the Old Southerner felt no need to explain himself.

This tendency was made manifest in the literature of the Old South—or, more precisely, in its absence. The truths and values of a society were most effectively encapsulated and made permanent through the written word, Page insisted. Though he recognized the existence of something approximating a southern literary tradition in essays such as "Authorship in the South before the War," Page found it wanting in terms of quality, quantity, and subject matter, concluding that any "discussion of Southern literature during the period which preceded the late war naturally resolves itself into a consideration of the causes which retarded its growth."[15] A literature might have provided a storehouse for the collected truths of the civilization, to be shared and enjoyed on both sides of the Mason-Dixon. Instead, the Old South's conspicuous lack of a regional literature—rooted in its disdain for self-representation, its preference for oratory, and its distrust of all things modern, in art as in everything else—rendered its political, social, and cultural theories evanescent and impermanent.[16]

This argument was not merely academic. In turning to the Civil War, Page insisted that it was not the institution of slavery, nor the superior force of northern arms, nor a loss of home-front will that doomed the Confederacy. Instead, Page tied the fate of the South directly to its literary shortcomings and its chronic failure to explain itself to those outside its borders. "Only study the course of the contest against the South," Page wrote, "and you cannot fail to see how she was conquered by the pen rather than by the sword."[17] It was northern inability to understand the nature of southern society that brought the nation to war, and it was the same failure on the part of the European nations that denied the Confederacy the global support it required. "Owing to the want of a literature at the South and to the ignorance and misapprehension of the South on the part of the world," Page wrote, the South "found itself forced into a position where it was confronted by the entire world and stood at the bar of Christendom without an advocate and without a defence."[18] Although every southern boy knew precisely what he was fighting for, the world at large had not the foggiest idea. Too self-assured to account for itself in a literature, the South did not attempt to explain its cause until it had already been lost. "It is almost incredible," Page concluded, "that a race so proud of its position, so assertive of its rights, so jealous of its reputation, should have been so indifferent to all transmission of their memorial."[19]

Page's conclusions regarding the southern past are easily summarized—stories matter. The Old South had failed to appreciate the power of culture and the importance of the written word, and it had suffered the consequences. The sectional conflict, Civil War, and southern defeat had each been a direct result of the South's studied refusal to explain itself to those outside its borders. This connection was direct, literal, and unimpeachable. Stories had brought about the downfall of the Old South. No further explanation was necessary. This belief formed the keystone of

Page's historical worldview, the conviction from which all others would flow and the driving force behind his literary productions. Stories had nearly ruined the South. Page's role, simply put, would be to make sure that it never happened again.

In his literary and historical work Thomas Nelson Page sought nothing less than a complete revolution in the nation's commonsense understanding of the "South." Page's plan for achieving this end reflected his unique understanding of the nature of public opinion and the process of cultural transmission. Though he seldom addressed such matters explicitly or systematically, the outlines of Page's vision are quite clear. As already mentioned, Page's worldview relied on an opposition between insiders and outsiders. Beyond this, however, Page held to a notion of public opinion that was vaguely conspiratorial and slightly paranoid. In any given circumstance, Page postulated, the North would choose to believe the worst about the South. Years of misdirection and misunderstanding had rendered outsiders positively incapable of understanding the society and history of the South. Left to their own devices, therefore, they would accept almost anything about Dixie, no matter how derogatory or far-fetched. Whether consciously or not, the world was out to get the South—to defile its name, to trample its reputation, and to undercut its civilization. The nation's default position regarding all southern matters, in other words, was fear and loathing. Given these circumstances, was it any wonder that the South had something of an image problem?

There was, however, a silver lining. The North had proven itself incapable of constructing an accurate picture of the South, but southerners might do that work for them. Though it was tempting to disregard northern public opinion entirely, past experience had proven the folly of such a course. Northern opinion must be cultivated, not ignored. Page was confident that with proper guidance the North might be brought to a truer understanding of the South. Yankees assumed the worst, but this was to be expected—they had never heard anything to the contrary. In the postwar period white southerners might remedy this imbalance, telling their own story in the hopes of helping northerners to a more complimentary view of the region. Northerners might never truly grasp the wonder of the South, but they could learn to leave the description to those qualified to make it.

At times Page's understanding of public opinion could seem purely mathematical, bordering on reductive. Cultural productions were divided into two types: those that were authored by southern insiders such as Page and those that were not. The crux of Page's project, quite simply, was putting more in column A than he found in column B. He would keep chipping away at the problem, offering his own explicitly and self-consciously *southern* visions of the South and southern history, until at some future date the South would wake up to find itself in complete control of its own image. It is in this context that we must understand Page's almost manic attempts to rewrite the nature of the South between 1885 and 1910. Everything he touched, he seemed to assume, would be safe from further misrepresentation. Everything he failed to address would be subject to all manner of confusion and falsehood. Each time Page wrote about a faithful slave or a fox hunt, each time he praised Robert E. Lee or his childhood Mammy, each time he put the South at the center of the nation's "discovery" and the American Revolution, each time he castigated Reconstruction or offered a white southern taken on the "Negro Question," he moved one step closer to his goal. Page was waging a war of cultural attrition, with each positive image of the South understood to counteract a deleterious one.

At the same time, however, Page's vision relied heavily on a process that might be termed "cultural alchemy," the mysterious means by which isolated stories became accepted fact. Page's stories were, after all, only a means to an end. In order for the New South to avoid the tragic fate of the Old, these stories would need to become something more substantial, accepted on both sides of the Mason-Dixon line as true-to-life depictions of southern society. Page could not control or predict this process, but he had seen it work before. Page found inspiration in the unlikeliest of places: Harriet Beecher Stowe's *Uncle Tom's Cabin,* a novel whose content he loathed but whose impact he could not help admiring. In Page's estimation *Uncle Tom's Cabin* "did more, perhaps, that any one thing that ever occurred to precipitate the war." The novel gave northerners a common language and set of images, one that "blackened the fame of the Southern people in the eyes of the North and fixed in the mind of the North a concept not only of the institution of slavery, but of the Southern people, which lasted for more than a generation, and has only begun of late, in the light of a fuller knowledge, to be dislodged."[20] The text unified northern public sentiment, creating an image that quickly became the commonsense understanding of the South and of slavery—the "truth" as antebellum and wartime northerners understood it. This movement, the abrupt shift to cultural fact, was precisely the alchemic reaction that Page hoped to replicate. If Harriet Beecher Stowe had made this process work to the South's detriment, could not Page make it work to its benefit? Eventually, Page was confident, his assorted images and snapshots of southern life would become—for the South, the North, and the world—the accepted truth.

Thomas Nelson Page was not a New South booster in the traditional historiographical sense of the term.[21] Although he practiced law, he was not a businessman. He never lived in Atlanta. He never planned a civic fair or state exposition. His only involvement with railroads was as a passenger. While Page could declare himself a member of the "new order of Southern life" and "one of those who can feel the thrill of new energies fill my heart," he was decidedly ambivalent about the vision of a business-oriented and modernizing South put forward by boosters such as Richard Hathaway Edmonds and Henry Grady. If he was not a New South booster, however, Page may have been something of a New South theorist. Page cherished his own vision of a New South, one more difficult to grasp but arguably more significant than our traditional understanding of that term. Page's could not be built, nor could it be bought, sold, or transported. In fact, it had no physical being at all, unless one counts the books and magazines out of which it would be constructed. His New South had a dual character, referring both to a cultural construct—a new image of Dixie to broadcast proudly to the world—and to the reformed and wide-awake society that would produce it. Southerners, for the first time in their history, would understand the power of public opinion and take active steps to shape it in their favor, claiming their past, present, and future and casting aside the outmoded, derogatory definitions that northerners unthinkingly accepted as the truth. Outsiders who did not know a magnolia from a dogwood would no longer define Dixie. Southerners would write their own story.

In this literary quest Page chose to begin at the beginning. There is a certain pleasing symmetry to Page's vision—his plan for the future was rooted in his understanding of the southern past; a reconsideration of that past, meanwhile, became a vital first step toward making that future a reality. Page's obsession with the Old South did not reflect a knee-jerk antimodernism.[22] It was, instead, rooted in a deep belief in the tangible importance of historical understanding to the health of a society. Page tended to view southern history holistically, making little distinction between the southern past and southern present. Although the Civil War marked a cataclysmic shift in the course of that history, it did not fundamentally disrupt the larger continuities. As such, Page could insist on various occasions that "the Old South made this people," that "the New South is, in fact, simply the Old South with its energies directed into new lines," and that "it is to the Old South that the New South owes all that is best and noblest in its being."[23] Slavery was gone, but the Old South lived on in its people. To discuss the southern past was to discuss the southern present, and vice versa. An engagement with the past was not a mark of disdain for the present, therefore, but of concern for it.

Despite the tangible importance of historical inquiry, Page found that "contemporary history is being recorded by writers organically disabled to comprehend the action of the South."[24] Because postwar southerners continued to display insufficient interest in reclaiming their past, northern writers dominated the historical landscape, just as they had before the war. The result, Page wrote, was a "strange and wondrous record" that "goes by the name of history" but "is no more like history than I to Hercules."[25] In the popular (that is, northern) understanding of the past, southerners stood "charged with the crime of attempting to perpetuate human slavery, and for this purpose with conspiracy to destroy the best government the world has ever seen," while "nearly everything that has counted for much in the history of this country, either sprung from or took its color from New England."[26] Such aspersions on the Old South bore directly upon the New. With such an ignominious past hanging over their heads, how could the postwar South be expected to thrive? Page complained that "we are paraded as still exhibiting unconquered the same qualities untempered by misfortune; as nullifying the Constitution, falsifying the ballot, trampling down a weaker race in an extravagance of cruelty, and with shameless arrogance imperiling the nation as much now as when we went to war."[27] The pressing threat of a misinformed but suffocating public opinion convinced him that, unless white southerners immediately reclaimed their past (and by extension their present), "in a few years there will be no South to demand a history."[28]

Page did not blame northerners for the negative images of the Old South that prevailed in American culture. "It is not their fault that our history has not been written," Page told a meeting of Confederate veterans in 1892. "Gentlemen, it is our fault."[29] Lacking any self-accounting from the South, the North "has recorded of us in the main only what it honestly believes."[30] Yankee defamations of the South were not rooted in spite or hostility but in ignorance—the issue was one of capability, not intent. The North simply had no business attempting to tell the story of the South. In Page's estimation, "no mind will be able to produce the delicate and subtle phases of that civilization but one that has received its spirit into the warp and woof of its thought."[31] Only a born southerner was capable of writing this history, for only a born southerner could comprehend it in all its glory. As such, Page urged his fellow white southerners to recognize the enormous stakes and to tell their own story to the world before it was too late. "If we are willing to be handed down to coming time as a race of slave-drivers and traitors, it is as well to continue in our state of lethargy and acquiescence," Page wrote. But "if we retain the instincts of men, and desire to transmit to our children the untarnished name and spotless fame which our forefathers bequeathed to us, we must awake to the exigencies of the matter."[32]

When Page called for a history of the antebellum South, it is important to note, he did not mean a bare recitation of the facts. He sought, instead, to elevate the more ethereal and abstract facets of southern society, those things that southerners intuitively grasped and northerners consistently failed to comprehend—the spirit of the period, its inner workings, its mind-set, its worldview, its soul. In stark contrast to the late-nineteenth- and early-twentieth-century movement toward scientific objectivity in historical philosophy and practice—a movement best exemplified by Herbert Baxter Adams's seminar at Johns Hopkins University—Page clung to an older model of historical practice, emphasizing atmospheric integrity over cold facts.[33] As such, Page did not consider historical and fictional writing to be opposing disciplines but saw them as allied tools to be used in tandem in his larger project.

At times Page even implied that literature was to be valued for its ability to paint a *truer* picture of the past than history, as when he claimed that since "no histographer [sic] has yet recorded the beautiful story of the Southern Civilization . . . it may be left for some writer styling himself a novelist to tell the story and perpetuate the life that is gliding so rapidly into the irrevocable past."[34] In the hands of an expert—that is, one who possessed the requisite local knowledge—literature could get at the colors of life much more effectively than history. What fiction lacked in terms of historical specificity and factual detail it more than made up for with spiritual investment. There were, Page might have suggested, things truer than facts.

The key point, then, was not *what* southerners wrote about the southern past but the sheer fact that they *were* writing about it. The particular shape of the Old South as Page chose to imagine it was actually somewhat incidental to his larger project. Page did not seek to impose a specific reading of the southern past upon the nation; instead, he sought to claim the exclusive right of white southerners to narrate that past. By definition, the result would be a depiction simultaneously more complimentary and more truthful. In this great project Page was more than willing to share the workload (and the spotlight). Any southerner—assuming he or she was white, of satisfactory breeding, and correct on the political issues of the day—was equipped to aid in the cause. In his speeches and writings Page enumerated a number of southern authors—including John Fox, Armistead C. Gordon, Joel Chandler Harris, Mary Murfree, and Amelie Rives—whom he took to be kindred spirits, whether they knew it or not.[35] Page recognized, of course, that the image of the South produced by Harris's dialect tales differed greatly from the South that appeared in John Fox's stories of the Kentucky mountains. From Page's viewpoint, however, which focused as much on the large-scale interplay between the sections as on the character of the particular images involved, these differences actually mattered very little. The important point was that southerners were writing the "South"—however they defined it individually—for a national audience.

The central premises of Page's vision were not just applicable to the antebellum period. Page also applied the same logic to more contemporary sectional concerns, focusing particularly on the ever-present "Negro Question." Page's views on this matter were predicated on a single (familiar) assumption: northerners were fundamentally unequipped to understand the intricacies of the problem and should, therefore, allow their southern white brethren to control matters. Disfranchisement, segregation, and even lynching were not northern concerns, Page insisted. As such, Yankees should leave the question to those who understood it. This line of argumentation should not be read as an attempt to reduce Page's literary and historical worldview to a mere cover for a contemporary white supremacist agenda. It should, instead, be taken as a reminder of the inextricable links between Old South storytelling and New South racial concerns and a testament to the central role of cultural considerations in the rise of Jim Crow.

Reconstruction was the glue that held together the southern past and the southern present, thematically as well as temporally. Like his vision of the Old South, Page's views on Reconstruction revolved around notions of regional self-definition and the proper relationship between insiders and outsiders. Reconstruction was, in effect, the exception that proved all of Page's rules, the paramount example of the dangers to be faced when insiders were not allowed to control what they knew best. Unlike many of his contemporaries, Page did not chalk up the extended orgy of misgovernment to vituperation or corruption on the part of northerners.[36] Page's Reconstruction was a tragedy, not an indictment. Ignorance, rather than sectional hatred, played the starring role. "The chief trouble that arose between the two races in the South after the war," Page wrote, "grew out of the ignorance at the North of the actual conditions at the South."[37] Yankees, who were "absolutely ignorant of the true relation between the old masters and slaves," entered Reconstruction with "a fixed idea that there could be no justice toward the Negroes in any dealings of their former masters."[38] Those northerners who "advised moderation and counseled with the whites were set aside. Bred on the idea of slavery presented in *Uncle Tom's Cabin* and inflamed by passions engendered by the war, the enthusiasts honestly believed that they were right in always taking the side of the down-trodden Negro."[39] The damage caused by this course was plain. Reconstruction, Page said sadly, was "a subject which called for the widest knowledge and the broadest wisdom"—attributes he understood to be the exclusive purview of white southerners—"and, unhappily, both knowledge and wisdom appeared to have been resolutely banished in the treatment of the subject."[40]

Page's most extended literary treatment of Reconstruction occurs in *Red Rock*, published in 1897 but likely started more than a decade earlier.[41] The text was Page's attempt to author the definitive southern view of the period so that its horrors and degradations would be known abroad. As such, the novel is thick with scheming carpetbaggers, rascally scalawags, and rioting freedpeople. Significantly, however, the novel ignores Washington politics almost completely, keeping its lens trained on a small section of an unnamed southern state. If Page's analytical accounts of the period focus on the larger sectional dynamics that produced Reconstruction in the first place, his novel provides an on-the-ground view of these dynamics in action. As depicted in *Red Rock*, the great travesty of Reconstruction is the illogical and immoral rule of the lowly, the weak, and the dishonest over the courageous, the cultured, and the intelligent: the overseer-turned-scalawag Hiram Still purchases the beautiful Red Rock plantation; Union army shirker–turned–carpetbagger Jonadeb Leech feels empowered to tear Confederate buttons from the chest of wounded hero Jacquelin Gray. Page believed, very simply, that bottom rails do not belong on top—top rails do. The best should rule; the rest should follow. Reconstruction was the converse of this natural order, and Page located the horror of the period in precisely this upside-down aspect.[42] The larger point, however, is that Page found the twin story lines of Reconstruction—northern control of the South on the national level and the tospy-turvy illogic of Reconstruction on the ground—to be inextricably linked. The confusion that had brought about Reconstruction in the first place was exactly mirrored by the chaos in the South. When southerners did not tell their own story (or were not allowed to tell their own story), the misadventures of Reconstruction were the inevitable result.

Page applied a similar logic to the so-called Negro Question of the 1890s and 1900s. As the very title of his 1904 book on the topic—*The Negro: The Southerner's Problem*—makes abundantly clear, Page's primary focus was to reserve for the white South the exclusive right to settle the race question. Page leaned heavily on the logic of Reconstruction to argue this point. The darkest period in the nation's history had arisen due to northern attempts to interfere in a racial regime it did not really understand. Did northerners really want to make the same mistake again? Moving from this starting point, Page's *book* is actually an extended meditation on sectional miscommunication. "Many, if not most, of the difficulties of the race problem since the war," Page insisted, "have been caused, or at least increased, by the ignorance of those outside the South, who, most cocksure of their positions when they were most in error, have tried to force a solution on lines contrary to natural and unchangeable laws."[43] White southerners and black southerners understood each other, Page argued. Problems arose when outsiders got involved, meddling with issues they could not understand. The take-home message in all of this was crystal clear: Dixie's racial future was to be the southerner's problem.

Something of a quid pro quo was at work, however. In return for their amenability in the small matter of Jim Crow, Page would offer northerners something infinitely greater—a stake in the South's glorious history. As he looked around in the last decades of the century, Page saw a new United States rising to a place of prominence in the world. As he put the matter in an 1888 speech, "A young giant stands among the peoples of the earth . . . the very perfection of physical life." Page worried, however, that the rising power lacked the heart to match its economic and political strength. "But what of the Spirit!" he asked. "What of that higher and finer existence without the aspirations for which Nations as well as individuals must after their brief day of glory go down to the earth like the beasts that perish?"[44] In their zeal to make money, Americans seemed willing to overlook the timeless virtues that guaranteed a civilization's lasting greatness. Page wrote that "the sacrifice of every principle to the Gilded god" threatened "to bring upon us the curse of Midas, and in the midst of rivers of gold menace us with intellectual starvation."[45] A nation with no sense of its own history and its place in the world could possess a greatness that was only fleeting, an importance that was no more than temporary.

Page offered a compelling answer to this dilemma. The South, in his estimation, possessed in spades precisely the soul, the passion, and the glamour that the nation at large seemed to lack. Having rescued the southern past from the clutches of northern misrepresentation, Page would allow the nation at large to claim a piece of that past and, in so doing, provide it with the romance and heroism it so desperately needed. Northerners would not just accept the South (as defined, of course, by white southerners such as Page) but embrace it, taking its unique history for their own. Looking forward to a day when the "name and fame of every worthy son of this land whether he be born in the North or in the South shall no longer be confined to the narrow limits of a single section, but shall be deemed the inalienable heritage of the Anglo-American race," Page came full circle.[46] His own hypersensitivity to issues of region led him to propose a new American nationalism, rooted in the southern past. Southerners would write the story of the South, but the nation could share in its glories. In this new arrangement sectionalism itself would disappear in a celebration of American nationalism, as the nation learned to love the South—or Page's version of it—as deeply as those who had been born and bred there.

NOTES

1. Assorted clippings, Thomas Nelson Page Collection, Duke University, Durham, N.C., box 17.

2. Joel Chandler Harris to Thomas Nelson Page, December 31, 1885, Thomas Nelson Page Collection, Duke University, box 1.

3. For examples of this sort of treatment, see Edward Ayers, *The Promise of the New South: Life after Reconstruction* (New York: Oxford University Press, 1992), 348–53; David W. Blight, *Race and Reunion: The Civil War in American Memory* (Cambridge, Mass.: Harvard University Press, 2001), 222–27; W. Fitzhugh Brundage, *The Southern Past: A Clash of Race and Memory* (Cambridge, Mass.: Harvard University Press, 2005), 16; Paul Gaston, *The New South Creed: A Study in Southern Mythmaking* (New York: Knopf, 1970), 167–75; Grace Elizabeth Hale, *Making Whiteness: The Culture of Segregation in the South, 1890–1940* (New York: Vintage, 1998), 51–59; and Nina Silber, *The Romance of Reunion: Northerners and the South, 1865–1900* (Chapel Hill: University of North Carolina Press, 1993), 113–15. For a less formulaic reading of Thomas Nelson Page, see Fred Hobson, *Tell About the South: The Southern Rage to Explain* (Baton Rouge: Louisiana State University Press, 1983), 129–57.

4. Thomas Nelson Page, *Red Rock: A Chronicle of Reconstruction* (1897; repr., New York: Scribner's, 1912), ix. On the "Lost Cause," see Blight, *Race and Reunion*, 255–300; Gaines R. Foster, *Ghosts of the Confederacy: Defeat, the Lost Cause, and the Emergence of the New South* (Baton Rouge: Louisiana State University Press, 1987); and Charles Reagan Wilson, *Baptized in Blood: The Religion of the Lost Cause, 1865–1920* (Athens: University of Georgia Press, 1983).

5. See Harriet R. Holman, "The Literary Career of Thomas Nelson Page, 1884–1910" (Ph.D. diss., Duke University, 1947).

6. Thomas Nelson Page, "Recollections and Reflections" (unpublished memoir), Thomas Nelson Page Collection, Duke University, box 17.

7. Thomas Nelson Page, "Authorship in the South before the War," in *The Old South: Essays Political and Social* (New York: Scribner's, 1893), 60.

8. "Marse Chan: A Tale of Old Virginia," "'Unc' Edinburg's Drowndin': A Plantation Echo," and "Meh Lady: A Story of the War" were collected in Thomas Nelson Page, *In Ole Virginia* (1887; repr., New York: Scribner's, 1908).

9. Hale, *Making Whiteness*, 55. See also Eric Sundquist, *To Wake the Nations: Race in the Making of American Literature* (Cambridge, Mass.: Harvard University Press, 1993), 324–47.

10. Thomas Nelson Page, "The Old South," in *The Old South,* 43.

11. Thomas Nelson Page, "Social Life in Old Virginia before the War," in *The Old South,* 167.

12. Page, "Old South," 48.

13. See Hobson, *Tell About the South.*

14. Thomas Nelson Page, "The Want of a History of the Southern People," in *The Old South,* 259.

15. Page, "Authorship in the South," 57.

16. Page's derision to the contrary, recent works by Eugene Genovese and Elizabeth Fox-Genovese and by Michael O'Brien have highlighted the impressive intellectual and literary accomplishments of the Old South. Elizabeth Fox-Genovese and Eugene D. Genovese, *The Mind of the Master Class: History and Faith in the Southern Slaveholders' Worldview* (Cambridge: Cambridge University Press, 2005); Michael O'Brien, *Conjectures of Order: Intellectual Life and the American South, 1810–1860* (Chapel Hill: University of North Carolina Press, 2003).

17. Page, "Old South," 50.

18. Thomas Nelson Page, "South as a Field for Literature," Thomas Nelson Page Collection, University of Virginia, Charlottesville, box 32.

19. Page, "Want of a History," 258.

20. Thomas Nelson Page, *Negro: The Southerner's Problem* (New York: Scribner's, 1904), 15. On the public reception of *Uncle Tom's Cabin,* see David S. Reynolds, *Mightier than the Sword:* Uncle Tom's Cabin *and the Battle for America* (New York: Norton, 2011).

21. See C. Vann Woodward, *Origins of the New South* (1951; repr., Baton Rouge: Louisiana State University Press, 1971); Gaston, *New South Creed;* Don Doyle, *New Men, New Cities, New South: Atlanta, Nashville, Charleston, Mobile, 1860–1910* (Chapel Hill: University of North Carolina Press, 1990).

22. Every major piece of fiction that Page authored before *Gordon Keith* (1903) took the antebellum South, the Civil War, or Reconstruction as its primary subject matter. *Gordon Keith* and *John Marvel, Assistant* (1909) moved to more contemporary subject matter, but Page published three works of nonfiction—*The Negro: The Southerner's Problem* (1904), *The Old Dominion* (1908), and *Robert E. Lee: Southerner* (1908)—between the novels, suggesting this his change of fictional focus may have had more to do with a recognition of changing public tastes than with a dimming of interest in southern history. See Hobson, *Tell About the South,* 153.

23. Page, "Old South," 40, 5; Page, "Want of a History," 268.

24. Page, "Want of a History," 268.

25. Page, "New South at Close Range," Thomas Nelson Page Collection, University of Virginia, box 31.

26. Page, "Want of a History," 266; Thomas Nelson Page, "The South," Thomas Nelson Page Collection, University of Virginia, box 33.

27. Page, "Want of a History," 255.

28. Ibid., 253.

29. Thomas Nelson Page, *Address by Thomas Nelson Page, LL.D., on the Necessity for a History of the South, Delivered before the Grand Camp of Confederate Veterans of the State of*

*Virginia, at Its Annual Meeting in the City of Roanoke, June 22, 1892* (Roanoke, Va.: Hammond's Printing Works, 1892), 4.

30. Page, *Address*, 3.

31. Page, "South as a Field for Literature."

32. Page, "Want of a History," 269.

33. See Peter Novick, *That Noble Dream: The "Objectivity Question" and the American Historical Profession* (Cambridge: Cambridge University Press, 1988), 21–61.

34. Page, "South as a Field for Literature."

35. Ibid. See also Harriet R. Holman, ed., *John Fox and Tom Page as They Were* (Miami: Field Research Projects, 1970). Page's inclusion of Murfree and Rives seems quite significant, given the patriarchal presumptions that underlay most of his fiction. Although he happily wrote African Americans and poor whites out of his very definition of southernness, Page appears to have reserved white southern women a place in his imagined literary coalition.

36. See Bruce E. Baker, *What Reconstruction Meant: Historical Memory in the American South* (Charlottesville: University of Virginia Press, 2007), esp. 1–89.

37. Page, *Negro*, 32.

38. Thomas Nelson Page, "The Southern People during Reconstruction," in *The Old Dominion* (1908; repr., New York: Scribner's, 1910), 265; Page, *Negro*, 34.

39. Page, *Negro*, 36.

40. Ibid., 34.

41. Holman, *Literary Career*, 75.

42. Such an understanding of Reconstruction was common among southern white conservatives in the years after 1877. See Joel Williamson, *The Crucible of Race: Black-White Relations in the American South since Emancipation* (New York: Oxford University Press, 1984), 79–80.

43. Page, *Negro*, 293.

44. Page, "South as a Field for Literature."

45. Ibid.

46. Ibid.

# Poison Stories

*A Rereading of Revolutionary Virginia's Baptist "Revolt"*

JEWEL L. SPANGLER

The 1792 poisoning of Virginia Baptist minister James Ireland had all the makings of a good story. There was a mystery: everyone from the victims to the district court judges was anxious to determine who put arsenic in the Ireland family's evening tea. The story had high drama. A roomful of people were sickened and a crowd of friends, neighbors, county officials, and medical specialists rushed to the scene to give aid and act as a posse to investigate the crime. The story had twists. While it initially seemed as if the Irelands had sweetened their tea with sugar from the Caribbean that slaves had tampered with, gradually people started to believe that the poison was local in origin—two of Ireland's house servants were suspected of trying very intentionally, if not very precisely, to kill the Baptist leader. There was tragedy. The only death in the incident was a three-year-old child who had sipped tea surreptitiously from an unattended saucer during the hubbub. The tale perhaps even had a hint of comedy. The diners all but rolled their eyes when Ireland, the first to feel ill, reacted to the poison's effects by leaping to his feet to run from the room, as he was known to be "addicted" to health complaints and had interrupted a few meals before. But then the whole group took sick all at once and "scattered off from the table, some hanging to the different door cheeks, and some in other postures, crying out, 'Hold my head, I shall die, give me drink, I am poisoned, etc!'"[1]

Two chapters of the preacher's published autobiography, *The Life of the Rev. James Ireland* (1819), sketch out this tale of attempted murder gone wrong. It is also relayed more briefly in the local Winchester newspaper, *Bowen's Virginia Centinel and Gazette,* and various Frederick County and district court proceedings.[2] Yet this story, like so many other personal dramas of the past, has largely been ignored by both professional historians and Baptists interested in their heritage. Their lack of interest in the poisoning is, of course, completely ordinary, as we remember and repeat over time only a tiny fraction of that which has been described in written source material. It is odd, however, that the poisoning is barely remembered when Ireland's autobiography is still read and used quite extensively by southern religious historians and American Baptist writers alike. For generations Ireland's memoir, the majority of which details the minister's high-spirited youth, his religious conversion, and the path he took to the pulpit in Revolutionary Virginia, has been an important primary source for those researching the origins of the Bible Belt and the founding of the Baptist faith in the southern United States.[3]

Popular versions of the Baptist founding story, largely written by Baptists themselves, tend to underscore the hardships the sect endured and overcame to spread the word of God. This literature draws from Ireland's autobiography mostly to recount a series of confrontations the minister had with colonial officials, culminating in his 1769–70 imprisonment in Culpepper County, Virginia, for preaching without a license (the Anglican Church was legally established in Virginia, and dissenting faiths could only practice at the pleasure of the colonial government). Descriptions in Ireland's memoir of his ongoing effort to preach from his jail cell window, even after the prison guard tried to silence him by suffocating him with smoke, exploding a homemade bomb in his cell, and poisoning his food, have facilitated the building of a narrative of the Baptists' rise in the United States as a product of hardship and brave perseverance. Ireland's confrontations, incarceration, and persecution are sometimes, and not inaccurately, linked by Baptist writers to the broader struggle for separation of church and state and religious freedom in the Revolutionary age, a linkage that underscores the fact that Baptists such as Ireland were important contributors to the American, and not just the Baptist, founding.[4]

Academics have focused on some similar features of Ireland's autobiography as they have formulated a "master narrative" of the rise of evangelical religion in the American South. That master narrative has cast early evangelicals as social and cultural outsiders in the Old Dominion, who faced off for their very survival against the planter elite and the institutions—such as courts and jails—that did their bidding. This narrative has described Baptists as challengers to colonial Virginia's class hierarchy because the faith allowed plain men to lead and to Virginia's patriarchal order because both women and slaves could assert themselves at least to a limited degree within Baptist congregations and households. Although, according to the standard narrative, Baptists ultimately threw their weight behind the planter-dominated social system of the Old Dominion in the nineteenth century, the rise of the Baptists is cast as a countercultural, "evangelical revolt."[5] James Ireland's story has figured in this narrative in key ways. Some have focused on the description of Ireland's torturous road to conversion in itself as emblematic of a broader cultural distinctiveness among Baptists that set them apart in an Anglican world religiously, if not necessarily socially.[6] Others have characterized Ireland's various persecution experiences as emblematic of a broader opposition that evangelicals faced because the Anglican establishment, the planter class, and government officials all were in some sense concerned that Baptists represented a threat to the social order in terms of race, gender, and/or class.[7]

This essay examines the "suppressed narrative" of the 1792 poisoning—a story that has long been available to, but remains largely unanalyzed by, both southern historians and those interested in Baptist heritage. It does not argue that this poisoning was particularly significant in itself—in my view the story does not "need" to be rescued and retold just for the sake of the telling. Nor will this essay focus on some of the most typical subjects associated with historical work on crimes and court cases, such as a consideration of motives for the poisoning or an assessment of these events as a direct window onto the world of those involved.[8] Instead, it asks whether Ireland's memoir might be read differently if the poisoning narrative were included—whether the master narrative of Baptist counterculturalism might in fact be problematized by a consideration of the entire memoir, rather than merely selected parts that best fit a story line of cultural outsiderism and class conflict. It employs a literary approach in an effort to read these chapters of the memoir not simply for their most overt and intended messages but also for more subtle meanings contained in the writer's word choices and story emplotment. The way that the 1792 poisoning story is actually told in print, its narrative structures, expresses in some sense the beliefs and assumptions of those who created the narrative—in this case both Ireland himself and a ghostwriter who finalized those chapters.

Analyzing Ireland's memoir both more completely and more closely does not uncover any great new truths and certainly does not overturn decades of historical writing on the rise of the Baptists. It does suggest, however, that contested narratives about the Baptists' rise were in play in the late eighteenth and early nineteenth centuries, allowing us to consider that story in more complex terms. Giving the neglected chapters on Ireland's poisoning a fraction of the attention that scholars have allotted to Ireland's conversion and persecutions, and directing that attention to the telling of the poisoning story itself, actually produces something of a counter-narrative to the standard historical interpretation of the rise of the Baptists in Virginia. This story of a slave and a servant's household rebellion invokes not social egalitarianism among the Baptists and challenges to the planters' patriarchal order so much as strict hierarchies of race and gender and strong proslavery messages.

~

By definition, to describe the Ireland poisoning is to fashion it narratively. Nevertheless, if the plot is to be considered, the basic contours of the story need to be fleshed out. A reading of the surviving source material that touches on the poisoning might invite historians to tell a story that goes something like this:

*On May 15, 1792, as the sun rose over the Valley of Virginia, Baptist minister James Ireland turned his carriage toward his home in Frederick County, having just completed visits to congregations he served in neighboring Shenandoah. He made a quick stop for supplies at a country store in Stoverstown (now Strasburg, Virginia) and then hurried on to his farm, where he was met by a swarm of children and his pregnant second wife. In addition to his preaching duties, Ireland produced foodstuffs on a homestead of 135 acres, primarily with family labor. His place was typical of the family farms that dominated the Shenandoah Valley, situated west of the Blue Ridge Mountains on the periphery of the slave society of the tobacco- and wheat-producing Tidewater and Piedmont regions that lay to the east.*

As Reverend Ireland passed through the doorway home, he could not have imagined that he was entering a crime scene in the making. At that moment, in his own kitchen, arsenic was steeping in boiling water that would be used to make him a pot of tea. Unaware that his late breakfast was intended to put an end to his life, he cajoled his daughter Jenny into leaving off from her chores to take tea with him. Both of them sipped the poison, and both became suddenly and extremely ill shortly after they set down their cups. Yet by the middle of the afternoon Ireland, at least, began to show signs of recovery. Foul play was not immediately suspected. That evening a pot of poisoned tea appeared on Ireland's table again, and this time the preacher, several members of his family, and even some visitors, partook, and all of them were soon violently sickened. Ireland's three-year-old son, William, died from the toxin the next morning, while Ireland himself, who rapidly drank two cups, was so severely sickened that he never fully recovered his health. A doctor was quickly sent for, and the rest of the victims gradually improved over the next two days. As news of the outbreak of illness spread, neighbors began to turn up as well. Even as the afflicted were treated with sweet oil, the growing crowd launched an investigation into what now had begun to look like a deliberate crime.

At first everyone seemed to assume that this was an act of deadly mischief rather than an attack on Ireland himself. It was widely believed that the poison had come into Ireland's house in some sugar that he had just purchased from a newly opened cask, as rumors had been circulating for some time that Caribbean plantation slaves were tampering with that product. Finding that no one else in the vicinity had fallen similarly ill from the same batch of sugar, the neighbors restarted their investigation, assuming now that the poisoning was a family affair. Ireland's household included one adult slave, a woman named Sucky, who worked in the kitchen and had been involved in at least serving the meals and beverages that were now suspected to have carried the poison. Neighbors questioned Sucky first, and their instincts were soon rewarded, as the slave offered something of a confession. On the road to the county jail in Winchester, however, they thought to inquire about how she had obtained the poison, and the plot thickened, as it were. Sucky implicated her *fellow kitchen servant, a local, Euro-American girl named Betsy Southerlin, whom she claimed had been the one to purchase the arsenic. When Betsy was questioned, she confessed her involvement.*

*At first everyone seemed to attribute the plot to Sucky and cast Betsy, the free girl, primarily as an accomplice. Ireland even kept Betsy out of jail for several days after her confession so that her friends could visit her and give comfort. Sucky was immediately tried in a court of oyer and terminer (consisting of a subset of the county justices and no jury, empowered to administer summary justice) because she was a slave and did not have the right to a jury trial. Upon hearing evidence, however, the justices were not immediately sure what to do and decided to delay making a determination about Sucky until after they had heard the case against Betsy. Betsy Southerlin then appeared before the full county court. The court determined that the case against her was in fact strong enough to send her back to jail until the district court met in the fall. Returning to Sucky's case, the pared-down court could not reach consensus and ultimately acquitted her by a narrow margin. In September Betsy faced the district court, where she was ultimately acquitted as well (on what grounds, we may never know). She left the county for good soon after, and no one was ultimately held responsible for the death of William Ireland.*

*Sucky, on the other hand, remained in the country jail for months after her trial in spite of her acquittal. Ireland paid out of pocket to keep her confined, and when she ultimately did return to Ireland's home, she was kept imprisoned in the preacher's tiny kitchen loft. After several months in the attic, Sucky asked Ireland to come to her little apartment to hear a confession that would allow her to be retried and executed. She repeated that she was responsible for the death of his child because she had been involved in the plot. Sucky did not get another day in court, but she was forced out of the Ireland household one way or another and may well have been sold out of the county entirely.*[9]

This story follows a narrative pattern that is repeated in the memoir as a whole and in Baptist writing of this period more generally and is emblematic of spiritual autobiography as a genre.[10] The poisoning story was added by the compiler, it is explained, not only because Ireland had himself written about it and therefore, one must assume, intended to have the story included but because, in the words of the compiler, to leave it out would "be depriving the friends of the blessed Redeemer (especially those of them who were personally acquainted with the subject of this history) of a very interesting part of the doings and sufferings of their departed friend." Ireland was "one among a thousand of the ministers of the Lord Jesus, who experienced the extremes of sorrow and joy, of tribulation and comfort," as biblically sanctioned in John 16:33: "In the world you shall have tribulation, but be of good cheer; I have overcome the world." The poisoning story was scripted as an object lesson for struggling Christians about God's aid to those of his servants in need. In this, the story echoes the broader autobiography. Ireland expressly saw his life-writing project as having a didactic purpose. He explained at the outset of the memoir that the aim of the volume was to "give a just relation of the wonderful dealings of the gracious God to me a sinner," in hopes that "it finds acceptance among the humble followers of the dear Redeemer, for whose comfort and encouragement in their heavenly pilgrimage, the work is undertaken."[11] Ireland plotted his memoir as a journey from emotional turmoil to inner peace, from sinner to saint, from detractor to Baptist leader. He highlighted his inner and external struggles expressly to send a message to readers about God's tests, God's abiding love, and the final victory in Christ—a typical narrative trajectory for many spiritual autobiographies of this period. Similarly, the earliest Baptist histories, written at about the same time, tended to be shaped as heroic tales of improbable beginnings, endurance through persecution, heroic leaders, and final victories with God's help.[12] In the end the hero, Ireland, surmounted difficult circumstances to prevail, as southern Baptists prevailed. In the specific case of the 1792 poisoning story, Ireland is described as having survived the attacks upon him (little William's death, while sad, was treated as tangential), having taken action to put his house to rights, and, in Sucky's final confession and pleas for death, having achieved a victory over the devil and his terrible test of Ireland's faith.

At the same time, the poisoning story asserts a narrative of patriarchal household order in a slave society that operates somewhat at odds with the master narrative of Baptist cultural "outsider-ness."[13] The story very directly describes Ireland as having distinctive relationships with Betsy and Sucky, which heavily underscores this point. At the most basic level the memoir casts Ireland as Betsy's gentle protector and Sucky's harsh master. The autobiography claims that when Ireland learned that Betsy Southerlin, the daughter of a neighboring family who had been hired into his household to help in the kitchen, was involved in the plot, he in essence came to her defense. First, he kept her out of jail for days after she confessed because he "would rather give her friends an opportunity of seeing her." After Sucky had been acquitted and Betsy, presumably now viewed as the primary poisoner, was remanded for trial, the autobiography tells us, the preacher chose not to hire a lawyer against her to present the case, which would have been standard procedure, and instead chose not to have all the evidence brought against her in court. That Betsy was ultimately acquitted, the narrative hints, might be attributable partly to his reticence to act. The autobiography explains that he made these choices in part to protect his young daughter from the trauma of testifying (something he ultimately was unable to prevent) but also because he simply "did not want to pursue the culprit Betsy with rigour."[14]

The description of his, and others', responses to the slave woman, Sucky, stands in stark contrast to Betsy's story. Hers is the tale of a dangerous slave, contained by Ireland and made to reveal herself as an agent of evil. While Ireland was too ill to act, the memoir tells us, his neighbors rapidly came to consider Sucky a prime suspect. They questioned her, rushed her out of the house, and stowed her in the jail. The memoir offers conflicting stories about Sucky's involvement, at once acknowledging that Betsy was the likely ringleader of the plot and at the same time persistently treating Sucky as the most guilty party, even while reporting that she had been legally acquitted. Once Sucky was let go by the court, the memoir reports, she continued to be treated as not only guilty of the crime but also as so dangerous that she had to be confined and isolated and so sinful that she "thought and affirmed that she saw the devil."[15] While the memoir posits that concern and protectiveness governed Ireland's choices with regard to Betsy, it frames Ireland as fearful and untrusting of Sucky, whom he rejected out of hand. Sucky is written as a dangerous and infectiously toxic force.

We cannot say with certainty whether there was in fact a differential reaction on Ireland's part with respect to the two women, followed by distinctive treatment—never mind what may have motivated the preacher along the way. Ireland's memoir, like all texts, is open to multiple readings that can be in conflict with one another and hardly correspond to the "reality" of Ireland's (or Betsy's or Sucky's) experience. But the memoir, supported by other sources, can be said to build a particular sort of story line of patriarchal household order in a slave society. The description of Ireland's response to Betsy's actions was consistent with contemporary understandings of Betsy's nature as a free "spinster" servant girl as well as her place in the Ireland family. Descriptions of Sucky in Ireland's memoir, on the other hand, conflict with a dominant narrative of both slaves' and women's passivity and touch on a deep-seated and pervasive fear of slave rebellion.[16] Ireland's "unfatherly" response to her might be read in that context. Descriptions of Ireland as a household head in this narrative, in sum, offer us a lens through which to view Baptists' articulation of their relationship to the social norms of their time. For what it's worth, those descriptions are at odds with a currently still popular narrative of the early Virginia Baptists as champions of a countercultural vision of human equality before God and equivocation on slavery.

Betsy Southerlin was a Frederick County native.[17] When Ireland contracted for her live-in services, he effectively promised her parents to bring her into his own household as a figurative daughter in much the way that apprentices in eighteenth-century workshops occupied a place of familial dependency. Descriptions of her in the memoir actually fit very nicely into the framework of expectations of fatherly household authority that prevailed in post-Revolutionary Virginia and with expectations of women's submissive dependency. Betsy is cast in the role of the passive female, directed and protected by others and virtually unable to act of her own accord. This characterization is curious because it develops alongside an emerging narrative of Betsy's culpability in the poisoning crime.[18] The autobiography presents us with a series of oppositions, defining Ireland in relationship to and against Betsy. It describes Ireland as authoritative, powerful, and in control and Betsy as a dependent whom he was in charge of. When Betsy's guilt came to light, according to the narrative, Ireland took action, setting the conditions under which Betsy would operate. He decided where Betsy would be in the days after the poisoning was discovered. He decided whether she needed the support of her friends. He decided how much of Betsy's life would be exposed to public view at trial. He decided whether enough evidence would be presented to convict her. In all of this, he is narrated as the household patriarch and she as the dependent.

The narrative characterizes Ireland as a rational "actor," while it imagines Betsy as being given over to her passions and at the same time curiously passive. She is portrayed as a creature of emotion, careening from one moment to the next by the force of her feelings. Ireland's autobiography tells us that Betsy, during the week before the poisoning, was an emotional wreck—depressed, reclusive, and tearful. Preparing for the crime had caused her to "struggle" with her conscience and drove her toward repeated emotional breakdowns. Conversely, Ireland appears in this narrative as someone, even under the extreme conditions of severe illness and loss, who is in full control of himself and operating from calm rationality. There are no tears, there is no anger, just steady action. Ireland has "preferences" and "wishes" in this narrative, not needs and impulses. If Ireland is the quintessential "agent," bringing order from the chaos caused by Betsy's impulsive poisoning plot, Betsy, strangely enough, is described as primarily a passive figure. A neighbor "instigated" her to "perpetrate the horrid crime"—the impulse came from outside of her, and she was the mere vessel or instrument of it, helpless to resist.[19] The framing of Betsy as passive here is interesting. Given that she emerges as the probable ringleader of a plot, she could easily have been described as active, self-directed, an agent. In fact, when Betsy appeared before the district court in the fall of 1792, now solely charged with the crime, even the court clerk framed her as passive. While she was charged with murder, with "malice aforethought" for "contriving and intending" to "deprive" Ireland of his life, he also described her as "not having the fear of god before her eyes, but being moved and seduced by the Instigation of the devil."[20] In sum, we could draw the conclusion from the tellings of this incident that Ireland was conceived of in terms of dominant masculinity—as active, rational, and in control. Betsy, by contrast, plays the role of the female dependent—weak, emotional, passive, a person to be controlled.

This is very much in keeping with the contours of hegemonic masculinity as historians have typically described it and is somewhat at odds with the work of a number of historians of early southern Baptists. It has long been noted that early Baptists allowed for a public space for women that was barred to them in secular life—that female Baptists found a voice and an agency and a public persona that defied gender norms of the period. It may not be possible to characterize early Baptists as "feminist," but the doctrine of spiritual equality before God has been described as setting the Baptists enough at odds with the dominant social order that there were outcries against them for disturbing familial harmony and upturning patriarchal authority. Similarly, the poisoning story fits a bit oddly with an emerging literature that posits a distinctive Baptist masculinity.[21]

The characterization of Sucky's involvement marks a dramatic contrast to that of Betsy. In theory Betsy and Sucky occupied similar positions in the Ireland household—both were dependents, and both were women.[22] In practice the language used to describe Sucky reveals a very separate and distinctive understanding of the slave woman in contradistinction to the free, Euro-American servant. While oppositions characterized Betsy's nature—she was weak, emotional, passive, and in need of protection, in contrast to Ireland's authoritative, rational ability—Sucky is cast as more similar to Ireland than different from him, necessitating that Ireland in essence go to battle with Sucky and defeat her to assert his household dominance. In the context of household crisis, Sucky was virtually "unsexed," and the protective elements of Ireland's received role as patriarch were concomitantly made inappropriate with respect to the rebellious slave under his roof.

In contrast to Betsy's passivity, Sucky is described as an actor in her own right—something that made her particularly dangerous (and contributed to her "unsexing"). While Betsy's agency in obtaining and using poison is balanced against her inner turmoil and her passive acceptance of others' commands, Sucky is described as being active in the plot. The narrative emphasizes, for example, Sucky's subtle efforts to allow the poisoning to go off successfully. Specifically, it highlights two occasions on which she lied to provide alternative explanations for the sudden onset of illness among the Irelands. Her untruthful reports are described as "artful," in other words carefully crafted and deliberate. She is labeled a "liar," a person invested with a negative form of agency that ran to the core of her identity.[23] Similarly, she is called a "murderer," an identity with unambiguous agency attached.

In a similar vein Sucky is imagined as focused and rational in her "artfulness." The autobiography does not suggest that she suffered from inner turmoil during the poisoning event or in its immediate aftermath. She is not characterized as a passive creature for others to activate but chose for herself. Finally, after a long confinement, the narrative tells us, Sucky did claim to become emotionally distraught—she had "seen the devil." When Betsy had seemed to show signs of religious conviction in the week before the poisoning, the narrative suggests that the whole Ireland family believed they should do everything in their power to encourage religious feeling and a resolution of spiritual anxiety in a conversion. When Sucky showed almost exactly the same signs of emotional turmoil with religious overtones, the source of the turmoil is given as the devil (the opposite of God's agency). And the stirring of religious emotion is characterized as an opportunity to reveal the culpability of the slave and drive her out of the narrative altogether (through execution). The narrative posits that, if a household head should expect to nurture and compensate for the emotional deficiencies of white female dependents such as Betsy and to guide them in spiritual matters, rebel slaves such as Sucky can be understood as unqualified for such treatment. Dependent women needed to be governed gently, but rebellious slaves needed to be brought firmly under control, and their inappropriate agency needed to be curtailed through forcefulness.

That Sucky was narrated as the "rebellious slave," the opposite of the "natural woman," is reinforced by the broader contours of the story as well. The first suspect in the crime, the autobiography and newspaper tell us, was not Sucky but slaves of the "West Indies." Everyone at the time must have understood that this was a reference to the massive slave uprising then going on in St. Domingue and concern that it would spread to other sugar islands. Once it had been determined that the freshly opened cask of sugar in Stoverstown was not the source of the poison, then all eyes are said to have turned to Sucky, as if she were the local individual most similar in their minds to their first suspects, a continuation of their initial train of thought.[24]

This connection makes some sense when it is recalled that the stories of the Ireland poisoning were told at the same moment that Frederick County residents were awash in news of the outbreak of the Haitian Revolution.[25] Story after story emphasized the physical horrors of the uprising, its escalating momentum, its increasing scope, and the complete inability of French forces to slow, never mind quell, the rebellion.[26] Reports also emphasized the notion that the revolt would not be contained on Hispaniola but was beginning to affect other slave societies, most particularly the British island of Jamaica.[27] Newspaper coverage also underscored the notion that free people on the island bore heavy responsibility for the revolt, in that divisions among them had emboldened slaves to act and made it difficult to put down the rebellion.[28] The newspaper additionally described a frightening surge in suspected slave conspiracies, revolts, and murders involving slaves within Virginia that year, a subtle suggestion that the uprising in St. Domingue might be felt closer to home.[29] By the end of 1792 Virginia's legislature would ratify their fears when it concluded a long debate by passing legislation to prohibit the importation of West Indian slaves to the state, a measure of the concern to prevent the "contagion of liberty" from infecting Virginia.[30]

In my view, when the poisoning narrative invoked the revolution in St. Domingue, it reinforced the story line that Sucky was a dangerous slave and that the poisoning may be read as slave rebellion. The fear of Sucky, the rebel slave, once called up, seemed very difficult to suppress. Like the rebels in the Caribbean, she was described as a danger and a contagion. Like them, she was interpreted as a force to be suppressed and quarantined.

These narratives of the Ireland household give us the briefest glimpse of Baptists telling one another stories about household governance and the mastery of slaves. But what about Baptists in Virginia more generally? Slavery was, in fact, an important issue that Baptists grappled with in the 1790s. The crisis in Ireland's household took place at a moment when the leaders of the church were actively discussing what their position on slavery should be. The Baptist General Association, which brought together ministers from the whole state of Virginia to organize political action on behalf of the congregations, sought to establish a Baptist position on slavery starting in 1785. This body, to which Ireland himself was a regular representative, ultimately proclaimed in 1790 that slavery was "a violent deprivation of the rights of nature and inconsistent with a republican government" and recommended to the Baptists of Virginia that they "make use of every legal measure, to extirpate this horrid evil from the land, and pray Almighty God that our honorable Legislature may have it in their power, to proclaim the general jubilee."[31] Two responses from regional organizations of Virginia Baptists to the statement of the General Association have survived—one issued before the St. Domingue uprising began, the other issued afterward, both disapproving of it.[32] In 1793 the General Committee voted that "the subject be dismissed from this Committee as it belongs to the legislative body." This was an important decision. In subsequent years several Baptist associations debated whether Baptists should promote some form of gradual abolition. In all cases these regional organizations quickly backed off, after polling the opinions of their individual congregations, all of them claiming that Baptists had no place, as an organization, interfering in this secular matter.[33] Starting in 1792, in other words, Baptist battles over slavery centered ever more tightly on the issue of the sacred and the secular. Slavery was judged a secular problem, to be settled by Richmond politicians (and perhaps by individual Baptist consciences), not a religious cause for Baptist preachers to place the weight of the whole church behind.[34]

None of the Baptist organizations left a record that they directly discussed slave rebellion in their decision-making processes, but, with the story of Ireland's choices about how to bring his house under control in mind, we might imagine some strong forces at work. In the previous generation Baptists had fought desperately to secure a position of legitimacy in Virginia against pointed opposition but then suddenly found traction in the years of the Revolution, when their own interests, as patriots and advocates of disestablishment, merged with the interests of the elite of the colony who led the rebellion. Baptists positioned themselves on the side of the patriot angels in the imperial struggle for their own reasons but reaped substantial rewards from upholding Virginia's rebelling government.[35] In the 1790s their newfound understanding of slavery as a secular problem might be understood not just as an effort to avoid alienating potential slaveholding converts but also, or even instead, as an effort to act in solidarity in a time of crisis, out of their own, well-developed fears.

The point here is not that the Baptists moved from antislavery to proslavery—clearly, evangelicals did not achieve unanimity of opinion on this issue either before or immediately after 1792. The point is to note that, just as the image of Sucky as a dangerous and rebellious slave, whether accurate or inaccurate, was called up by Ireland and his ghostwriter, so too might that image have occupied the thoughts of at least some of the men in charge of making Baptist social policy in the 1790s and beyond. We know that Baptists were increasingly willing to define slavery as a secular issue and to avoid taking institution-driven action against it starting in the 1790s. Ireland's story of household rebellion cannot speak directly to this issue, but it gives us occasion to at least imagine that, at a time when slavery seemed to pose particular dangers and solidarity among the free seemed particularly important to achieve in light of the revolution then under way in the Caribbean, Baptists as a group could have had a similar image of the slave rebel in mind. In their "retreat" from antislavery, we might posit, Baptists could have been acting from the same impulses as slaveholders and did not have to give in or be brought around.

It has been a recent development in the historiography of the early Baptists of the American South to note both how these evangelicals challenged dominant values and also how they undergirded them.[36] A new tolerance for ambiguity and conflicting narratives has begun to break down the old, oppositional framework that dominated scholarship for more than a generation. At the same time, recent work has begun to consider the contested nature of relations between slaves and free people within Baptist congregations and to conceive of the development of proslavery Christianity as in part a response to free peoples' lived encounters with slaves in biracial congregations.[37] Rereading *The Life of the Rev. James Ireland* can reinforce these themes of conflict and ambiguity. Probing the stories of Ireland's life deeply enough to get beyond the most direct and self-consciously constructed arguments of the memoir reveals assumptions about gender and race that are difficult to square with Ireland's self-conception as a "Baptist for the people." Taking in Ireland's story in its entirety—both for its narratives of inner turmoil, social conflict, and public persecution and also for its story of a Baptist slaveholder asserting conventional household order when under siege—undermines the old master narrative and introduces in its place multiple ways of telling a Baptist story. It suggests something about the dangers of privileging some stories over others, or turning a deaf ear to those that do not conveniently fit our purposes.

NOTES

1. James Ireland, *The Life of the Rev. James Ireland Who Was, for Many Years, Pastor of the Baptist Church in Buck Marsh, Waterlick and Happy Creek, in Frederick and Shenandoah Counties, Virginia* (Winchester, Va.: James Foster, 1819), 203 (hereafter cited as *Life of Ireland*).

2. *Life of Ireland*, 199–209; *Bowen's Virginia Centinel and Gazette; or, The Winchester Political Repository*, May 21, June 4, and September 3, 1792; Frederick County Court Minute Book, 1790–1793, 195–99, Library of Virginia; Frederick County Court Order Book no. 23, 1791–92, microfilm reel 76, 467–70; loose papers in Frederick County District Court End Causes, September–December 1792, box 6, Library of Virginia.

3. Ireland's memoir is now easily accessible to scholars and the general public, which no doubt helps explain why it has been used so extensively. It was not always clear, however, that Ireland's story would survive at all. The preacher dictated the autobiography from his deathbed in 1806, and the manuscript languished until Ireland's son prevailed upon an unnamed compiler to take the scribe's work and shepherd it into print. The 1792 poisoning story itself was in fact effectively written by this compiler, primarily drawing from Ireland's written notes on the event, supported by personal knowledge and conversations with Ireland's wife and friends (*Life of Ireland*, 197, 198). The book finally appeared in 1819, making it just barely eligible for reproduction by the Readex microform project, *Early American Imprints*, ser. 2: *Shaw-Shoemaker, 1801–1819*, which placed it in many American research libraries, where it became easily accessible to scholars. The book has now come full circle, with two new hard copy editions for general audiences in the last generation (*Concise History of the Ketocton Baptist Association & Life of James Ireland* [Harrisonburg, Va.: Sprinkle University Press, 2002]; Keith Harper and C. Martin Jacumin, eds., *Esteemed Reproach: The Lives of the Reverend James Ireland and Reverend Joseph Craig* [Macon, Ga.: Mercer University Press, 2005]).

4. For early Baptist treatment of Ireland's struggles, see, for example, James B. Taylor, *Lives of Virginia Baptist Ministers*, 2d ed. (Richmond: Vale and Wyatt, 1838), 114–25. Three excellent examples of Ireland's usefulness to Baptist historians in the last century are Lewis Peyton Little, *Imprisoned Preachers and Religious Liberty in Virginia* (Lynchburg, Va.: J. P. Bell Co., 1938); and H. Leon McBeth, *The Baptist Heritage* (Nashville: Broadman Press, 1987), 271; and Keith E. Durso, *No Armor for the Back: Baptist Prison Writings, 1600s–1700s* (Atlanta, Ga.: Mercer University Press, 2007), 239–47. It should be noted that Durso does mention the 1792 poisoning in a descriptive paragraph. The Center for Baptist Heritage Studies has used Ireland's persecution story in various ways in an effort to educate children and the general public about the early history of Virginia Baptists. See, for example, "James Ireland," *Heritage Seekers*, vol. 1 (2006); excerpts from "Our Story," a DVD educational tool produced by the Virginia Baptist Historical Society, at www.baptistheritage.org/OurStory/tabid/225/ Default.aspx; and "Acorns to Oaks," www.baptistheritage.org/AcornstoOaks/tabid/122/Default.aspx. The society also commissioned a painting of Ireland preaching from his jail cell as part of a thirty-six-panel mural depicting key moments in Baptist history by important historical artist Sidney E. King. The story of Ireland's struggles now reaches a non-Baptist popular audience as well. Colonial Williamsburg, for example, has staged "impersonations" of James Ireland, at which he discusses "his conversation, trials, temptations and eventual redemption in a time of political upheaval and revolution" (Colonial Williamsburg website, www.history.org/Foundation/press_release/displayPressRelease.cfm?pressReleaseId=931).

5. Rhys Isaac, "Evangelical Revolt: The Nature of the Baptists' Challenge to the Traditional Order in Virginia, 1765 to 1775," *William and Mary Quarterly* 31 (1974): 345–68. Many historians have, in some measure, described early southern evangelicals in socially oppositional terms. See, for example, Wesley Gewehr, *The Great Awakening in Virginia, 1740–1790* (1930; repr., Gloucester, Mass.: P. Smith, 1965); Donald G. Mathews, *Religion in the Old South* (Chicago: University of Chicago Press, 1977); Rhys Isaac, *The Transformation of Virginia, 1740–1790* (Chapel Hill: University of North Carolina Press, 1984); James D. Essig, *The*

*Bonds of Wickedness: American Evangelicals against Slavery, 1770–1808* (Philadelphia: Temple University Press, 1982); Christine Leigh Heyrman, *Southern Cross: The Beginnings of the Bible Belt* (New York: Knopf, 1997); Janet Moore Lindman, "Acting the Manly Christian: White Evangelical Masculinity in Revolutionary Virginia," *William and Mary Quarterly* 57 (2000): 393–441; Thomas Kidd, *The Great Awakening: The Roots of Evangelical Christianity in Colonial America* (New Haven: Yale University Press, 2007), 247–48; and Monica Najar, *Evangelizing the South: A Social History of Church and State in Early America* (New York: Oxford University Press, 2008). Some recent work has offered a more nuanced interpretation, without fully abandoning the received narrative. See particularly Charles Irons, *The Origins of Proslavery Christianity: White and Black Evangelicals in Colonial and Antebellum Virginia* (Chapel Hill: University of North Carolina Press, 2008); Janet Moore Lindman, *Bodies of Belief: Baptist Community in Early America* (Philadelphia: University of Pennsylvania Press, 2008); and Randolph Ferguson Scully, *Religion and the Making of Nat Turner's Virginia: Baptist Community and Conflict, 1740–1840* (Charlottesville: University of Virginia Press, 2008).

6. For sustained discussions of Baptist conversion that use Ireland's narrative, see, for example, Philip N. Mulder, *A Controversial Spirit: Evangelical Awakenings in the South* (New York: Oxford University Press, 2002), 46–47, 49–50; Rodger M. Payne, *The Self and the Sacred: Conversion and Autobiography in Early American Protestantism* (Knoxville: University of Tennessee Press, 1998), 85–91; and Spangler, *Virginians Reborn: Anglican Establishment, Evangelical Dissent and the Rise of the Baptists in the Late Eighteenth Century* (Charlottesville: University of Virginia Press, 2008), 175–79. For briefer mentions, see Lindman, *Bodies of Belief,* 58, 66; Scully, *Religion and the Making of Nat Turner's Virginia,* 77.

7. Jerry L. Tarver, "Baptist Preaching from Virginia Jails," *Southern Speech Journal* 30 (1964): 139–48; Isaac, "Evangelical Revolt," 345–46, 365–66; Sandra Rennie, "Virginia's Baptist Persecution, 1765–1778," *Journal of Religious History* 12 (1982): 48–61; James D. Essig, "A Very Wintery Season: Virginia Baptists and Slavery, 1785–1979," *Virginia Magazine of History and Biography* 88 (1980): 176–77; Heyrman, *Southern Cross,* 17.

8. A number of excellent studies have recently focused on crime, trials, and their popular press coverage. See, for example, Melvin A. McLaurin, *Celia: A Slave* (Athens: University of Georgia Press, 1991); Sean Wilentz and Paul Johnson, *The Kingdom of Matthias: A Story of Sex and Salvation in 19th-Century America* (New York: Oxford University Press, 1995); and Patricia Cline Cohen, *The Murder of Helen Jewett: The Life and Death of a Prostitute in Nineteenth-Century New York* (New York: Knopf, 1998). This essay is not a microhistorical study of that sort.

9. In addition to the sources cited in n. 2, this narrative was based on *Bowen's Virginia Centinel and Gazette,* March 18, 1793, 3; and Frederick County Personal Property Tax Book, 1793, microfilm reel 124.

10. For a discussion of spiritual autobiographies and their narrative forms, see, for example, Peter A. Dorsey, *Sacred Estrangement: The Rhetoric of Conversion in Modern American Autobiography* (University Park: Pennsylvania State University Press, 1993), esp. 17–42; Payne, *Self and the Sacred;* and Daniel B. Shea Jr., *Spiritual Autobiography in Early America* (Princeton: Princeton University Press, 1968).

11. Ireland, *Life of Ireland,* 7, 197, 198.

12. See, for example, Robert B. Semple, *A History of the Rise and Progress of the Baptists of Virginia,* rev. and extended by G. W. Beale (1819; repr., Richmond: Pitt and Dickinson, 1894); and William Fristoe, *A Concise History of the Ketocton Baptist Association* (Staunton, Va.: William Gilman Lyford, 1808).

13. For a discussion of the style of patriarchal governance, see Kathleen M. Brown, *Good Wives, Nasty Wenches, and Anxious Patriarchs: Gender, Race, and Power in Colonial Virginia* (Chapel Hill: University of North Carolina Press, 1996), 334–42; Mark E. Kann, *A Republic of Men: The American Founders, Gendered Language, and Patriarchal Politics* (New York: New York University Press, 1998), 5–29; and Carole Shammas, *A History of Household Government in America* (Charlottesville: University of Virginia Press, 2002).

14. Ireland, *Life of Ireland,* 208.

15. Ibid., 208, 209.

16. For a discussion of the idea of the rebel slave and gender, see, for example, Rebecca Hall, "Not Killing Me Softly: African American Women, Slave Revolts, and Historical Constructions of Racialized Gender" (Ph.D. diss., University of California at Santa Cruz, 2004); and Maggie Montesinos Sale, *The Slumbering Volcano: American Slave Ship Revolts and the Production of Rebellious Masculinity* (Durham: Duke University Press, 1997). For a discussion of widespread fear of rebellion, see Brian Ray Gabrial, "'The Melancholy Effect of Popular Excitement': Discourse about Slavery and the Social Construction of the Slave Rebel and Conspirator in Newspapers" (Ph.D. diss., University of Minnesota, 2004).

17. There was a Southerlin family living in the same district of the county as Ireland in 1792 (Frederick County Personal Property Tax Book, 1792, microfilm reel 124). Ireland's autobiography reported that when Betsy was questioned about the poisoning, she described purchasing the arsenic from an apothecary who knew her and her mother. It was claimed that she used that familiarity to her advantage, convincing him to sell her the arsenic by reminding him that her mother had previously used it to kill rats and asserting that she was purchasing it for her mother's use (Ireland, *Life of Ireland,* 200).

18. Other sources repeat this tendency to push Betsy's active role in the poisoning to the background even while developing a narrative of her culpability. The local newspaper reported the poisoning as the "supposed" act of "a mulatto female servant," without any mention of Betsy at all, and then followed up two weeks later with a report that Sucky was tried on the charge of "administering poison," while Betsy was "examined" "as an accomplice." In the fall the paper reported that the grand jury had found a "true bill" against Betsy "for being concerned in administering poison." *Bowen's Virginia Centinel and Gazette,* May 21, 1792, 3; June 4, 1792, 3; and September 3, 1792.

19. Ireland, *Life of Ireland,* 204–5, 208.

20. Frederick County District Court End Causes, box 6, September–December 1792, Library of Virginia.

21. On evangelical southern women, men, and gender relations, see, for example, Heyrman, *Southern Cross;* Lindman, "Acting the Manly Christian"; Blair A. Pogue, "'I Cannot Believe the Gospel That Is So Much Preached': Gender, Belief, and Discipline in Baptist Religious Culture," in *The Buzzel about Kentuck: Settling of the Promised Land,* ed. Craig Thompson Friend (Lexington: University Press of Kentucky., 1999), 217–42; Lindman,

*Bodies of Belief,* 112–33; and Najar, *Evangelizing the South,* esp. chap. 2; and Scott Stephan, *Redeeming the Southern Family: Evangelical Women and Domestic Devotion in the Antebellum South* (Athens: University of Georgia Press, 2008). It should be remembered that while Betsy Southerlin was herself not a converted Baptist, the poisoning story does narrate Ireland as a Baptist head of household.

22. Sucky was probably born in North America, as there are no indications otherwise in the narrative, and at one point she is described in the newspaper as a "mulatto." Ireland had paid personal property taxes on her for several years before 1792 as well as on her young child.

23. The *Oxford English Dictionary* gives an eighteenth-century definition for *artful* as "Skilful in adapting means to ends, so as to secure the accomplishment of a purpose, adroit; passing gradually into: Skilful in taking an unfair advantage; using stratagem, wily; cunning, crafty, deceitful."

24. Philip D. Morgan briefly mentions a connection between the 1792 poisoning story and West Indian slaves (see *Slave Counterpoint: Black Culture in the Eighteenth-Century Chesapeake and Lowcountry* [Chapel Hill: University of North Carolina Press, 1998], 619), but the link to the Haitian Revolution has been left largely unexplored in the historical literature.

25. The newspaper noted that conflict among free people had surfaced there with the outbreak of the French Revolution, at once echoing the divisions of that revolution, reinforcing class divisions within the colony, and opening up for debate the place of free people of color. They learned that in August 1791 slaves dramatically entered the contest, launching a violent uprising of enormous proportions, which plunged St. Domingue into war. When Ireland's poisoning took place, French troops had arrived in the Caribbean to enter the fray, but the conflict still raged out of control. The United States was sending supplies to support the French effort, and some American politicians (such as secretary of state Thomas Jefferson) were actually urging a negotiated peace with the rebels that included limited emancipation, to stave off the complete destruction of slavery in St. Domingue. At that moment the specter of general emancipation loomed large, but it would not come to fruition (for a time) for another year, releasing a flood of refugees into U.S. ports in 1793. For a good overview of the revolution in St. Domingue in the early 1790s, see David Patrick Geggus, *Haitian Revolutionary Studies* (Bloomington: Indiana University Press, 2002). For the American reaction to the Haitian Revolution, see Alfred N. Hunt, *Haiti's Influence on Antebellum America: Slumbering Volcano in the Caribbean* (Baton Rouge: Louisiana State University Press, 1988); and Tim Matthewson, *A Proslavery Foreign Policy: Haitian-American Relations during the Early Republic* (Westport, Conn.: Praeger, 2003).

26. A January 1792 report out of Providence, Rhode Island, for example, brought news from the island that a "party of French horse had been attacked by the revolted Negroes and about 40 of the former killed, which had given great spirits to the blacks; that the whites had abandoned Curacole and Jaquize, and that the former was in flames" (*Bowen's Virginia Centinel and Gazette,* January 7, 1792, 2). Midway through the year Frederick County residents read that the situation had only worsened. An extracted letter from "Cap Francais" noted "when peace will be restored to this unhappy place God only knows. I have witnessed more misery in the last six months than, perhaps, was ever exhibited in any place" (*Bowen's Virginia Centinel and Gazette,* May 21, 1792, 2).

27. In January 1792, for example, Frederick residents read a letter from Jamaica that "the spirit of revolt among the negroes had at length reached that island . . . inhabitants were sincerely alarmed for their safety, had proclaimed martial law, and were taking every precaution in their power to prevent a general insurrection" (*Bowen's Virginia Centinel and Gazette,* January 7, 1792, 2). In April they read of troops arriving in Jamaica to "awe the negroes from a tendency to insurrection" (*Bowen's Virginia Centinel and Gazette,* April 16, 1792), 2.

28. See, for example, *Bowen's Virginia Centinel and Gazette,* May 21, 1792, 2. Frederick County residents also learned that the uprising could have impacts much closer to home when they read that the insurrection threatened to undermine a contract between the United States and St. Domingue for the purchase of fine and superfine flour, which Frederick County residents were involved in supplying (see *Bowen's Virginia Centinel and Gazette,* February 11, 1792, 3).

29. A report from the eastern shore of Virginia in May announced, for example, that "a very dangerous insurrection among the negroes on the Eastern-Shore" was under way, in which "about 900 assembled in different parties, armed with muskets, spears, clubs, &c. and committed several outrages upon the inhabitants." A later article revealed that the first report had been vastly exaggerated (see *Bowen's Virginia Centinel and Gazette,* May 28, 1792, 2; June 4, 1792, 3).

30. Hunt, *Haiti's Influence,* 108–9.

31. *Minutes of the Baptist General Committee at Their Yearly Meeting, Held in the City of Richmond, May 8th, 1790* (Richmond: T. Nicolson, n.d.), 7.

32. The Roanoke Baptist Association rejected the statement in 1790 because of fear that a hasty emancipation would deprive slaveholders' children of their livelihood. They did not, however, question the right of Baptists to consider and take positions on slavery. See Roanoke Baptist Association, Minute Book, 1789–1831, MS, Virginia Baptist Historical Society, 38 (June 1790). Strawberry Baptist Association came out against the General Committee's statement the same month as Ireland's poisoning. The statement was not very specific—they "answered thus; we advise them [the General Committee] not to interfere in it." Here we begin to get a hint that perhaps opinion was moving against the church taking positions on slavery at all. See Strawberry Association Minute Book, 1787–1822, photostat, Virginia Baptist Historical Society, 45 (May 1792); *Minutes of the Baptist General Committee, Holden at Muddy-Creek Meeting-House: Powhatan County, Virginia, May 1793* (Richmond: T. Nicolson, 1793), 4. The Roanoke association had also claimed that it might not be the mandate of a religious body such as the General Committee to address a general emancipation, but rather than simply say that the subject was not "religious" and belonged strictly to the legislature, the association explained that its reasoning was that the issue was very complex, that it was not completely clear what God intended with respect to such institutions of human inequality, and that individuals should be left to act at their own discretion.

33. *Minutes of the Baptist Dover Association, Held at Bestland Meeting-House, Essex County, Virginia, October 14th 1797* (Richmond: John Dixon, n.d.), 5; *Minutes of the Ketocton Baptist Association, Held at Thumb Run, Fauquier County, Virginia, August 1796* (Dumfries, Va.: Printed by Thomas Thornton[?], 1796), 4, 5; *Minutes of the Ketocton Baptist Association Held*

at Frying-Pan, Loudoun County, August, 1797 (n.p., n.d.), 4, 6; *Minutes of the Ketockton Baptist Association, Continued at Broad-Run Meeting-House, Fauquier County, Virginia, August 4, 1798* (Winchester, Va.: Richard Bowen, n.d.), 3–4; *Minutes of the Kehukee Baptist Association Holden at Parker's Meeting-House, on Meherrin, Hertford County, North Carolina, September, 1796* (n.p., n.d.), 4; *Minutes of the Kehukee Baptist Association, Holden at Cashie Meeting-House, Bertie County, N. Carolina, Thursday, September 20, 1798* (n.p, n.d.), 3.

34. This move toward defining slavery as a governmental problem beyond the purview of the church has been beautifully highlighted by Monica Najar. See "'Meddling with Emancipation': Baptists, Authority, and the Rift over Slavery in the Upper South," *Journal of the Early Republic* 25.2 (2005): 157–86.

35. Spangler, *Virginians Reborn*, esp. 195–229; Charles F. Irons, "Believing in America: Faith and Politics in Early National Virginia," *American Baptist Quarterly* 21 (2002): 397.

36. See particularly Irons, *Origins of Proslavery Christianity*; Lindman, *Bodies of Belief*; and Scully, *Religion and Nat Turner's Virginia*.

37. See particularly Irons, *Origins of Proslavery Christianity*; and Scully, *Religion and Nat Turner's Virginia*.

# "And Bid Him Bear a Patriot's Part"

*National and Local Perspectives on Confederate Nationalism*

ORVILLE VERNON BURTON *and* IAN BINNINGTON

Hail, lone and lovely Star! thy rays
Shall kindle in each Texan heart,
Once more the old heroic blaze.
And bid him bear a Patriot's part

—*Edgefield Advertiser*, February 19, 1862

Albert Padgett, sixteen years old in 1860, opposed secession. Padgett, a native of Edgefield District, South Carolina, was attending Dickinson College in Pennsylvania when South Carolina seceded. As a college student, he wrote of the men who advocated it that they, "as Milton expresses it—'Had rather rule in Hell, Than serve in Heaven,'" and they "ought never to be favored by the true Southerner." His attitude changed just a few months later, however, when war came. He returned to South Carolina and transferred to his denominational (Methodist) college, Wofford, in Spartanburg District. He joined many of his classmates in the "Spartan Rifles" and marched with them to Virginia. After his initial duty, Padgett re-enlisted. Yet, at the same time that his Confederate national sentiment was growing, he chose to move his enlistment closer to home. He joined an Edgefield company known as the Saluda Riflemen, of the Seventh South Carolina regiment, "to be with his neighbors."[1] Even though his home district of Edgefield was less than sixty miles from Spartanburg, his growing sense of Confederate nationalism did not diminish his preference to be with a company even more closely associated with his local identity. Both local affiliation and national vision worked within Albert Padgett, as they did with so many other Confederate southerners.

On September 17, 1862, Corporal Padgett, fighting beside his friends, relatives, and neighbors at Sharpsburg, was shot while aiding a fallen comrade. As the Confederate army retreated into Virginia, Padgett was left behind with other wounded. Eighteen years old, he died on January 3, 1863, and was buried far from Edgefield and South Carolina in Mount Olivet Cemetery, Frederick City, Maryland. After news of his death reached them, the Saluda Riflemen published a "Tribute of Respect" to young Padgett in the *Edgefield Advertiser*. The student who had once opposed secession was now a martyr. Padgett "died like a Christian hero, worthy of the great cause in which he was engaged." Padgett's death, explained his comrades, "can have no other effect than to alienate our affections towards the invaders and sow deep in our bosoms an undying hatred." His death invited others "to the banquet of blood prepared by Lincoln and his fiendish Cabinet for the brave defenders of our home to pour out, as a sort of panacea for all our heart-burning and desire for revenge in this our struggle for National Liberty."[2] For Edgefield, in death and memory Albert Padgett became a symbol of Confederate nationalism.

While historians of the South and the Civil War have discussed the question of Confederate nationalism, many of their studies have concentrated on the role of nationalism in Confederate defeat. With exemplary scholarship historians have shown how states' rights and pervasive localism sowed the seeds of defeat—seeds that could not sprout into the strong Confederate nationalism needed to win the Civil War. Historians have often jumped to the end of the story, though, using loss of popular will and military defeat as the lens through which to assess Confederate nationalism.[3] In so doing, they have tended to underemphasize the extraordinarily rich theoretical literature on nationalism. Instead, Confederate nationalism and nationalism studies generally need to be reintegrated, so that we may fully realize Drew Faust's suggestion that we take Confederate nationalism "on its own terms" and examine it as an attempt "to represent Southern culture to the world at large, to history, and perhaps most revealingly to its own people."[4]

Historians have debated when the South, in opposition to the non-South, was created; the words *South, Southrons,* and *Southerners* were meaningful and common terms long before the firing on Fort Sumter, before a Confederate state existed. Yet allegiance to the "South" over and above allegiance to a local community was not predominant.[5] Before the Civil War, according to William Freehling, "if asked to describe his primary allegiance to others," a southerner "would not likely have said that he was above all an American or a Southerner or a South Carolinian or even a resident of Colleton County. Rather, he was proud to be from Whippy Swamp."[6] Yet, as the example of young Padgett illustrates, the meaning of *southerner* and the actions of a true scion of the South could change dramatically in a short span of time. By late 1862 that same Whippy Swampian, or Edgefieldian, would have described himself un-self-consciously as a Confederate, a partisan of the new Confederate nation.

Any effort to analyze the meaning of Confederate nationalism is daunting because *nationalism* as a term of analysis resists easy definition. As Philip Curtin has noted, the concept of nationalism "has long since expanded into a cloud of loose implications and emotional overtones."[7] Scholars have proposed definitions ranging from Ernest Renan's abstract assertion that a nation is "a soul, a spiritual principle," to Anthony Giddens's sociopolitical belief that a nation is "a bordered power-container," to Walker Connor's characterization of a nation as "a self-aware ethnic group."[8] By contrast, historian Robert Wiebe has called for scholars of nationalism to recognize that nationalism "arises out of a cluster of shared beliefs that are always contested, always labile, always in the process of re-creation."[9] Similarly, according to Benedict Anderson's influential theory, the nation is "imagined as a *community,* because, regardless of the actual inequality and exploitation that may prevail in each, the nation is always conceived as a deep, horizontal comradeship."[10] In Anderson's formulation the national and the local are directly linked through what he calls "print culture," but the locus of nationalism is never made explicit. Does the imagined community descend from placeless literary abstractions, or does it ascend from the experiences of ordinary people at multiple local sites? Addressing this question, other scholars have argued that, while nationalism begins "in the imagination," it is also the case "that local persons and material conditions can and did affect those imaginings in profound ways."[11] Although a nation is collectively imagined in the abstract, therefore, connections at the national level work in similar ways to more intimate, backyard bonds of comity. The national "imagined community," ultimately, only makes sense because it is built upon the *local* imagined community.[12]

To provide a framework for explaining the way that men and women forged links between community and nation, we invoke the work of historian David Potter, who has succinctly argued that people base their devotion to the nation on the belief that the nation protects that which is dear to them. The viability of Confederate nationalism, therefore, depended critically on the Confederate States of America's ability to convince southerners that it embodied and protected their values,[13] including home, hearth, community, white supremacy, and slavery. In this context preexisting loyalties, principally those of local community, began to expand within the lived experiences of war, to encompass more than they had before, ultimately expanding so far as to embrace the idea of nation itself. Hugh Seton-Watson has described Russia's state-centered attempts at nation building as "stretching the short, tight, skin of the nation over the gigantic body of the empire."[14] Borrowing this formulation and applying it to the South's local peculiarities, we exchange *community* and *nation* for Seton-Watson's *nation* and *empire* and see the Confederacy from a different perspective—that is, "stretching the short, tight, skin of the *local community* over the gigantic body of the *nation*." Nation building, in other words, is a process by which a people's mental topographies connect concrete, local identities to an abstract, national identity.

Writing on late-nineteenth-century German nationalism, Alon Confino has addressed the multiple loci of nation building by arguing perceptively that historians must find a "remedy to the artificial dichotomy between nationalism from above and from below."[15] We echo this assertion and seek to examine the multiple levels of nation building. Therefore, we believe that an examination of Confederate nationalism in the Civil War South can benefit from a two-pronged approach, one that juxtaposes a local perspective, on the one hand, and a regional literary perspective, on the other. In the local approach we look for evidence of Confederate nationalism "from below" in a particular local community, specifically the slave-owning community of Edgefield District in upcountry South Carolina; in our analysis of nationalism "from above," we examine literature aimed at a pan-southern readership as a way of cementing the national imagined community. Ultimately, we hope this analysis opens up a new understanding of the ways in which both the ground level of experience of civil war in a specific community and the abstractions of Confederate literature helped solidify the amorphous entity that became Confederate nationalism.

First and foremost, southerners understood the unfolding political drama through events in their own local society. The aggregate of communities that came together to form the Confederacy were far from monolithic; local society and community varied enormously. While the Edgefield District was not "typical," however, of *the* Confederate community, any more than Albert Padgett was typical of *the* Confederate soldier, it can act as one particular lens to focus our attention. On the western border of South Carolina, across the Savannah River from Augusta, Georgia, midway between the Blue Ridge Mountains and the Atlantic Ocean, Edgefield District was only touched by actual fighting at the very edges of the large piedmont district. Yet Edgefieldians experienced the war in many ways. Soldiers fought in many theaters and countless battles and skirmishes, while their relatives at home worried and lived amid the turmoil of wartime.[16]

Along with this local lens, we analyze the creation of national identity in literature, especially novels, of the Civil War South. This literature, often published in Richmond or Mobile, was produced less for a specific local community and more for an abstract body of Confederate readers. While the leading scholar of Civil War popular literature, Alice Fahs, effectively mines Confederate periodical literature, her analysis of the extant collection of wartime Confederate novels is more limited. The only Confederate novel that appears (and then briefly so) in her text is Augusta Jane Evans's *Macaria*.[17] Our analysis, though, includes a more systematic examination of wartime Confederate literature as a genre, taken on its own terms as a literary expression of southern nationalism. Study of these Confederate novels opens up a valuable window onto the process by which some Confederate literary elites tried to articulate the founding principles of their nation in a fictional form. Literature is essential for an analysis of nation building's multiple levels because it straddles the artificial boundary between the intelligentsia as nationalist producer and the citizen as nationalist consumer (one model of nationalism-in-formation): author and reader cooperate in the shared act of writing and reading, distant in time and sometimes in understanding yet united in the creation of a shared meaning.

Writing a constitution, like creating an army, navy, or system of currency and taxation, is nation building of a sort. But this state-focused approach is not enough to create allegiance to a nation; rather, the people's support is an essential element. This is a crucial point because it is apparent in the local context that a sense of Confederate nationalism based on political apparatus was not the reason so many young southern boys volunteered to fight or that so many southern girls urged them to go. Initially, the Civil War was a local affair, and their response to the war was an affirmation of community identity. Community and family went hand in hand as families often settled near one another and attended the same church in what was termed their "settlement." With the first call to support a war for southern independence, Edgefieldians interpreted the meaning of the conflict and reacted to its demands from the perspective of their own families, relatives, friends, and local community. Although slavery defined the southern way of life (and words such as *liberty* and *independence* must be read in that context), even the white plain folk who had no slaves and little or no wealth had stakes in the community. For them the war was a matter of honor, a fight to protect community values.

Thus, at the war's outset Confederate nationalism did not spring up fully formed. Instead, layers of meaning built upon each other as people developed an understanding of war and nation in relation to local community. Lincoln's victory in November 1860 caused country villages, just like the state assembly in Columbia, to debate the question of secession. Emulating their Revolutionary grandparents and ancestors, companies of "Minute Men" formed throughout Edgefield District; on November 10 the Hamburg Minutemen concluded an evening of fireworks and political speeches by burning Lincoln in effigy. Six hundred people turned out at Edgefield Court House on November 13 to hear the report of the "Committee of Fifty," citizens who had been chosen eight days earlier and charged with drawing up resolutions for public discussion. This local committee emphasized South Carolina's independence, recommending that "secession of the state from the Federal Union is the proper mode of resistance."[18] On December 20 the secession convention in the state capital fulfilled the wish of the editor of the *Edgefield Advertiser*, who had hoped to publish the good news not that South Carolina was part of a new nation or confederacy but that it was "a free and independent republic."[19]

Even then, however, nationalistic demonstrations were not absent from communities such as Edgefield. In one case an Edgefield citizen linked home, community, and country, writing under the bold title "Awake! Awake!": "Come from the rivers, hills, valleys and plains. Come to the rescue of our country from the dangers that threaten our wives, our children and our domestic peace. Come without prejudice to any man, and let us reason together as patriots and not as partisans."[20] The calls to come together as a community reflected the same attitude at the start of the Mexican War. In May 1846 Joseph Abney suggested the primary reason that Edgefieldians volunteered for that war and, we believe, for the Civil War as well. "The blow has been struck . . . and whether she be right or wrong, we go for our country with all our mind, and with all our heart. . . . The man that pauses now to ask, who brought about the conflict, is like the man, who, when his neighbor's house is on fire, cries 'stop the incendiary,' whilst the devouring flames roll on unrestrained, and wrap the noble tenement in destruction and ashes. . . . We are truly proud to see our countrymen, from all quarters rushing with he[roi]c ardor to the conflict—it do[e]s honor to them as Americ[an]s,—it does honor to the country they call their own."[21] Initially, Edgefieldians went to war—and thus answered the call of the Confederate nation—from a sense of local pride, honor, and duty. But the experience of going to war expanded the ideological horizons of those young men and, at least to a certain extent, the horizons of those they left at home. The decision to act locally had nationalist implications.

This process was not without controversy, however. Even those willing to defend South Carolina were not necessarily willing to defend a new Confederate States of America. In May 1861 a regiment stationed on the South Carolina coast was split so that some members of Edgefield companies were assigned to a regiment being sent to Virginia. Of a thousand soldiers in the regiment, not more than one hundred were willing to leave South Carolina. In a letter to the Edgefield paper, the captain of the group that refused to go sought to explain why "a large majority of the Commissioned and Non-Commissioned officers and privates . . . declined to follow Col. [Maxcey] Gregg to Virginia." The captain reminded readers that these civilian soldiers had left "businesses, homes and families at a few hours notice" and rushed to Charleston in the first week of January 1861, before there was a Confederacy and before any other state had seceded. "During the whole period we had never dreamed of leaving our own State—one acre of whose soil is dearer to many of us than the balance of the continent—the *possibility* of being required or asked to do, had never been hinted to us by those in authority." Connecting family to community and the state, the captain described Gregg as a "man without family" who "could not appreciate the conflicting emotions which stirred the breasts of his command." The captain accused Gregg of incorrectly attributing the negative response to his call to mere "cowardice." He further charged Gregg of plying troops with liquor to entice them to follow him.[22] The Edgefield Riflemen who did accompany Gregg to Virginia took umbrage at the notion that they drunkenly volunteered under the sway of Colonel Gregg, yet they defended those who had refused to leave South Carolina because they had done so in the "defence of their country."[23]

For some wealthy Edgefieldians and political elites, the ability to envision and support a Confederate nation early in the war was less difficult. James Henry Hammond, who famously declared, "Cotton is King!" in the U.S. Senate, demonstrated an early willingness to make sacrifices on behalf of the war effort.[24] Likewise, James B. Griffin, a wealthy Edgefield planter, wholeheartedly supported the Confederate cause. In June 1861 Griffin showed no reluctance to go beyond Edgefield and even South Carolina to fight for the southern nation when he was appointed a cavalry major in Wade Hampton's legion and left for Virginia. In a February 1862 letter to his wife he described his nationalistic determination: "If the unprincipled North shall persist in her policy of Subjugating the South, that we, who are able to resist them, will continue to do so, until we grow old and worn out in the service, and that then, our Sons will take the arms from our hands, and spend their lives, if necessary in battling for Liberty and independence." Griffin even accepted that their infant son, "yes darling little Jimmie," would eventually "take his Father's place in the fields, and fight until he dies, rather than, be a Slave. *Yea* worse than a Slave to Yankee Masters."[25]

Over time the experience of fighting a war invoked local expressions of nationalism that echoed Griffin's enthusiasm, rather than the provincialism and reluctance characteristic of soldiers' reactions in the war's early stages. The *Edgefield Advertiser*, for instance, published poems that extolled southern pride for the cause of the Confederate war effort. On February 19, 1862, the *Advertiser* published "Twilight Prayer for Our Country," which clearly defined its readers' country as the Confederacy by calling on "*every* Southron" to protect the country.[26] "The Volunteers," published on April 30, 1862, is written from the perspective of volunteers heeding "our country's call," who promised not to return to "dear ones" at home until the Yankees were defeated.[27] During the war years the commitment of the *Edgefield Advertiser* to publish nationalist literature that invoked the defense of southern homes in the fight against the "Northern horde" was fairly consistent with the only two major exceptions consisting of the periods following important Confederate defeats, at Gettysburg and Vicksburg in the summer of 1863 and at Atlanta in the autumn of 1864.[28]

Women were instrumental in writing much of the literature in the *Advertiser,* and many of the pieces published during the war years deployed commonly understood gender roles in order to advance the Confederate cause. As Drew Faust has noted, southern women writers supported the war effort by urging men to leave the "home front" to go off and fight.[29] Edgefield writers employed this trope throughout the war. In its early years they portrayed women cheering the "sons of southern soil" who heeded their "country's calling" by meeting in battle the northern soldiers who had crossed the "border line" and trod on southern land.[30] Later on, women were called upon to find the soldier's "empty sleeve" an attractive badge of honor,[31] and they were urged to shame deserters.[32] Local writers portrayed mothers and widows as valiantly sacrificing their sons and lovers to the war effort,[33] although this duty seemed to become more burdensome as the military losses became more devastating.[34] Increasingly, women tied their fate to the national project as they wrote about the incredibly emotional impact of a war to protect southern soil, a war whose effects literally hit close to home.

Certainly, on the local home front in Edgefield, writers were employing print as one way to begin to forge a national identity and thus connect with the Confederacy. In order to understand more broadly the way that literature conceptualized the imagined community of the Confederate nation and its relationship to local communities, we turn now to an analysis of literature produced for a more general southern readership. Historians have noted that antebellum novelists such as John Pendleton Kennedy, William Gilmore Simms, and Nathaniel Beverly Tucker sought to "restore order and purpose to an increasingly Yankee world" through southern sectional literature. Similarly, during the war years novelists continued seeking this distinct sense of order and purpose as they tried to imagine a Confederate national identity. In the antebellum years Simms had felt that the route to nationalism lay in sectionalism—that "devotion to the nation stemmed from loyalties that were immediate and local."[35] Likewise, during the Civil War Confederate novelists sought to foster loyalty and devotion to the new Confederate nation. As Benedict Anderson noted for the seventeenth and eighteenth centuries, "print-capitalism" provided a root from which nationalism emerged, and the intellectual elite of the Confederate South were very interested in promulgating nationalism through literary culture. Alice Fahs notes that "in both North and South, popular war literature was vitally important in shaping a cultural politics of war." War literature "did not just reflect a new united nationhood; it attempted to imagine such unity into being rhetorically."[36]

Early on, a number of southern commentators were impatient for a body of literature that would enable the production of a common identity at both the local and the regional levels. Writing just before the war, Henry Timrod bemoaned the lack of a truly national, southern voice in literature: "No one who does not speak for himself can speak for his country, and therefore, no imitator can be national."[37] Five years later, in January 1864, Frank H. Alfriend, the new editor of the *Southern Literary Messenger*, stressed the importance of literary expression for national power. "Where is the nation," he asked, "which in any age, in any department or arena of action, has ever attained a position of eminence or even respectability among its compeers, that is not under the heaviest obligation of gratitude to its Historians, its Poets, and its Novelists?"[38] By this time, however, Timrod admitted that he saw the stirrings of southern literature amid the fires of war. Writing for the Columbia newspaper the *Daily South Carolinian,* he noted that "the great and troubled movement through which we are passing has stirred the Southern mind to an unwonted activity. . . . we perceive the national mind struggling to find fit and original expression."[39]

Proclamations about the necessity of national literature aside, the relationship between a burgeoning corpus of this literature and a particular locale, such as Edgefield, must proceed from a series of informed assumptions. First, the act of writing is an individual, particularistic cultural expression, but it also claims an audience in a wider cultural milieu than can be encompassed by the individual; it is in that sense an act of community. Second, the act of publishing is a commercial enterprise that mediates between cultural expression and profit. Publishers believe there is a market for what they have to offer, that the community will purchase and read it. Third, the act of reading can be individualistic and private, but it can also be communal and public. Writing represents an act of community that includes author, publisher, and public collaborating in the cultural enterprise.[40] Writing on "The Civil War as a Popular Literary Event," Fahs makes the point that authoring, publishing, and reading became vitally important acts of nationalism in the context of the Civil War. For Confederates, in particular, "the act of reading itself now took on a strongly ideological cast. . . . Suffused with nationalistic aims, reading was less a private than a public, patriotic act."[41]

Reading thus reinforced a sense of nation linked to community and helped bridge the gap between the experienced reality of everyday life and the emotive abstraction of a national life. In the America of the 1860s most classes of white people had the opportunity to participate to some extent in the "taking of the news," which often included novels, many of which were first printed as serials in the leading newspapers or journals of the day, offering another way to reach less developed rural locales in the South. Reading the news was often a public and participatory affair. Newspapers were readily available in taverns, where they were often read aloud to attentive and sometimes fractious crowds.[42] Similarly, community members read aloud as an accompaniment to such patriotic activities as preparing comfort packages for the troops. Shortages of paper during the war also meant that people read to each other and shared most print media. Within the home families read aloud to each other as a form of entertainment. The entire family shared newspapers, and, although there was a commonly held notion that politics was a male preserve, by the middle of the nineteenth century women's interest was becoming more overt. Women's magazines were extremely active, and women were increasingly targets of subscription drives.[43]

In these ways contemporary print media were a primary means of transmission for a nationalist ethos in the making. Mistakenly, though, much of the scholarship on reading during antebellum and Civil War America does not focus on southern states because of prevalent stereotypes of southern illiteracy. The idea of an illiterate antebellum white South was propagated for their particular purposes both by the North and the planter class, and that idea is still widespread. Ronald J. Zboray, for example, who argues that "as industrialism spread in antebellum America, the printed word became the primary avenue of national enculturation," downplays the place of the South in the developing national consciousness. Zboray calls attention to the South's low literacy rates, yet his figures point to a literacy rate among white adult southerners at 93.8 percent—fifteen of sixteen white southerners were literate.[44] Indeed, according to James McPherson, Civil War armies, including the Confederacy's, were "the most literate in all history to that time." Elisabeth Muhlenfeld concurs; she found that southern soldiers craved all forms of print media, and "novels were usually read literally to pieces."[45]

Although we have not found a particular reader in Edgefield who was reading a particular "Confederate" novel,[46] we know that the people of Edgefield read avidly. When Robert Mills conducted a survey of the state of South Carolina in 1825, he noted that "a taste for reading has been manifested by the ladies of the village of Edgefield, who, with several gentlemen, constitute a society, which is called the Edgefield Female Library Society." White Edgefieldians also belonged to book clubs and other organizations, such as the Beech Island Farmers' Club, which regularly presented papers and discussed books.[47] Citizens of Edgefield also devoured newspapers. With less than three thousand white households, the subscription rate to the *Edgefield Advertiser* was at fifteen hundred in 1853.[48] As indicated earlier, the *Edgefield Advertiser* regularly featured poems, short stories, and other occasional pieces, edited and sometimes written by a local woman, Clara V. Dargan. Nearly every issue advertised "literary journals."

Taking into account this strong local context of readership, we are able to draw historical conclusions about the impact of Confederate novels at the local level. Our assessment of Civil War Confederate literature corresponds with that of Amy M. Thomas, writing of the thirst for reading material among the people of Edgefield in the mid-1850s, that "what remains unrecorded—their words and thoughts about reading—must be imaginatively reconstructed."[49] Therefore, while specific reader responses to a particular text are largely unrecoverable by historians, possible readings of the same text are open to historical reconstruction through the application of reasonable assumptions about contemporary conventions, culture, and ideology. In an environment beset by war and privation, some individuals chose to write about the war, and others chose to read about it. In particular, literary expression sought to validate the sacrifice and to bind the community together, indeed to awaken a sense of a wider community than the local area.

Our analysis at the regional level focuses especially on the novel. Narrative can be a particularly effective tool for building national loyalty, insofar as it is more gripping than reasoned analysis. During the nineteenth century, moreover, the novel came into its own as a literary form and as a primary form of entertainment and instruction. The genre of wartime Confederate literature, defined as novels written by southerners, published during the war, and dealing directly with the war, consists of seven works, more than half of them written by women.[50] Although the genre of the Confederate novel was relatively small in size, it compensated through its unadulterated nationalism. One way that these novels posited a national identity was by portraying a "mythic present,"[51] which in turn depended on an ideal, glorified, and fundamentally ahistorical past. In a sense all nationalisms speak to a Golden Age, to an idyllic picture of national strength, honor, and unity; remembered pasts are based on the desires, needs, values, and truths of the current culture, a vision of what should be true. The Confederate mythic present had a number of constituent parts, but it was usually defined in opposition to the alien culture of the Republican North. By this logic white Confederate nationalists created the saga in which *they* were the innocent victims of northern, Republican perfidy and tyranny, enslaved African Americans were happy and satisfied, white southerners were honorable and valorous to the Cause, and God was on their side to ensure ultimate victory.

Southern authors publishing in 1863 and 1864 evoked this mythic present and encouraged their readers to identify with Confederate nationalism by demonstrating its superiority to crass, Yankee materialism. Four interrelated binaries stand out: liberty versus abolitionism, freemen versus hirelings, pureblood versus ethnic, and civilization versus barbarity. Novels imagine the Confederate protagonist as a champion of liberty, which in this case appears to mean a champion of the rights of white individuals free of externally imposed controls. The northern "Other" is imagined as a fanatical abolitionist, one who wants not only to eradicate slavery for his own selfish and arrogant ends but also to eliminate liberty. Not admitting that the South was fighting to preserve slavery, novelists portrayed southern characters as fighting explicitly for "liberty" and "freedom," by which the novelists meant implicitly the freedom to enslave others.[52] At the same time, despite historical understanding that for most northerners the war was initially about Union and not about slavery, Confederate novelists represented abolitionism as the major reason for northern aggression.

First of all, Confederate novelists differentiated southern freemen from northern hirelings. Southern defenders of liberty are cast as freemen who *choose* to defend family, neighborhood, and community out of a sense of honor, duty, and nationalism. By contrast, the northern abolitionists do not choose to fight; they send into battle their hirelings, who, with no sense of honor, fight for monetary reward. (In this formulation, though, Confederate novelists ignored the use of hired substitution in southern as well as northern armies.) Another assumption reinforces this juxtaposition: the hireling is ethnically alien. Not loving members of kith and kin, the northern hordes are depicted as Irish or Dutch (meaning German). In contrast to the enemy's repeated ethnicization, writers never explicitly address Confederate white ethnicity. Instead, it is an ideological given that "Southron" must be a white ethnicity of pure and noble derivation. Finally, unlike white southerners, gentlemen all, Yankees as portrayed in novels are barbarous, insensible to polite and humane rules of civilized warfare, the very antithesis of the concept of community. The idealized, literary southerner is the epitome of contemporary manliness, while the stylized northerner plays Mr. Hyde to the South's Dr. Jekyll, employing brute force and rapacity rather than humanity and civility. It is easy to caricature the vaudevillian and simplistic binaries between southern good and northern evil, but the pervasiveness of these tropes suggests something significant at work. Authors and Confederate political leaders had to convince themselves, their peers, and white southern men and women that loyalty to the *new* nation superseded loyalty to the *original* American nation.

The three Confederate novels examined here, by Sally Rochester Ford, Mary Jane Haw, and James Dabney McCabe, are representative of the genre. During the Civil War, Confederate novelists sought to foster loyalty and devotion to the new Confederate nation. Southern literati promulgated the idea that this war was a battle between good, which the people should support, and evil, which the people should reject. In Sally Rochester Ford's novel *Raids and Romances; or, Morgan and His Men* (1863) the description of General Morgan borders on adulatory—his horsemanship is elegant, his features confirm "daring and determination," his mustache is "trimmed with exquisite precision." He manifests "manly dignity."[53] His men and his Cause are blessed on high, and their conduct befits civilized gentlemen. In stark contrast to the chivalrous Morgan and his men, Yankees are characterized as "hordes of blue-coated Abolitionists" whose "polluted feet [are] desecrating the streets of our city." They are "jail-birds and wharf rats" commanded by destitute and selfish men "devoid of honesty and patriotism." These men shoot stretcher bearers, and "with low and cruel mockery" they taunt their "helpless prisoners."[54] These hordes of abolitionists are not even Americans. Ford describes the Union soldiers as "ignorant Irish and Dutch Lincolnites." Moreover, they "cared no more about the Constitution . . . than did the perjured tyrants at Washington."[55] (Once again, it was adherence to constitutional norms that makes a citizen.) In no way do Union troops act like civilized human beings, like free men, like good republican men, like Southrons. Instead, they insult ladies, abuse the elderly, and even desecrate the Holy Bible. Ford's message was clear: we cannot submit to such men; put your allegiance behind the Confederate nation.

Similar binaries infuse Mary Jane Haw's novel *The Rivals* (1864). Federals are "hordes of ruthless and barbaric hirelings," represented by "dirty Dutchmen," capable of communicating only through "a volley of coarse oaths, uttered in broken English or low Dutch." These Yankees despoil graves and abuse the very African Americans they are supposedly liberating. The tragic hero of Haw's novel is a turncoat Virginian, Walter Maynard, who retains his commission in the United States Army for purely mercenary reasons. In choosing to fight for the Union, Colonel Maynard was treacherous "to his friend and to his country," but he is redeemed in death. In advancing upon Richmond in June 1862, amid extreme danger, he gives no heed to his safety because he is suffering from a guilty conscience. Haw makes her point that Maynard's country is not the United States of America; he owes fealty to the Confederate nation. Maynard thanks the Lord for the Confederate victory at Richmond, is forgiven by his friend and the woman they both love, and dies, having "sinned and suffered his last on earth."[56]

The master of hyperbolic patriotism was James Dabney McCabe. In *The Aid-de-Camp* (1863) McCabe shows Lincoln and his cronies creating an army of the "scum of the North and West," a mob of "miserable specimens of humanity." McCabe, echoing the Saluda Riflemen's Memorial description of Abraham Lincoln, reserves some of his choicest vitriol for the chief conspirator. An uncouth, furtive character with his feet rudely up on the table, McCabe's Lincoln is close to powerless. Although wishing he had not been elected, Lincoln follows Seward's determination: "I must stick to it. Seward says we must run the machine as we found her, if we bust her; and I'll do it."[57] *Machine* is not incidental usage. As an aggregate of rural communities such as Edgefield and others, the South imagined itself as rural and pastoral rather than cold and mechanistic. Southerners imagined the industrial North, by contrast, as a hard conglomeration of grasping, community-less individuals, much like a piece of equipment.

The machinations of Lincoln and his men are observed in the Cabinet Room by the young protagonist, Edward Marshall, whom a friend ushers through a secret tunnel into the White House and thence through a series of secret passages to a concealed gallery overlooking the Cabinet Room. This labyrinth suggests the distance between the obscure secrecy of shady leaders and those they govern while offering readers the fantasy of spying, along with Marshall, on the Republican Cabinet's sordid deliberations on the need to instigate war. McCabe's descriptions of the Cabinet members, though, contrast starkly with his depiction of southern general P. G. T. Beauregard. Whereas Beauregard creates devotion and patriotism in his wake, Lincoln's ignorant and sinister gang leaves in their wake oppression, deception, and unbridled self-interest; while Beauregard is a member of a wider community, Lincoln and his ilk reject such ties. Secretary of the Treasury Salmon Chase is "a keen, shrewd Yankee sharper" whose features "told of trickery and deceit." The "dark and gloomy" Montgomery Blair, postmaster general and native Marylander, has a "bitter and malignant expression," and his manner toward the president betrays "a strange mixture of fawning servility and contemptuous hate." Secretary of War Simon Cameron "was a great villain." Secretary of State William Seward, "the master spirit of the Cabinet, the true Ruler of the Union," is the greatest scoundrel, "utterly destitute of principle and integrity." Readers are told that "ambition was his God, and that he feared nothing, scrupled at nothing, in his efforts to gratify his absorbing passion."[58]

McCabe and other Confederate novelists do not lay the war's opening shots upon the South at Fort Sumter. The Cabinet's April 7 discussion centered on the need to manufacture a war with the South to satisfy the presumed desires of the northern electorate and the depraved ambitions of Seward. McCabe has Seward, without any reference to the preservation of the Union, looking instead to preserve Republican political power: "If we yield to the South, the people will drag us from power. There is a strong anti-slavery sentiment in the country, which will sustain us in a war. . . . We are pledged to carry on the war against slavery, and we have tried the ballot-box long enough. We must now use the sword." As McCabe writes in 1863, Secretary Cameron admits the war would be "long and bloody," but he does not mind; because the North had greater resources and manpower, McCabe has him say, "we shall finally hold the Southern States as conquered Provinces."[59]

Confederate writers presented a clear message. And although we do not want to exaggerate the compliance of readers, many white southerners reading this and similar Confederate novels would note the dark, scowling, self-serving, and malignant secrecy of the Republican North against the background of the "fair" (both white and just), open, selfless leadership of the Confederate South as a source of swelling patriotic pride. Evidence from the *Edgefield Advertiser* demonstrates, moreover, that at the local level writers and readers perceived northern political leaders as despicable. A humorous story published early in 1861 portrayed Lincoln as a machine politician laboriously doling out patronage appointments to loyal office seekers. When a barely literate southerner drives them off, Lincoln tries to thank him by offering him a post as Cabinet minister; the righteous southerner, though, claims that he only wants a "good sound administration" that allows states to secede from the Union.[60] Elsewhere the local paper denounced Lincoln as a "Babboon [sic]" and imagined a docile slave denouncing Lincoln as one of the devil's own.[61] In this view the northern leader clearly did not have the South's best interests in mind.

Producers of literary Confederate nationalism "from above," as well as "from below," very much understood that nationalism was linked to community. Confederate novels, in the nineteenth-century Romantic style, include numerous evocations of place. Authors used specific names early in the novels to create a connection between the real and fictional South, broadly conceived to include non-Confederate slaveholding areas. Readers in communities such as Edgefield, South Carolina, could feel a connection with characters standing beneath a large elm tree in Jefferson County, Kentucky, or on the thoroughfares of Baltimore or near the old Washington Henry Academy in Hanover County, Virginia.[62] At the same time that they provided local color, the authors evoked family ties. The opening lines of Ford's *Raids and Romances* reveal that the hero went to war only after he received the blessings of his reluctant father. Other novelists used similar settings. Augusta Jane Evans's *Macaria* starts with a scene between the hero and his mother; Florence O'Connor's *Heroine of the Confederacy* begins with a scene between the heroine and her guardian.[63]

This brief consideration of southern novels written during the war years demonstrates a construction of abstract national identity written by an intelligentsia and aimed at a general southern readership. Writers presented stories that could have been set in readers' own localities in order to create a sense of allegiance to a Confederate nation. This literature pairs an elite nationalist narrative with a popular family and community backstory; the characters make sense to the reader because they are rooted in a local context. The literati and intelligentsia who were so vital in promulgating the nationalist ethos worked in the abstracted context of print culture. In turn, however, the reading public used this literature to inform and consolidate their own identities as Confederates and as community members.

Some of the same forces were at work in the lyrics of a proposed Confederate national anthem, penned by St. George Tucker early in the war. In his second verse Tucker shared with Confederate novelists the binary idea of the southern self and the northern Other.

How peaceful and blest was America's soil,
'Till betrayed by the guile of the Puritan demon,
Which lurks under Virtue, and springs from its coil,

To fasten its fangs in the life-blood of freemen.
Then loudly appeal to each heart that can feel,
And crush the foul viper 'neath Liberty's heel;
And the Cross of the South shall forever remain
To light us to freedom and glory again.[64]

The northern other, the "Puritan demon" juxtaposed to southern free men, is the betrayer of America's soil and will be defeated by the crushing heel of Liberty. In short, this southern script for the war is a self-justificatory explanation of innocence. They, white southerners, are the aggrieved, and the Confederate nation, which corrects that egregious situation, deserves the people's allegiance.[65]

Tucker's song, to the same tune as Francis Scott Key's anthem for the United States, also draws a map for the future:

And if peace should be hopeless, and justice denied,
    And war's bloody vulture should flap its black pinions.
Then gladly to arms, while we hurl in our pride
    Defiance to tyrants and death to their minions,
With our front in the field, swearing never to yield,
    Or return, like the Spartan, in death on our shield,
And the Cross of the South shall triumphantly wave
    As the flag of the free and the pall of the brave.[66]

Or as Key put it, writing at Fort McHenry in September 1814:

Oh! thus be it ever, when freemen shall stand
    Between their loved homes and the war's desolation!
Blest with victory and peace, may the heaven-rescued land
    Praise the Power that hath made and preserved us a nation.
Then conquer we must, for our cause it is just,
    And this be our motto: "In God is our trust."
And the star-spangled banner forever shall wave
    O'er the land of the free and the home of the brave![67]

The distinction here, though, runs to the heart of Confederate nationalism, in literature or anywhere else: there is a world of difference between the flag flying over the *home* of the brave and the flag acting as the *pall* of the brave.[68] In Key's verse the flag welcomes home the still living defender of the free; in Tucker's it decorates the fallen soldier's coffin and greets his grieving relatives and friends. The vision in Tucker's anthem is of a hell in which southern bravery and fortitude might carry the day but at a tremendous cost; Key's earlier vision is of a land blessed by peace and justice, looked over favorably by the Almighty.

Over time literature in the *Edgefield Advertiser* replaced South Carolina's "palm-wreathed flag" with the Confederacy's "stars and bars" as the banner under which soldiers fought.[69] Ironically, though, even as the Confederate flag became a much more prevalent sight in southern locales as a coffin's pall toward war's end, overt displays of patriotism became more common. On March 22, 1865, very near the end of the Confederacy's existence, South Carolina's General Stephen D. Lee was in nearby Augusta, Georgia, to collect men furloughed and otherwise absent from the army. According to the *Edgefield Advertiser,* "General Robert E. Lee's amnesty proclamation, and, above all, the re-instatement of Gen. [Joseph] Johnston, has caused absent soldiers to flock to their commands by regiments." Stephen Lee gathered between eight and ten thousand men, and, as the group camped nearby, the residents went out to celebrate the troops, the women cheering and throwing flowers—"no less than one thousand million Jonquils and Daffodils have been sacrificed (and nobly) in the cause."[70] Even though these troops were not from Edgefield, the local community identified them with the Confederate cause and welcomed them as the town's own. A similar broadened perspective was on display earlier in the war when the *Advertiser* celebrated the Confederate soldiers fighting for "Liberty" in Texas.[71]

The dull routine of life on the home front and the barrenness of rural existence also encouraged Edgefieldians to look outward, toward a broader national identity. In early 1865 one young woman whose brother was serving in the Confederate army wrote about the nation in her diary. "Times are dull and dark," she intoned, "when we lie down at night in ignorance of what may be the news from the army, our hearts go up in prayer to Almighty God that he will 'Deliver us from evil' both as a nation and individually." In another entry she wrote about two soldiers from Texas passing through South Carolina. Even though she referred to them as "strangers," she and her father recognized a common national identity and sense of community with these two Confederates and invited them to stay a few days. She later recorded, "Their coming was a pleasing variety to our monotonous lives."[72]

This bird's-eye view of one community shows that, as the war heated up, people were swept into the broad cauldron of the nationalist project. In the process they left something of their local selves behind; however, they did not leave all of it behind.[73] The formation of nationalism was not a simple dichotomy between the local community and the national state. More of one did not necessarily mean less of the other. In the Confederacy, as in the United States before and after, the ties of community served a nation, and national interest served local political affairs. Sometimes at odds, at other times localism and nationalism worked hand in hand, nationalism growing out of localism rather than opposing it. Edgefieldians remained Confederate nationalists, even when they were upset with military matters or bureaucratic policies. Even Confederate deserters largely wanted the Confederacy to win the war; they had merely lost the enthusiasm, impetus, or sense of duty to risk dying for that cause. Men who initially refused to leave Edgefield or South Carolina eventually did leave and fight for the Confederate nation. The men who fought, and their families and communities, grew in support of the Confederate nation. This trajectory was not always smooth, and pro-national sympathy, as opposed to local allegiance, fluctuated over the course of the war. At the beginning Edgefieldians sought to protect their homes; as the war concluded, they recognized that protecting their homes meant supporting the nation.

The sense of Confederate nationalism was at least as powerful after defeat as it was before the war's end. When news of Confederate defeat reached Turnwold, Georgia, some one hundred miles from Edgefield, on May 2, 1865, Joseph Addison Turner, the editor and proprietor of the local journal the *Countryman,* noted, "The whole southern country is now one gigantic corpse, and a black pall lies listless on its lifeless limbs."[74] Three weeks later, however, Turner proposed to breathe life back into this ravaged carcass with a bold five-point plan for reconciliation with the northern victor:

1.—A new flag.—Our people have so long fought against the United States flag, and it has waved over the bloody graves of so many of them, and over so many of their ruined homes, and burned towns, and villages, that you cannot expect it to command their hearts and heads, though you do their hands, in its support.

2.—A new constitution should be agreed upon, because the old one is not sufficiently explicit as to our rights.

3.—A full and complete acknowledgement of our state rights, and state sovereignty should be accorded us—together with a complete recognition of our institution of slavery.

4.—An abnegation of the idea that our people became rebels, or were guilty of treason when they seceded, and waged war against the north—they owing allegiance to their respective states alone.

5.—A consolidation of the war debt of the two sections.

Turner conceded that chances of this plan finding favor in Congress were limited but nevertheless felt that the goals of defeated Confederate nationalism should hold sway.[75] In spite of abject and public defeat, Turner gave little sign of being conquered intellectually or morally. Turner wanted a new flag and constitution (once again, the fascination with documents is telling of the American experience), acknowledgment that secession was legitimate, that states' rights, including slavery, were paramount, and that there was in fact no inclusive "American" nation at all.

The complexity of identity was manifestly apparent after the war. In 1866 and 1867 Union veteran John De Forest served as a Freedmen's Bureau agent in Greenville, South Carolina, about fifty miles north of Edgefield District. Reflecting on localism and white southern pride, he wrote about a friend's assertion that, if South Carolinians discovered heaven was outside the state, "they would not want to go to it." Less than two years after the war, De Forest reported an often repeated declaration by a "sturdy old planter," who explained his multiple allegiances and loyalties. "I go first for Greenville, then for Greenville District, then for the upcountry, then for South Carolina, then for the South, then for the United [S]tates; and after that I don't go for anything. I've no use for Englishmen, Turks, and Chinese."[76] A half-century later another voice from the Civil War spoke on the question of nation and locality. C. Irvine Walker of Camden, South Carolina, a self-confessed "old veteran of the Sixties," offered his services in recruiting efforts for the world war, describing how he had "the respect and confidence of the Vets of our State and of the entire South."[77] Even though he was specifically offering his services for recruiting in South Carolina, Walker still regarded the "South" as an entity worthy of his loyalty. Walker devoted a considerable portion of his postwar career to the preservation of the Confederacy's memory.

St. George Tucker's proposed Confederate anthem anticipated the common postwar ideology of the "Lost Cause" by implying defeat at the very moment that it trumpeted the cause of nation. Ironically, while Confederate nationalism was not powerful enough to ensure victory, a popular version of Confederate nationalism grew stronger when a Confederate state no longer existed, becoming more fervent in defeat.[78] When the mythic present became the mythic past, tropes developed in Confederate novels became the prototypes of the influential Lost Cause literature most commonly associated today with Thomas Dixon's *The Clansman* and Margaret Mitchell's *Gone with the Wind*. While those defeated rarely get to write the history of the war, Confederate novelists began a tradition of the noble Confederate cause that has dominated the memory of the Civil War. Indeed, in the aftermath of the defeat, these stories of Confederate innocence perhaps played a more important role in how white southerners remembered and came to memorialize the war than did actual experience.

Nationalism is a complicated component of human identity. Conventionally, nationalism is often identified in parallel with ethnic, linguistic, religious, or other cultural traits, while it also has the power to transcend those limitations. Nationalism, though, does not have to be a function of community identity; it can be the bedrock of the community itself. Evidence shows that, although the process was not single nor simple, local and abstract Confederate allegiances built upon and shaped each other. Over the course of the war nationalist sentiment was created from above and from below, and the "short, tight, skin of the *local community*" did increasingly come to stretch "over the gigantic body of the *nation*."[79] Confederate nationalism rose too fast, in straitened circumstances, in the midst of war, based on the ignoble and oppressive foundation of racial slavery. But white southerners of varied social classes, economic backgrounds, and political persuasions did briefly come together to extend the boundaries of their communities beyond the local and beyond the state, to define a nation in what had been a region. Even today, long after the war's end, southern nationalism is still dynamic, expressed in theme parks, novels, movies, revisionist histories, political pressure groups, and a real estate stampede that threatens to turn the region into a simulacrum of itself. This South is a replica not of what it was but of what it is imagined to be.

NOTES

*Epigraph:* "Address to the Texas 'Lone Star,'" *Edgefield Advertiser,* February 19, 1862. Less than a year after the firing on Fort Sumter, at least some Edgefieldians were feeling a connection to their Texan Confederate brethren.

1. Albert Maxmillion Padgett to Mahlon Mouzon Padgett, December 17, 1860, June 30, and September 29, 1861, Padgett Papers, D. A. Tompkins Memorial Library, Edgefield. "Tribute of Respect," *Edgefield Advertiser,* May 5, 1863. His father, Mahlon Mouzon Padgett, in 1860 was forty-seven years old and owned land valued at $5,120 (among the top quarter of those who owned any land). Twelve enslaved persons accounted for most of his $15,800 (among the top 14%) personal estate. The Padgetts were Methodists, and Wofford was a Methodist school.

2. "Tribute of Respect," *Edgefield Advertiser,* May 5, 1863.

3. For the debate on Confederate nationalism and popular will, see, for example, Richard E. Beringer et al., *Why the South Lost the Civil War* (Athens, 1986); Paul Escott, *After Secession: Jefferson Davis and the Failure of Confederate Nationalism* (Baton Rouge, 1978); William W. Freehling, *The South vs. the South: How Anti-Confederate Southerners Shaped the Course of the Civil War* (New York, 2001); Gary W. Gallagher, *The Confederate War: How Popular Will, Nationalism, and Military Strategy Could Not Stave Off Defeat* (Cambridge, 1997); George C. Rable, *The Confederate Republic: A Revolution against Politics* (Chapel Hill, 1994); and Emory M. Thomas, *The Confederate Nation: 1861–1865* (New York, 1979); and *The Confederacy as Revolutionary Experience* (Englewood Cliffs, 1971). There have also been thorough examinations of dissonance between the experience of the people and the promises and duties of the government; see, for example, William A. Blair, *Virginia's Private War: Feeding Body and Soul in the Confederacy* (New York, 1998); Wayne K. Durrill, *War of Another Kind: A Southern Community in the Great Rebellion* (New York, 1990); Peter Wallenstein, *From Slave South to New South: Public Policy in Nineteenth Century Georgia* (Chapel Hill, 1987); and David Williams, *Rich Man's War: Class, Caste, and Confederate Defeat in the Lower Chattahoochee Valley* (Athens, 1998).

4. Drew G. Faust, *The Creation of Confederate Nationalism: Ideology and Identity in the Civil War South* (Baton Rouge, 1988), 6–7.

5. John McCardell, *The Idea of a Southern Nation: Southern Nationalists and Southern Nationalism, 1830–1860* (New York, 1979); Orville Vernon Burton, "Sectional Conflict, Civil War, and Reconstruction," in *Encyclopedia of American Social History,* ed. Mary Kupiec Cayton et al. (New York, 1993), 1:131–57. In his novels Sir Walter Scott used the term *Southron* to refer to an Englishman, distinguishing him from a Scotsman. White southerners in the United States applied the term to themselves. John William De Forest, *A Union Officer in the Reconstruction,* ed. James H. Croushore and David Morris Potter (New Haven, 1948), 159 n. 1.

6. William W. Freehling, *The Road to Disunion: Secessionists at Bay, 1776–1854* (New York, 1990), 41.

7. Philip D. Curtin, "The Black Experience of Colonialism and Imperialism," in *Slavery, Colonialism, and Racism,* ed. Sidney W. Mintz (New York, 1974), 20.

8. Ernest Renan, *Qu'est-ce qu'une nation?* trans. Ida Mae Snyder (Paris, 1882), 26; Anthony Giddens, *A Contemporary Critique of Historical Materialism,* vol. 2: *The Nation-State and Violence* (Cambridge, Eng., 1985), 119; Walker Connor, "A Nation Is a Nation, Is a State, Is an Ethnic Group, Is a . . . ," *Ethnic and Racial Studies* 1.4 (1978): 388. In thinking about nationalism as process, Tom Nairn suggests that it tells progressive narratives through regressive means by constructing usable pasts, by "resurrecting past folk-heroes and myths . . . and so on." Nairn, *The Break-Up of Britain* (London, 1977), 348.

9. Robert H. Wiebe, "*Imagined Communities,* Nationalist Experiences," *Journal of the Historical Society* 1.1 (Spring 2000): 53–54.

10. Benedict Anderson, *Imagined Communities: Reflections on the Origins and Spread of Nationalism* (London, 1983), 6–7.

11. Trish Loughran, "Virtual Nation: Local and National Cultures of Print in the Early United States" (Ph.D. diss., University of Chicago, 2000), 4.

12. Celia Applegate, *A Nation of Provincials: The German Idea of Heimat* (Berkeley, 1990); Alon Confino, *The Nation as a Local Metaphor: Württemberg, Imperial Germany, and National Memory, 1871–1918* (Chapel Hill, 1997); Abigail Green, *Fatherlands: State-Building and Nationhood in Nineteenth-Century Germany* (Cambridge, 2001).

13. David M. Potter, "The Historian's Use of Nationalism and Vice Versa," *American Historical Review* 67.4 (July 1962): 924–50.

14. Hugh Seton-Watson, *Nations and States: An Inquiry into the Origins of Nations and the Politics of Nationalism* (Boulder, 1977), 148.

15. Confino, *Nation as a Local Metaphor.*

16. Orville Vernon Burton, *In My Father's House: Family and Community in Edgefield, South Carolina* (Chapel Hill, 1985).

17. See Alice Fahs, *The Imagined Civil War: Popular Literature of the North and South, 1861–1865* (Chapel Hill, 2001), 116, 136, 143, 146.

18. *Edgefield Advertiser,* November 14, 1860.

19. Ibid., December 19, 1860.

20. Ibid., October 31, 1860.

21. Ibid., May 20, 1846. For other communities, see Mary Elizabeth Massey, *Ersatz in the Confederacy* (Columbia, S.C., 1952), 6; Clement Eaton, *A History of the Southern Confederacy* (1954; repr., New York, 1965).

22. F. F. Warley, "By Request of the Edgefield Riflemen," *Edgefield Advertiser,* May 15, 1861; J. William Harris, *Plain Folk and Gentry in a Slave Society: White Liberty and Black Slavery in Augusta's Hinterlands* (Middletown, Conn., 1986), 146; J.F.J. Caldwell, *The History of a Brigade of South Carolinians, Known First as "Gregg's," and Subsequently as "McGowan's" Brigade* (Philadelphia, 1866); Milledge Louis Bonham, "The Life and Times of Milledge Luke Bonham," MS, in Bonham Papers, South Caroliniana Library, University of South Carolina, 742.

23. "Replies to Capt. Warley," *Edgefield Advertiser,* May 29, 1861; see also F. F. Warley, "For the Advertiser," *Edgefield Advertiser,* June 5, 1861.

24. Drew Gilpin Faust, *James Henry Hammond and the Old South: A Design for Mastery* (Baton Rouge, 1982), 370–74; Harris, *Plain Folk and Gentry in a Slave Society,* 162–63; Bonham, "Life and Times of Milledge Luke Bonham," 724, 727–78.

25. James B. Griffin to Leila Griffin, February 26, 1862, in Judith N. McArthur and Orville Vernon Burton, *"A Gentleman and an Officer": A Military and Social History of James B. Griffin's Civil War* (New York, 1996), 163.

26. "Twilight Prayer for Our Country," *Edgefield Advertiser,* February 19, 1862.

27. "The Volunteers" ("By an Old Soldier"), *Edgefield Advertiser,* April 30, 1862.

28. See "The Butler Sentinels" (by "The Young Volunteer"), *Edgefield Advertiser,* November 13, 1861.

29. Drew Gilpin Faust, "Altars of Sacrifice: Confederate Women and the Narratives of War," in *Divided Houses: Gender and the Civil War,* ed. Catherine Clinton and Nina Silber (New York, 1992), 177–82.

30. "Sweethearts vs. War," *Edgefield Advertiser,* April 24, 1861; "War Song," *Edgefield Advertiser,* July 10, 1861; "A Woman's Spirit," *Edgefield Advertiser,* June 18, 1862.

31. Dr. G. W. Bagby, "The Empty Sleeve," *Edgefield Advertiser,* January 21, 1863; Clara V. Dargan, "Gone to the War," *Edgefield Advertiser,* February 18, 1863.

32. A. B. Meek, "War Song," *Edgefield Advertiser,* August 13, 1862; Hapsdale, "The Deserter's Wife," *Edgefield Advertiser,* July 20, 1864.

33. S.A.L., "A Mother's Prayer," *Edgefield Advertiser,* February 6, 1861; B.A.S., "Female Patriotism," *Edgefield Advertiser,* July 24, 1861; "The Patriot's Mother" (reprinted from the *Richmond Enquirer*), *Edgefield Advertiser,* July 16, 1862; "Reading the List," *Edgefield Advertiser,* September 3, 1862.

34. See F.J.M. Jr., "A Story of the War," *Edgefield Advertiser,* January 4, 1865, in which a maiden dies after hearing of her loved one's death.

35. John McCardell, *The Idea of a Southern Nation: Southern Nationalists and Southern Nationalism, 1830–1860* (New York, 1979), 176, 144; Elisabeth Muhlenfeld, "The Civil War and Authorship," in *The History of Southern Literature,* ed. Louis D. Rubin Jr. (Baton Rouge, 1985), 180.

36. Benedict Anderson, *Imagined Communities,* 36; Fahs, *Imagined Civil War,* 1–2, 63.

37. Henry Timrod, "Literature in the South," *Russell's Magazine* 5 (August 1859): 385–95.

38. "Editor's Table," *Southern Literary Messenger* (January 1864): 63.

39. Henry Timrod, "Southern Literature," *Daily South Carolinian* (Columbia), January 14, 1864.

40. Robert Darnton, "What Is the History of Books?" in *Reading in America: Literature and Social History,* ed. Cathy N. Davidson (Baltimore, 1989): 27–52; and Robert A. Gross, "Texts for the Times: An Introduction to Book History" in *Perspectives on American Book History: Artifacts and Commentary,* ed. Scott E. Casper et al. (Amherst, 2002), 1–16.

41. Alice Fahs, "Commentary: The Civil War as a Popular Literary Event," in Casper et al., *Perspectives on American Book History,* 214.

42. Thomas C. Leonard, *News for All: America's Coming-of-Age with the Press* (New York, 1995), 12. The *Memphis Appeal* editor was "mindful of the illiterate Grandmother Pugh and those unable to afford a paper who depended on others to read the news and views to them. He wanted parlor and tavern orators to make the rafters sing when they read his work aloud." Ellis, *Moving Appeal*, 52. Editors included comments with the local news to keep their readers' interest (Eleanor Elizabeth Mims, "The Editors of the Edgefield *Advertiser*: Oldest Newspaper in South Carolina, 1836–1930" [Master's thesis, University of South Carolina, 1930], 54).

43. Tama Plakins Thornton, *Handwriting in America: A Cultural History* (New Haven, 1996), 59.

44. Ronald J. Zboray, *A Fictive People: Antebellum Economic Development and the American Reading Public* (New York, 1993), xvi, 197–98. Among the works on New England are Richard D. Brown, *Knowledge Is Power: The Diffusion of Information in Early America, 1700–1865* (New York, 1989); and William J. Gilmore, *Reading Becomes a Necessity of Life: Material and Cultural Life in Rural New England, 1780–1835* (Knoxville, 1989). There are no comparable monographs on the South. Sylvia Scribner and Michael Cole, *The Psychology of Literacy* (Cambridge, Mass., 1981), and Brian Street, *Literacy in Theory and Practice* (Cambridge, 1985), refute the literacy/modernization thesis. For literacy in Edgefield, see Burton, *In My Father's House*, 80–90. High literacy rates attributed to the North may have been overstated. During the antebellum period theology students traveling through New Jersey complained about illiteracy among "poor" rural whites. See David Paul Nord, "Religious Reading and Readers in Antebellum America," *Journal of the Early Republic* 15 (1995): 241–72; Harvey J. Graff, *The Literacy Myth* (New Brunswick, N.J., 1991), app. B, "Literacy and the Census," 329–33.

45. James M. McPherson, *What They Fought For, 1861–1865* (Baton Rouge, 1994), 4; Muhlenfeld, "Civil War and Authorship," 182.

46. The wartime *Advertiser* contained no novel reviews, a genre that is generally absent from Confederate newspapers and periodicals. Nina Baym, *Novels, Readers, and Reviewers: Responses to Fiction in Antebellum America* (Ithaca, 1984).

47. Deed Book 1: 1786–89, Edgefield County, S.C., October 27, 1789; *Edgefield Advertiser*, October 1, 1856, January 29, 1920; Robert Mills, *Statistics of South Carolina, Including a View of Its Natural, Civil, and Military History, General and, Particular* (Charleston, 1826), 351; Farmers Club, Beech Island, Records of the ABC Farmers Club, South Caroliniana Library; Library File, D. A. Tompkins Library.

48. Burton, *In My Father's House*, 20. The wartime *Advertiser* contained no novel reviews, a genre that is generally absent from Confederate newspapers and periodicals; Nina Baym, *Novels, Readers, and Reviewers: Responses to Fiction in Antebellum America* (Ithaca, 1984).

49. James L. Machor," Historical Hermeneutics and Antebellum Fiction: Gender, Response Theory, and Interpretive Contexts," in *Readers in History: Nineteenth-Century American Literature and the Contexts of Response*, ed. James L. Machor (Baltimore, 1993), 55, 78; Amy M. Thomas, "Reading the Silences: Documenting the History of American Tract Society Readers in the Antebellum South," in *Reading Acts: U.S. Readers' Interactions with Literature, 1800–1950*, ed. Barbara Ryan and Amy M. Thomas (Knoxville, 2002), 111, 115–16, 132.

50. Alex St. Clair Abrams, *The Trials of the Soldier's Wife: A Tale of the Second American Revolution* (Atlanta, 1864); Napier Bartlett, *Clarimonde: A Tale of New Orleans Life, and of the Present War* (Richmond, 1863); Augusta Jane Evans, *Macaria; or, Altars of Sacrifice*, 2d ed. (1863; repr., Richmond, 1864); Sally Rochester Ford, *Raids and Romances; or, Morgan and His Men* (1863; repr., New York, 1866); M. J. (Mary Jane) Haw, *The Rivals: A Chickahominy Story* (Richmond, 1864); James Dabney McCabe, *The Aid-De-Camp: A Romance of the War* (Richmond, 1863); and Florence J. O'Connor, *Heroine of the Confederacy; or, Truth and Justice* (London, 1865). Many of these novels continued in publication after 1865, often issued by presses in the northern states. Fahs, *Imagined Civil War*, has Haw and McCabe in her bibliography but not in the text in any systematic fashion. Ford is absent altogether.

51. Ian Binnington, "'They Have Made a Nation': Confederates and the Creation of Confederate Nationalism" (Ph.D. diss., University of Illinois at Urbana-Champaign, 2004).

52. Although not about the causes of the war, one Confederate novel about slavery's role in Confederate nationalism is E. W. Warren, *Nellie Norton, or Southern Slavery and the Bible; a Scriptural Refutation of the Principal Arguments upon Which the Abolitionists Rely: A Vindication of Southern Slavery from the Old and New Testaments* (Macon, 1864). Overall, discussion of slavery is rare.

53. Ford, *Raids and Romances*, 28. John Grant Wilson and John Fiske, eds., *Appleton's Cyclopedia of American Biography* (New York, 1888), 2:501; John W. Leonard, ed., *Who's Who in America: Biographical Dictionary of Notable Living Men and Women of the United States, 1901–1902* (Chicago, 1901), 390; Lucian Lamar Knight, ed., *Biographical Dictionary of Southern Authors* (1929; repr., Detroit, 1978), 151; Taryn Benbow-Pfalzgraf, ed., *American Women Writers: A Critical Reference Guide from Colonial Times to the Present*, 2d ed. (Detroit, 2000), 3:61–62.

54. Ford, *Raids*, 12–13, 23–24, 57, 75.

55. Ibid., 81. See also 121–23, 284, 317.

56. M. J. Haw, *The Rivals: A Chickahominy Story* (Richmond, 1864), 43, 48, 52, 53, 43–44, 54, 58. The Online Computer Library Center (OCLC) cites a notice in the *Magnolia Weekly*, March 19, 1864, stating that the *Illustrated News* of Richmond awarded Haw a thousand dollars for this novel.

57. James Dabney McCabe, *The Aid-De-Camp: A Romance of the War* (Richmond, 1863), 28, 40, 42, 20, 21. The *Magnolia Weekly* originally serialized *Aid-De-Camp*. Wilson and Fiske, eds., *Appleton's Cyclopedia of American Biography* (New York, 1888), 4:74; Knight, *Biographical Dictionary of Southern Authors*, 271.

58. McCabe, *Aid-De-Camp*, 21, 22.

59. Ibid., 23–24, 25.

60. Artemas Ward, "Artemas Ward on a Visit to Abe Lincoln," *Edgefield Advertiser*, January 30, 1861.

61. Big Dan, "Song for the Times," *Edgefield Advertiser*, September 4, 1861; "A Southern Scene from Life," *Edgefield Advertiser*, October 23, 1861.

62. Ford, *Raids*, 5; McCabe, *Aid-De-Camp*, 7; Haw, *Rivals*, 3.

63. Ford, *Raids*, 5; Augusta Jane Evans, *Macaria; or, Altars of Sacrifice* (Richmond, 1864), 5–8; Florence J. O'Connor, *Heroine of the Confederacy; or, Truth and Justice* (London, 1865), 2–7.

64. St. George Tucker, "The Southern Cross," dated February 22, 1861, printed in the *Southern Literary Messenger* 32 (March 1861): 189.

65. A similar preoccupation with northern culpability comes through in another proposed Confederate national anthem, "God Save the South," published anonymously in the *Countryman* in September 1862. Lacking Tucker's eloquence, this unnamed author was equally clear about blame for the war:

> War to the hilt,
> Theirs be the guilt
> Who fetter the freeman,
> To ransom the slave.
> Then still be undismayed,
> Sheathe not the battle-blade,
> Till the last foe is laid,
> cold in the grave.
> —"The Southern National Anthem," *Countryman*, 3,
>       no. 1, September 29, 1862, 5

66. Tucker, "Southern Cross."

67. Francis Scott Key, "The Star Spangled Banner," September 20, 1814, University of Oklahoma Law Center, www.law.ou.edu/hist/ssb.html.

68. In this context a "pall" means "a cloth, usually of black, purple, or white velvet, spread over a coffin, hearse, or tomb. Also: a shroud for a corpse." *Oxford English Dictionary*.

69. Contrast S.A.L., "To the 'Edgefield Riflemen' Whose Term Expires on the First of July," *Edgefield Advertiser*, June 26, 1861, with "A Banner Song for the South—Our Southern Flag" (from the *Charleston Portfolio*), *Edgefield Advertiser*, September 11, 1861; and W. Lafayette Simmons, "The Soldier to His Wife" (from the *Jackson Mississippian*), *Edgefield Advertiser*, February 18, 1863.

70. "Eight Thousand Veterans and Wagons Innumerable," *Edgefield Advertiser*, March 22, 1865.

71. R. W., "Address to the Texas 'Lone Star,'" *Edgefield Advertiser*, February 19, 1862.

72. Ella Watson Diary, January 25 and March 8, 1865, typescript 5 and 10, in the Papers of Harry Watson, South Caroliniana Library.

73. Burton, *In My Father's House*, 225–27.

74. Robert E. Lee surrendered to Ulysses S. Grant on April 9, 1865; on April 18 Joseph E. Johnston surrendered the remaining Confederate army to William Tecumseh Sherman. Joseph Addison Turner, "The State of the Country," *Countryman* 20, May 2, 1865.

75. Turner, "The Five Points," *Countryman* 20, May 23, 1865.

76. De Forest, *Union Officer in the Reconstruction*, 177.

77. C. I. Walker to D. R. Coker, August 10, 1917, in the Papers of David R. Coker, South Caroliniana Library. Walker wrote a history of the regiment, *Rolls and Historical Sketch of the Tenth Regiment, So. Ca. Volunteers, in the Army of the Confederate States* (Charleston, 1881). Cornelius Walker (1842–1927) graduated from The Citadel on the eve of the Civil War and enlisted immediately. A veteran of the Tenth South Carolina Infantry and a longtime mem-

ber, and sometime commander, of the United Confederate Veterans, he was seventy-five years old in 1917. Obituary, *Camden Chronicle*, November 11, 1927.

78. This essay is no apologia for the Confederacy of the 1860s nor a testament of faith for the neo-Confederate movement of more recent times. Recognizing that Confederate nationalism was founded on the unpalatable, the unjust, and the downright wrong is the historian's responsibility, one from which we should not retreat.

79. Seton-Watson, *Nations and States*, 148.

# Her Life, My Past

*Rosina Downs and the Proliferation of Racial Categories after*
*the American Civil War*

JIM DOWNS

I want to begin with a story about a girl who traveled from New Orleans to Philadelphia in the immediate aftermath of the American Civil War. Her story contains fractions of a broken genealogy that have passed through the historical record with scant clues detailing America's obsession with color. For a brief moment she was a celebrity, and while many of the details of her later life remain unknown, she has over the past few decades made cameo appearances in scholarly articles and discussions as one of the most recognizable faces of the "white slave children."[1] She has fascinated audiences then and even now because she represents a surprising aberration in the history of slavery: she is by all accounts of African descent but appears white. Due to the development of racial ideology in the United States, she was marked as "black," although she could clearly pass as "white." Often the story of her travail tells of her being paraded from the plantations of the Deep South to the elite drawing rooms of the postwar North and meditates on the ways in which white northerners would have been intrigued by the progeny of interracial sex or potentially seduced by the prurient fascination with "light-skinned" women that characterized much of the domestic slave trade of the antebellum period.

I want to break free from this narrative and instead consider how the experience of this young girl calls for a reconsideration of how racial categories developed in the United States. I want to argue that the American fascination with her developed as a result of a broader discourse about color that can be traced to the emergence of the African diaspora in the seventeenth century. I want to rethink the formulation of racial categories by decentering the United States as the site of the formation of racial ideology. Instead, I want to reveal how the existence of racial categories in places such as Brazil and the West Indies informed ordinary Americans' understanding of racial categorization that began to be discussed during the colonial period but became codified when four million people were liberated from chattel slavery at the end of the American Civil War. Finally, I want to uproot the unspoken and cryptic narratives of racial passing that have broadened the gap between past and present, between the Caribbean and the United States, between the story of a young girl and a historian who shares her name.

According to the surviving sources, we know this: her name was Rosina Downs, referred to at times as Rosa in the northern press and as Rosie in a longer family lore. We know that she was born a slave in New Orleans in the 1850s and was emancipated when Union forces took over control of New Orleans in 1862. We can assume that she was quarantined in a refugee camp in 1862, when Union general Benjamin Butler took control of the city and divided whites from blacks, the freeborn from the enslaved.[2] We know that she was the daughter, according to an article in *Harper's Weekly*, of a "bright mulatto" woman and a father who served in the Rebel army. But this is where it gets tricky.[3] There are many Downses to whom she could have been related. Was she related to Henry Downs, a freeborn black physician employed by the Union army in Louisiana, who is described in the Freedmen's Bureau records as part of the African Corps?[4] Or was she the distant offspring of the Louisiana senator Solomon W. Downs?

A clue to unraveling this puzzle might be found in figuring out how Rosa became part of this campaign. According to *Harper's Weekly*, Rosa and two others—Rebecca Huger and Charles Taylor—were brought to New Orleans by Colonel Hanks and Philip Bacon. Bacon, a teacher, followed the Union army to New Orleans in 1862 to establish the first school for freed children, where he presumably came into contact with Downs, Huger, and Taylor and became intrigued by their color. Bacon, along with Colonel Hanks, in an effort to raise money for schools in the South, then paraded the children throughout the North as the unofficial poster children for the establishment of a school system. An editorial in *Harper's Weekly* mentions that photographs of the so-called white slave children could be purchased from the New England Freedmen's Aid Society (NE-FAS).[5] Despite the fact that this was a flagrant case of exploitation based on the children's color, that the NEFAS promoted this cause suggests that the children's parents may have agreed to it—because throughout the postwar period the aid society consistently operated as an organization deeply committed to the improvement of freed slaves' conditions during and after the Civil War.[6] So, if Rosa's parent or parents did in fact consent to her travels to the North, it suggests that perhaps Rosa was connected to reform-minded people who understood her travels as a part of a larger social project to ameliorate the conditions of former slaves in the South. If this is the case, it reveals Rosa was not just a naive child taken from the refugee camp in New Orleans but part of a larger plot orchestrated by members of the Downs family, who understood their responsibility to their race.

But back to the images, to the portraits of these former slaves showcased from New Orleans to New York. The first image presents the children dressed in Victorian clothing, while the headline reads, "Slave Children from New Orleans." The size and style of the photograph, better known as a "carte de visite," reveals that this was an image easily circulated and therefore accessible to a mass audience. The headline provides the most historically telling detail. To a northern audience, the reference to slave children coming from New Orleans would have set off an alarm— throughout the decades leading up to the Civil War, the slave population dramatically shifted from the Upper South to the Mississippi Valley— marking New Orleans as the central hub of the domestic slave trade.[7] That freed slaves were now being advertised in the reverse route suggests that this campaign about education formed a mere facade that masked a deeper concern about the implications of emancipation. According to the logic of the photograph, the doors of the slave markets in New Orleans had been blown off, but the children's dress suggests that emancipation had not set loose thousands of untamed freed slaves, as antebellum proslavery advocates had warned, but genteel and polite children who were in simple need of education. While the children's Victorian clothing counters the deep-seated nineteenth-century imagery of the African as barbaric, naked, and destitute, it begins unwittingly to promote its own racial logic. Their identification as "white slave" children might have served as a warning to northern viewers that could read, "Beware—some of the slaves are white." Marking the children as white and circulating an image that conforms to Victorian notions of civility might encourage northern audiences to broaden their understanding of what constitutes a slave, what it means to be, in the nineteenth-century nomenclature, a "negro." For northern, and even in certain cases southern, audiences that had had little exposure to plantation life, an image of people who appeared as white but had black ancestry was an entirely foreign concept. So, readers needed to be told in some way, or even warned, about this phenomenon, which invariably fueled nineteenth-century paranoia surrounding miscegenation.[8]

In an effort to accentuate Rosa and her contemporaries' "fair" complexions, the editors at *Harper's Weekly* sketched an image of the children next to a group of "darker black" people dressed in servants' clothing. Placing the children alongside the others presented a stark contrast and in so doing relayed to northern audiences the gradations of race. In this context *white* meant "Victorian," whereas *black* signaled those who served. But as the story of Rosa's trip unfolds, her arrival in Philadelphia invalidated the distinction. When the management of a Philadelphia hotel, the Continental, discovered that Rosa and the others had been born as slaves, they were asked to leave immediately. Despite Rosa's fancy hat, Rebecca's elegant cape, and Charley's dapper suit, the children were thrown out of the hotel, onto the streets.

The story of Rosina Downs, Rebecca Huger, and Charley Taylor reveals the most fundamental component of racial formation that continues even today: it is not one's identity that matters but rather how one is identified. Although Rosa could have easily disclosed a genealogy that connected her to a white Louisiana senator or even a free black doctor, it did not matter; she could still be identified as a slave, no matter how genteel or elegant her appearance.[9] Within the history of the United States, racial slavery derived from colonial law that deemed a child born of an enslaved woman was automatically enslaved. The passing of this legislation naturalized the institution of slavery by defining reproduction as the foundation for modern slavery.[10] The outgrowth of this codification led to the marking of children born of enslaved women, and oftentimes white men, as slaves. Within the confines of plantation communities both slaves and members of slaveholding families easily recognized these offspring of slaves, regardless of their color.[11]

The use of the term *mulatto* can be traced to seventeenth-century British North America and the creation of manumission laws.[12] An entire set of legal codes developed in order to distinguish the manumitted mulatto from the white population and to place the mulatto in a separate category that disavowed any white ancestry and accentuated his or her black origins. Furthermore, from the seventeenth through the early nineteenth centuries, classification regarding color did in fact appear in court cases, local and state laws, and popular discourse. Runaway-slave ads and municipal records, for instance, include many references to "mixed-race" people. Similar to the post–Civil War period, these references to people of mixed racial background often resulted from legal, social, and political questions about how these people would fit into the broader society or functioned as markers of racial classification.[13]

When the American Civil War ended in 1865 and emancipated slaves fled from southern plantations, references to color exploded. Beleaguered military officers and anxious state leaders systematically used color at the federal level to establish order in the postwar South. When Union army commanders devised policies on how to handle fugitive slaves that crossed their lines for protection, they often referred to the color of the emancipated bondsperson. When federal government agents mediated contracts between disgruntled planters and unpaid freedmen, they too documented the color of the former slaves. When state government officials in places such as Florida and Mississippi outlined black codes to define the meaning of freedom, they made a distinction between "mulattoes" and "black" people. When census takers in 1870 collected data about residents in the United States, the category created to classify freed slaves was "color," not "race." As a result, many census recorders made further distinctions according to gradations of color.[14]

Further, when municipal authorities sanctioned marriages between freedwomen and men, they noted not only the newlyweds' color but also that of their parents.[15] When state and in some cases federal administrators visited the newly constructed schools for the children of freed slaves, they often remarked on the color of the pupils. When journalists, travelers, and ordinary white Americans encountered newly emancipated slaves in the countryside, at work in a home, on a plantation, or arriving on the streets of a northern or even a southern town, they consistently commented on the color of the former slaves.[16] Finally, when freedpeople themselves created their own bank, the Freedmen's Savings and Trust Company, they too followed a system of classification that emphasized color, detailing the complexion of each of their patrons for identity purposes.[17]

While references to color certainly appeared in seventeenth- and eighteenth-century statutes, laws, and other forms of public and popular discourse, the increased use of these definitions proliferated in response to the crisis that emancipation sparked in 1862. Documenting and referring to former slaves in terms of color became a way to confront the confusion of the postwar period. The deployment of crude terms such as *mulatto, quadroon,* and *octoroon* or even the reproachful adjectival descriptions of freed slaves as "light," "high yellow," or "fair," reveals a postwar crisis over who was of African descent. The use of the terms was highly arbitrary and only reproduces a false racial taxonomy that does not denote any kind of biological reality. As historian Barbara J. Fields has brilliantly argued, race is not a concept like the speed of light, nor is it a quantity that can be measured like the value of the mathematical symbol pi.[18] Instead, race is the outgrowth of very specific historical circumstances that shape its meaning and its value.[19]

Without this codification of racial categories, the idea of "race" as a distinct concept may have dissipated in the postwar period, but it instead was reified. After the Civil War, for example, when interviewing former slaves in New Berne, North Carolina, Vincent Colyer remarked, "I have had men and women apply for work who were so white that I could not believe they had a particle of negro blood in their veins."[20] If those of African descent showed no visible "trace of negro blood," as Colyer's comment suggests, then why continue to define freed slaves as black?

While capitalistic imperatives, not racist ideology, necessitated the creation of a dependent class in the postwar South, one must not overlook the ways in which racism operated within this system.[21] Noting the color of freed slaves in a number of settings from schools to federal debates to employment contracts solidified the assumption that if a dependent class needed to return to the plantation South, then those transported back to the fields would be black. Thus, when color is noted in these varied and seemingly innocuous contexts, while often distant from the fields of the postwar South, it served to reassert that racial categories determined who could be used as dependable labor.

## Color in Response to a Crisis

The ending of slavery thus represented a crucial, and often overlooked, watershed in the history of racial classification. The Civil War and Reconstruction era created for many white Americans—in both the North and in the South—an epistemological crisis on how to respond to the emancipation of well over four million people. In an effort to address the chaos and confusion that accompanied the destruction of slavery, local, state, and federal authorities attempted to reinscribe slavery onto the bodies of freedpeople by constantly documenting color at every turn that former slaves made on their road to freedom. While many historians have treated the collapse of slavery in terms of the political debates and economic struggles that ensued, they have overlooked the ways in which the Civil War created an epistemological crisis over the question of who, in fact, was black. Before the Civil War slaveholders could easily keep a record of slaves' descendants, their ancestry, and their physicality; in fact, such information was often marshaled in an effort to earn a higher profit when slaves were bought, bartered, and sold to work on neighboring and distant plantations. Yet when slavery ended during the Civil War, so did the ability of the nonblack community to keep accurate tabs on who was of African descent. The marking of freed slaves as mulatto, quadroon, and octoroon increasingly became a way for those in power to address the epistemological crisis over who was black.

Employing a system of racial classification based on color also became a way to restructure a society that otherwise relegated people of African descent to isolated plantations.[22] With the exception of what they encountered—a handful of broadsides, a dozen cartoons, and a score of abolitionist writings—many white people in the United States had little or no understanding of black people or the manifestations of race.[23] Before the war, slaves were confined by the rigid parameters of the plantation gates, but emancipation shattered those boundaries and placed former slaves in direct contact with whites. Listen to the description that a contributor for *DeBow's Review*, a southern periodical, gave in 1866 regarding the condition of emancipated women he encountered: "Some three hundred women, and children between the ages of six and sixteen—all as idle as the dogs, which are quite as numerous as the negroes, for they all love dogs and take care of them, however much they may neglect their children. These three hundred 'Amazonidee' are under the especial charge of the Richmond Bureau. They constitute a zoological garden independent of Mrs. Gibbons' zoological gardens. They are of all colors, from ebony-black to almost pure white; and of all races, except the pure Caucasian."[24]

Just as sixteenth- and seventeenth-century travel writers, voyaging throughout the Atlantic world, encountered Native peoples in the Americas and commented copiously on their bodies, culture, and behavior,[25] so, too, did writers in the nineteenth century follow a similar discursive pattern in their observations about the color of emancipated slaves with whom they came in contact after the Civil War. At a church meeting in Washington, D.C., in 1862, a journalist for the *Chicago Tribune* reported on a group of slaves and free blacks who had gathered to hear a speech about the coming of emancipation; he described the members of the audience as "partly white; many were mulattos, quadroons, and octoroons."[26] Also reporting on a political gathering of freed slaves, a reporter for the progressive black newspaper the *Christian Recorder* depicted the audience in terms of color. "They were of every hue from the light octoroon to the deep black. They were such a looking body of men as might pour out of a market-house or a courthouse at random in any Southern State. Every Negro type and physiognomy were here to be seen, from the genteel serving man to the rough hewn customer from the rice or cotton field. Their dress was varied as their countenances."[27]

Racial classification developed as a way for nonblack people to negotiate the uncertain social relations that emancipation engendered. An established criteria of racial classification developed that infiltrated everything from the writing of legal documents to the recording of census data to the ordinary customs of social discourse. Take, for example, the constant references in the nineteenth-century press about Frederick Douglass as a "mulatto" or even Homer Plessy's identification as an "octoroon" in the 1896 landmark case *Plessy v. Ferguson* legalizing segregation. That two of the most widely known African American men of the nineteenth century, Frederick Douglass and Homer Plessy, were both identified as mixed-race is not coincidental and indeed illustrates the overwhelming and intense preoccupation with color that dominated the United States in the nineteenth century. That both men have entered the historical record with references to their color and by extension their genealogy exemplifies how many nineteenth-century white Americans used color as a way to make distinctions among freedpeople.

Furthermore, the distinction made between Douglass as mulatto and Plessy as octoroon challenges the prevailing interpretation of the "one-drop rule," which classifies race according to a simple bifurcated system of black or white—when, in fact, throughout the postwar period the varied designations of color connoted different and profound meanings to white Americans who attempted to gain a profile and understanding of freed slaves.[28] The lighter and more fair-skinned people of African descent were perceived as intelligent and were also, to borrow the oft-quoted nineteenth-century term, "handsome," compared to their "darker" contemporaries. At the same time, references to quadroons and octoroons seemed frequently to denote the freed slaves' potential to be subversive. An 1887 issue of the Cleveland Gazette, for instance, tantalized its readers with the headline story of "Victims of a Handsome Quadroon." The article detailed one Mary Robinson, who allegedly traveled through various parts of Virginia seducing male companions to accompany her across the state—where she promised them great fortune that was awaiting her. Yet according to the article, Robinson gave one of her male companions "the slip" and was, as the newspaper warned, "believed to be in Philadelphia."[29]

In many other newspaper stories and accounts, so-called quadroons appeared as deceptive and subversive, tricking and seducing people with their allegedly concealed African identity. While it is difficult to measure how many nonblack people in the nineteenth century associated quadroons with being manipulative, a clue to solving this quandary can be found in the 1868 San Francisco minstrel aptly titled "The Charming Gay Quadroon."[30] The creators of this minstrel, in following with the genre's often satiric style, identify the leading character as both "charming" and "gay" in an effort to overturn the otherwise widespread popular conception that quadroons were inherently deceptive and subversive.[31]

Nevertheless, the fascination with identifying people of African descent as "black, mulattoes, quadroons, and octoroons" resulted from a number of different factors. While it could be flatly read as northerners' prurient fascination with the "exoticness" of southern former slaves, it seems more likely to represent the nineteenth-century belief that appearance mattered. Throughout the postwar period and even earlier, appearance, according to many in the nineteenth century, revealed one's social class, personal character, moral code, and even medical condition.[32] Part of the campaign involving the aforementioned "white slave children," for example, centered on dressing the children in elegant clothes in order to directly counter the prevailing image of slaves as savages.

Documenting gradations of color thus became a way to understand freed slaves during a period when much was unclear about their character and their fate; color was the first characteristic that many people who placed value on appearance would notice. The historian Winthrop Jordan claimed that despite distinctions made between "mulattoes and Negroes," the evidence does not indicate that "mulattoes' status was higher and demanded different treatment" or "that mulattoes were preferred as house servants or concubines."[33] Yet evaluating the use of the idiom *mulatto* only in terms of social status and treatment ignores the context in which the word emerges. The word *mulatto* does not initially get deployed in response to an effort by slaveholders to create divisions of labor, from arduous plantation work to the seemingly less straining domestic work, but rather the term emerges because of a question or a shift in the political and social order, largely stemming from manumission laws. The term also develops at first as a way to identify the offspring of an interracial couple. Whether that offspring is excused from slavery or is confronted with the conditions of a child born of two slaves is only the result of the more primary concern of how first to identify this child. Similarly, when the use of the term *mulattoes* enters into the legal code, it does not matter; even if we accept Jordan's claim that mulattoes were not afforded different status or treatment from full-blooded black people, the issue nonetheless is that the presence of mulattoes called for a legal declaration of their status. Just because state or local officials determined not to offer mulattoes a better status or treatment does not mean that mulattoes were seen as similar to full blacks in the first place. The very act of distinguishing between the two suggests an effort to create a social order based on color.

Consequently, the deployment of terms such as *mulatto* and *yellow* that marked and quantified color ranged from isolated legal incidents regarding the status of a manumitted slave to political questions about the offspring of an interracial couple to the more widespread emancipation of four million slaves during the American Civil War. As such, references to color in the historical record should not be simply interpreted as markers of elevated status or preferred treatment but rather as by-products of a social and political system that attempted to respond to legal questions or a social crisis.

### The Federal Codification of Color

The federal government's uncertainty surrounding emancipation led to the organization of interviews, surveys, and commissions that visited communities of former slaves and evaluated their color.[34] Of the many different organizations that reported on the conditions of former slaves during the Civil War and Reconstruction period, the most significant was the Office of the American Freedmen's Inquiry Commission (AFIC), which was founded by the secretary of war, Edwin M. Stanton. In a series of reports aimed at evaluating former slaves' labor power, the federal agents often turned their attention to issues relating to color. At first they were fascinated by the mere presence of mixed-race people in communities of former slaves. In their initial report filed in 1863, they detailed the presence of a "mulatto" in a family of "black" people.[35] By the end of their tour their intrigue with color had morphed into a full-blown investigation into the so-called medical realities of people with "mixed blood." In fact, in the final part of their last report, published in 1865, the federal agents included a section aptly titled "The Future of the Color Race," containing quotations made by physicians about the physiological attributes of mulattoes.[36]

In the AFIC's first report, published on June 30, 1863, six months after the formal issuance of the Emancipation Proclamation, the investigators reported on the ways in which "a mulatto girl deemed it beneath her to associate with her half-sister, a black and the daughter of her mother's husband, her own father being a white man."[37] The commissioners who drafted the report refer to this incident in order to inform Stanton that "many colored women think it more disgraceful to be black than to be illegitimate."[38] That the said "mulatto girl" would prefer to disavow her own family and be perceived as "illegitimate," rather than be marked as black, revealed to the federal commissioners that gradations of color mattered. They used this incident to explain to Stanton that he need not worry about hiring guards to patrol the villages where freed slaves lived, as "there are no sentinels so strict as the negroes themselves."[39] Learning about how this particular mulatto girl refused to associate with members of her own family because they were darker than she was suggested to the federal agents that a hierarchy based on color existed within freed-people's communities and could be used by the government to negotiate the uncertain terrain that emancipation posed. It is important to note, however, that these agents failed to realize that this racial hierarchy did not originate among slaves but was a system of classification that southern slaveholders had created.[40] The federal agents further failed to realize that this former enslaved girl was the exception, not the rule—many former enslaved people did not subscribe to the same prejudicial ideas about color that she did.

The description of the girl as mulatto as well as references to her family as black nonetheless provided Stanton and other readers of the report with a formal lesson on the various ways in which color could vary. The explanation of her genealogy attempts to explain to readers of the report the common organization of former slave family units that dominated the antebellum South and were making their ways toward freedom. As the first report published by the AFIC, this document reveals the extent to which leaders in the top echelon of the federal government were made aware of color as they initially learned about the effects of emancipation.

Throughout the war the AFIC's obsession with color intensified. Deeply concerned with the implications of emancipated, mixed-race people in the United States, Samuel Howe, one of the authors of the initial report, traveled to Canada in order to gain a sense of the condition of freed slaves who had migrated north before the war. While evaluating the status of refugee slaves in Canada, Howe claimed that emancipation would ultimately lead to extinction of the "black race." Focusing entirely on color, Howe noted the presence of "pure Africans, half-breeds, quarter-breeds, octoroons, and of others who the dark shade grows fainter and fainter" in Canada and claimed that this "mulattoism" would ultimately eliminate the black race.[41]

While so-called scientific writers had made claims about the inferiority of mulattoes since the early nineteenth century, Howe's claim, articulated under the aegis of the AFIC, had a much greater impact on the lives of freedpeople than the antebellum articulations on this topic.[42] In the early nineteenth century discussions of mulattoes as distinct and inferior buttressed a proslavery rhetoric but were often challenged by fiery rebuttals leveled by abolitionists and northern thinkers. By the midcentury, however, the stakes were much higher; discussions about mulattoes did not just support a proslavery parable but actually determined if the federal government would amend the Constitution by defining former slaves as citizens and extending voting privileges to them.[43] Put another way, those who propagated ideas about racial inferiority of mulattoes in the nineteenth century were ill-informed thinkers whose message gained momentum among southern slaveholders and impressionable northerners who sought an "empirical" and "objective" justification for enslavement. In the years 1863 to 1865 federal agents conveyed ideas about the racial inferiority of mixed-race people to the war secretary and to members of Congress, who read and cited the AFIC's conclusions. Congressmen such as Samuel Cox, a Democrat from Illinois, ultimately used these claims about racial inferiority to argue that former slaves were, in fact, "dying out" and cautioned members of Congress not to violate the Constitution by providing federal assistance to them.[44]

Throughout the postwar period, discussions of color gained even more momentum, becoming an integral way that those in power defined former slaves. Although eighteenth- and nineteenth-century doctors made references to mixed-race people and their alleged inferiority, these ideas circulated at most on the pages of medical journals.[45] By the late 1860s references to mulattoes began to appear in the federal government's official documentation of the medical consequences of the war. From discussions of disease transmission to investigations of pulmonary capacity and even to measurements of mulatto people's bodies in comparison to white, black, and Indian bodies, nineteenth-century doctors, working under the auspices of the federal government, produced reports that detailed the physiology of mixed-race people. The proliferation of these reports further bolstered a proslavery parable that made distinctions among black people based on gradations of color. These reports, while intended to provide an encyclopedic analysis of health conditions of soldiers during this period, in actuality produced an official statement by the federal government that solidified the importance of distinguishing people based on color. Moreover, the federal classification of "mulattoes" and "black people" also became a way for doctors and federal leaders to understand an entire population of emancipated slaves by drawing divisions among them based on their body size, health, and susceptibility to disease.[46]

## The Color Line beyond the United States

The proliferation of classifications of color after the Civil War also brought to the surface a number of ideas that had circulated throughout the United States and the Atlantic world in the two centuries that predated the destruction of slavery. In the seventeenth and eighteenth centuries references to color appeared idiosyncratically. The constant use of the word *mulatto* in the postwar period resulted from the impact of the African diaspora throughout the Atlantic world. The term *mulatto* derives from a word in the Spanish language meaning "small mule" and was first used by Spanish slaveholders in the Caribbean and South America to describe the offspring of interracial couples. American slaveholders later adopted the term—revealing a commonality that connected plantations from Cuba to the Carolinas.[47] Nevertheless, throughout much of the Atlantic world mulattoes often represented people who were perceived as having African ancestry but were considered in some way different from those who were enslaved. Thus, government officials and colonial administrators often developed a separate category of classification to demarcate those of perceived or mixed African ancestry from those who were defined as "full-blooded" Africans.[48]

Often neither freed nor enslaved, mulattoes' questionable presence led to the declaration of various laws specifically designed to address their political and legal status. In eighteenth-century Martinique colonial authorities established distinct laws across a range of activities that targeted mulattoes, barring them from walking on public streets and forbidding them to be called "Monsieur" or "Madame."[49] A law passed in Jamaica in 1761, for example, affording mulattoes the legal rights to own property and slaves created fear among the landed white gentry that such a stipulation "tends to destroy the distinctions requisite and absolutely necessary to be kept up in this island between white persons and Negroes."[50] Meanwhile, in Trinidad in 1824, John Baptista Phillip, a "mulatto," addressed colonial authorities, advocating for the mulatto population on the island to have the same rights and privileges as their white contemporaries.[51] Perhaps the most famous case is that of the mulattoes of St. Domingue, whose questionable political position eventually led Pierre Victor Malouet to draft a proposition providing mulattoes with the same privileges enjoyed by British colonial officials.[52] In an effort to gain political recognition, the free mulattoes of St. Domingue pressured the French General Assembly in Paris to grant them political participation. Although the General Assembly eventually acceded to the mulattoes' claim, the French planters in the colonial threshold of St. Domingue refused to acknowledge the ruling. An insurrection thus erupted, which impelled the otherwise robust French colonials to turn to British colonial officials in the neighboring island of Jamaica for support. British officials helped the French planters, yet the free mulattoes continued to demand political recognition. Malouet thus proposed a specific article to address the status of free mulattoes on the island.

In many other, albeit less explosive, cases the presence of people of mixed African ancestry gave way to continued usage of the idiom *mulatto* that attempted to maintain a certain degree of social order among the freed and the enslaved. While many countries in the Atlantic world did not specifically employ the term, they often created a similar one that defined those of mixed racial ancestry. In Venezuela, for example, government officials established the category of "pardo" to categorize those of African, Indian, and European ancestry, while Colombians on the Atlantic coast defined their mulatto population as "costeños." In Brazil, Cuba, and other parts of Central and Latin and America the category of "mulatto," or mixed race, appeared in colonial statues and laws in order to maintain social relations.[53]

Consequently, when emancipation erupted in the United States, federal officials did not simply rely on a southern U.S. definition of race and color in order to rebuild the South, but rather, they tapped into a larger discourse about color that permeated the Atlantic world through the African diaspora. Throughout the early part of the nineteenth century Americans had read about the news of the Haitian rebellion in the northern press, and the proponents of the insurrection, the "free mulattoes," subsequently became part of the American public imagination. The idea that mulattoes, not full-blooded African slaves, had spearheaded the revolt buttressed American readers' own conceptions, their ideas and social practices, that distinctions needed to be made among those of African descent. In 1796 readers of the Philadelphia newspaper the *Pennsylvania Gazette*, for example, learned that a mulatto by the name of Lafond, whom the paper described as "one of the worst subjects of Petit Guave," was killed by "negro pioneers."[54]

Throughout much of the reporting on the Haitian Revolution, accounts such as this proliferated that portrayed the leaders of the insurrection as mulatto, which was then followed with a description that attempted to evoke fear in the minds of the reader, in this particular case the reference to Lafond "as one of the worst." After such accounts there often appears an effort by the writer or reporter to mark a difference between the said named mulatto and the nameless yet unified group of "negroes." While the terms *mulatto* and *negro* certainly conjured different meanings in the minds of American readers, the outcome, nevertheless, was that a distinction was made about black people—and that distinction was based on color.

Employing many of these widely accepted tropes about color, Mary Hassal, an American traveler, recounted a story from the Haitian Revolution and distinguished throughout the letter "mulattoes" from "people of color" when she wrote to her uncle Aaron Burr, who was then vice president. She wrote, "In the first days of the massacre, when the negroes ran through the town killing all the white men they encountered, a Frenchman was dragged from the place of his concealment by a ruthless mulatto, who, drawing his sabre, bade him prepare to die."[55] Hassal then explained to Burr that the Frenchman had pleaded for his life and promised the mulatto his riches if he would return him to his home. Once the Frenchman entered the home, Hassal introduced the other key character. She writes:

> While they were disputing, a girl of colour . . . entered, and having learned the story, employed all her eloquence to make the mulatto relent. She sunk at his feet, and pressed his hands which were reeking with blood. Dear brother, she said, spare for my sake this unfortunate man. He never injured you; nor will you derive any advantage from his death, and by saving him, you will acquire the sum you demand, and a claim to his gratitude. She was beautiful; she wept, and beauty in tears has seldom been resisted. Yet this unrelenting

savage did resist; and swore, with bitter oaths to pursue all white men with unremitting fury. The girl, however, hung to him, repeated her solicitations, and offered him, in addition to the sum proposed, all her trinkets, which were of considerable value.[56]

Hassal's letter to her uncle reveals the extent to which Americans throughout the nineteenth century, particularly those in positions of power and influence, slowly became aware of color distinctions made throughout the broader Atlantic world. In particular, her letter illustrates how the distinctions made between *mulatto* and *girl of color* carried particular meaning. That mulattoes, not simply black people or freed slaves, organized such a campaign and then executed it with such vengeance set in motion a belief that those of mixed blood should not be trusted. Meanwhile, the reference to the "girl of colour," who is clearly not a participant in the revolt, indicates that distinctions did exist among those of African descent—that some could be allies, while others were the enemy. The reference to how the girl of color manages to assuage the mulatto's threat by calling him "brother" perpetrates the idea that all people of African descent, regardless of where they fall in terms of color, or in this case which side they take in the revolt, are ultimately united by their shared African ancestry. And as a result, the idea of "brotherhood" strengthens the notion that color is not an imagined or arbitrary characteristic but a palpable and concrete trait.

In fact, once the Civil War broke out in the United States in 1861, Americans referred to the Haitian Revolution and evoked the classification of the mulatto as a way to predict black participation in the war.[57] In an editorial titled "Will the Blacks Fight?" published in the *New York Evening Post* in July 1862, the author relayed the history of the Haitian Revolution to the mostly northern readership. He claimed that the incident in St. Domingue revealed how black people of different colors found a common brotherhood and joined forces against those who oppressed them. The author further claimed that the action of their so-called brothers in St. Domingue would inspire northern blacks to join the Union army and help emancipate their enslaved southern contemporaries— just as mulattoes and enslaved blacks had joined forces during the Haitian Revolution. Using the Haitian case, he also underscored how black people inherently possessed the capability to wage successful military campaigns. The author nonetheless reinscribes the primacy of color by referring to the agents of the insurrection as the "unorganized mulattoes in the south of St. Domingo."[58] By constantly referring to the revolutionaries as "mulattoes," he signals to northern readers the continual need to maintain a system of racial classification in the United States that ranks enslaved people based on their color, which, according to his particular logic, defines their military prowess.

The idea that mulattoes would be vital to the Civil War effort was a popular theme in American letters and discourse that originated from the Haitian Revolution. Stationed in a former plantation district in South Carolina, Charlotte Forten Grimké, a leading black social reformer from Philadelphia, served as a schoolteacher to newly emancipated slaves. In a diary entry from November 1862 Grimké wrote of telling the students about the Haitian Revolution and of Toussaint Louverture, the former slave who led the revolt. "I long to inspire them," she wrote to her diary, "with courage and ambition (of a noble sort,) and high purpose." While the story of the Haitian Revolution was meant to inspire the students, Grimké's hopes seem to dash when she looked across the crowded schoolroom and noticed "how very few mulattoes there are here." Forten further lamented, "Indeed in our school, with one or two exceptions, the children are all black."[59] According to the underlying logic of Grimké's entry, the fate and future of the emancipated population did not lie in the education she provided but rather in the color of the pupils.

From white editorialists to black social reformers many Americans seemed to emulate the so-called mulattoes of the Haitian Revolution. They viewed them as heroes who could address the uncertainty of the Civil War and Reconstruction. The success of the mulatto population in Haiti, achieving rights and becoming the first black republic in the Atlantic world, thus supported the American idea that color mattered and could be used as a way to structure a society no longer organized around the institution of slavery. Certainly, classification according to color can be traced to the colonial period, but the confusion of the postwar period surrounding emancipation, combined with the broader discourse about color in the Atlantic world, led to an increased use of this form of categorization.

## The Rise of Racial Classification after Emancipation in the Atlantic World

The phenomenon of classification by color, which exploded in the United States after the Civil War, is not that uncommon within the broader context of the African diaspora. In many places in the Atlantic world, when a crisis erupted or a major transformation in the social and political order occurred, classifications based on color proliferated. After the end of slavery in Brazil, for example, categories of color predominated. While Brazil since its colonial period had had a special category that designated persons of color, "pessoas de cor," the destruction of slavery wrought a proliferation of related categories, including "preto" (black) and "pardo" (mulatto), African or Brazilian born, and slave or free.[60]

Similarly, after the declaration of emancipation in Jamaica in 1838, the category of "colored" began to appear in demographic charts of the island's population.[61] Although colonial and state officials in Jamaica had acknowledged the presence of "mixed-race" people since the 1793 publication of Bryan Edwards's *History, Civil and Commercial of the British Colonies in the West Indies*, the historical accounting of so-called colored people as a distinct category appeared formally in 1844—a few years after the 1838 abolition of slavery.[62] According to this chart that details the island's population from 1673 to 1793, only the term *black* was used; after 1793 the next year to appear on the chart was 1844, at which time the category of "colored" was included in addition to the continued use of "black." Furthermore, the formal marking of people of African descent into two separate categories, "black" and "colored," not only illustrates how categories based on color proliferate during a moment of crisis but, in the case of Jamaica, how state officials endorsed and propagated such classification in order, as historian Aline Helg argues, "to form a buffer between free blacks and slaves." Yet much to the dismay of colonial administrators, mulattoes and slaves rejected such an artificial marker of difference and instead recognized a shared identity that enabled them to unite in a political campaign against British authority on the island.[63]

As Afro-Jamaicans rejected the distinctions made between those of African descent, throughout the rest of the Atlantic world the reinscription of racial categories predominated as, with the collapse of the institution of slavery, the crisis over "who was black" continued. This crisis illuminates at the most basic level the absurdity of racial characteristics in the first place.

Furthermore, the story of the Civil War period is often told as one that unfolds purely within the national boundaries of the United States, and so, by extension, the history of the African diaspora remains very much outside the purview of this otherwise truly nationalistic story about the clashes between the North and the South. Yet once the issue of slavery and emancipation takes center stage as the fundamental cause of the war, we then need to think more critically about the African diaspora. Both before and after the war, Americans concerned about the fate of freed slaves looked beyond the national borders of the United States as a way to think about the end of slavery. And in so doing, the issue of color once again appeared as the organizing principle around which to imagine a world no longer organized by slavery. In an effort to settle the question of what to do with freed slaves, James Mitchell of the American Colonization Society (ACS) wrote to President Abraham Lincoln during the Civil War to advocate for the removal of former slaves to "tropical areas" in the Western Hemisphere that included populations of mixed-race people. Framing his argument around ideas of "mixed blood," Mitchell identified Mexico as an appropriate place for the colonization of freed blacks because the country had for generations had large populations of mixed-race people:

> The shorter the journey the more likely are we to succeed in the work of removal, so that of the several places eligible—South America, Central America, or Mexico, the latter is the most eligible on this account although the quality of the final neighbor might not be so agreeable, yet as we are struggling for life we should wave that reflection or objection—Mexico can hardly be called a Tropical country, but it has already become the home of the mixed bloods of North America; where the partial assimilation of the colored races has been progressing for many generations so that of the 7,000,000 population in that country not more than 1,500,000 can be regarded as of Castilian blood, and it is questionable whether there is the half of that uncorrupted— yet notwithstanding this large preponderance of mixed bloods the population is heterogeneous and factious, so that the annexation of this Country or its people to ours is not safe, if we wish to perpetuate unimpaired our institutions, for no part of a true republic could be constructed out of a land thus encumbered with mixed bloods, it being a condition precedent that the in-

habitants shall be homogeneous, either originally or by assimilation, through the amalgamation of races. But Mexico is now and has been peopled with a factious mixed and consequently revolutionary race, and we fear will remain so for ages to come.[64]

Before the Civil War, in fact as early as 1816, the architects of the ACS had promoted Africa as the site where manumitted and free black people should return after slavery. Yet as Marshall's letter to Lincoln suggests, Mexico is not only a closer and a more manageable location than Africa to finance a resettlement effort, but it also is a more suitable place because of its long-standing history of "mixed blood" inhabitants. Fifty years earlier, colonization advocates had seen a direct relationship between slaves in the American South and black people in Africa. Yet the outbreak of the war and the gradual emancipation of the slaves caused Marshall to rethink the physiognomy of American slaves in the South. Emancipation thus revealed to many Americans, including Marshall, that American slaves were of so-called mixed blood. According to the underlying logic of Marshall's letter, a common bond therefore no longer existed between the enslaved people of the American South and Africans.

This transformation in the ACS's claim that American slaves would be better suited for settlement in Central or South America can be traced to the society's awareness of racial categories that existed in other parts of the Atlantic world. A few years before Marshall's statements about the removal of mulattoes to Mexico, Angelina Grimké Weld, a prominent social reformer, wrote to her southern relative Theodore Grimké about the excitement that boiled over at a meeting of the ACS in 1832 in which members debated the issue of amalgamation. In response to the pending question of the fate of "mulattoes" if emancipation took hold in the United States, Grimké asked her brother a series of questions about the presence of mulattoes and the outcome of amalgamation in other parts of the Atlantic World—evincing an awareness about the categories of color that existed outside the borders of the United States. She asked, are "people in the West Indies principally mulatto? And how is it in South America? Did they not amalgamate there? Did not the Helots, a great many of whom were Persians, etc., taken in battle, amalgamate with the Grecians, and rise to equal privileges in the State?"[65] As a result of questions like this, by 1861, after decades of debate over the character and fate of freed slaves, the ACS, one of the leading advocates of black liberation, overhauled its mission and central tenet due to the growing obsession with color and the powerful system of social classification of freed slaves as mulatto or mixed blood that came to dominate the Civil War era.

Nevertheless, Marshall's earlier designation of Mexico also reveals the extent to which Americans in the nineteenth century conceptualized race and color outside of the narrow national parameters of the United States. Leaving aside the exaggerated and erroneous history that Marshall propagates, his letter nevertheless decenters the United States, in particular the American South, as the site of racial formation. Instead, his letter reveals the extent to which nineteenth-century Americans imagined the historical construction of racial formation in other parts of the Atlantic world that long predated the arrival of Africans to Jamestown in the seventeenth century. More important, Marshall's letters illustrate how Americans relied on this more global understanding in order to make sense of mixed blood people and color classification.

Although Marshall's efforts to create a settlement for freed slaves in Mexico never materialized, the issues of mixed blood that galvanized his campaign remained alive throughout the 1860s and 1870s. While census recorders used color to classify residents of the United States and members of federal and state agencies continually relied on color categorization in their reporting and documenting of freed slaves' lives, the preponderance of this system ultimately began to reveal its weaknesses. Because the whole system of color classification was arbitrary, artificial, and lacked scientific validity, those in power began to see its flaws. In the United States Army, for instance, Private Charles R. Pratt, an enlisted man whom military officials presumed was white, requested permission to transfer to a black regiment. "I am a colored man, and my position as a private in a white Regiment is very unpleasant," Pratt explained. He further added, "My feelings are constantly outraged by the conduct of those who have no respect for my race."[66] Pratt's story illustrates, like many novels that dominated the literary landscape of the late nineteenth century, how some people of African descent who could have bypassed color classification refused and instead willingly and publicly declared their heritage.[67]

With the exception of those who claimed their African ancestry, problems nevertheless developed as those in power attempted to maintain a social order by employing a system that relied on color classification. Government officials struggled to determine who was, in fact, black after the Civil War. A case brought before the Supreme Court in Michigan in 1866 involving William Dean, who voted in an election as a "white man," provides a potent example of the fallacy inherent in the system of color classification. According to an article in the *Chicago Tribune,* "Witnesses were introduced to determine the shade of Mr. Dean's complexion, the kinkiness of his hair, the shape of his nose, and also to trace his pedigree."[68] Witnesses that testified from Dean's home state of Delaware identified him as a mulatto, as the definition of *black* in that state translated to having one drop of Negro blood. Yet in Michigan having one-sixteenth of black blood meant that he was black. In order to determine if he was one-sixteenth black, medical authorities were called in, and Dean was "put through all medical tests known to the profession." While the doctors claimed that his skin color was no darker than that of a pure Caucasian, one physician measured the cartilages on his nose and concluded that Dean was one-sixteenth black. The court ignored this testimony and eventually ruled in favor of Dean, claiming that a person who had less than a quarter of African blood was white.[69]

Although the Supreme Court in Michigan ultimately established a barometer for how to evaluate color in 1866, the years following Reconstruction would witness a more dramatic turn. The Jim Crow period, which both by law and custom segregated blacks from whites, relied heavily on the postwar fascination with color. Without the demarcation of color in the United States, which in many ways was informed by the impact of the African diaspora throughout the Atlantic world, the effort to mobilize such a widespread and effective system of segregation might not have been possible. Jim Crow restrictions succeeded because a code based on the gradations of color already existed as a fundamental and often articulated part of many social institutions, government methods of classification, and popular discourse.

The travels and travails of Rosina Downs and the other "white slave children" indicate the extent to which ideas about color developed as a result of a larger social crisis. The constant references to the color of former slaves in the historical record point less to the issue of whether some former slaves enjoyed better treatment or elevated status, but rather, as Downs's story reveals, to a change in the social and political order—in this case what should happen to those who look white but were born enslaved. Furthermore, the focus on Downs's color is not entirely coincidental within the larger discourse of the Atlantic world and the African diaspora. From the late eighteenth century to the years leading up to the U.S. Civil War, Americans read about "mulattoes" and those of various colors who lived in places such as Brazil and the West Indies. So, when Downs first began to appear in the headlines in the northern press, her presence as a "white slave child" or as a "mulatto" evoked categories of classification that came to represent people of African descent from other parts of the globe—which explains in part why and how northern audiences eventually accepted her identification as a former slave.

Yet haunting both this story and the historical record in the United States and in other parts of the Atlantic World are the harrowing and intangible stories of racial passing. Rosina Downs appears in the press after the war but then passes through history with very little of an archival trace. Her story is told and retold but is often not written down. Instead, it is hidden and sometimes secretly celebrated behind closed doors in rooms where color no longer seems to carry a currency—because, in part, this was the plan. Yet her discovery in a newspaper that matches the now-bent carte de visite found in an old shoebox among cards and letters, notes and diaries, reveals what got caught between slavery and freedom.

Knowing that she cannot speak to me across generations of silence, and feeling that only my hands will lead to a resurrection of the forces that shaped her life, I will position her as my muse, my light, my clue to unraveling a history that extends from Africa to the Caribbean to New Orleans to Philadelphia. Yet the insistent application of categories of color will cut across time, flatly identifying her as my kin, my past.

NOTES

1. Gregory Fried, "True Pictures," *Common-place* (American Antiquarian Society) 2.2 (January 2002), http://www.common-place.org/vol-02/no-02/fried/; Mary Niall Mitchell, "'Rosebloom and Pure White,' or So It Seemed," *American Quarterly* 54.3 (September 2002): 369–410.

2. For more on Butler's occupation of New Orleans, see James Parton, *General Butler in New Orleans. History of the Administration of the Department of the Gulf in the Year 1862: With an Account of the Capture of New Orleans . . .* (New York: Mason Brothers, 1864).

3. "White and Colored Slaves," *Harper's Weekly*, January 30, 1864, 71.

4. Assistant Commissioner Report, "List of Employees," Medical Division of the Freedmen's Bureau, RG105, Louisiana; Henry Downs (alias Henry Hunt), Application no. 1161403, Certificate no. 1061520, Pension Files, RG 15, National Archives, Washington, D.C.

5. "White and Colored Slaves," 71.

6. For the role that the NEFAS played in the postwar South, see Second Annual Report of the New England Freedmen's Aid Society (Boston: Published at the Office of the Society, 1864), 35, Massachusetts Historical Society. Also see Jean Fagan Yellin, *Harriet Jacobs: A Life* (New York: Basic Civitas Books, 2004).

7. For more on the domestic slave trade, see Walter Johnson, *Soul by Soul: Life inside the Antebellum Slave Market* (Cambridge, Mass.: Harvard University Press, 1999).

8. Certainly, some nineteenth-century white Americans interacted with biracial people. More to the point, white Americans would have also read novels and stories that included biracial characters, but my sense is that the fascination with mixed-race people skyrocketed after the war due to emancipation: white northerners faced the prospect of mixed-race former slaves entering their cities and towns. Moreover, even some black people, who may have certainly understood the variations of racial classification, worried about the influx of former slaves in their communities. On northern black fears of the arrival of southern slaves, see Abby Howland Woolsey to Harriet Gilman, March 9, 1865, in *Letters of a Family during the War for the Union, 1861–1865,* vol. 2 (New Haven, Conn.: Tuttle, Morehouse & Taylor, 1899). In this letter Woolsey explains how former slave Harriet Jacobs had to ease the anxiety that northern blacks had about the effects of emancipation. On representations of interracial characters in American literature, see Werner Sollor's authoritative book, *Neither Black nor White yet Both: Thematic Explorations of Interracial Literature* (New York: Oxford University Press, 1997).

9. I am indebted to Barbara J. Fields's lucid and cogent writings on the vexed subject of the history of racism. See Fields, "Whiteness, Racism, and Identity," *International Labor and Working-Class History* 60 (Fall 2001): 48–56; Fields, "Of Rogues and Geldings," *American Historical Review* (December 2003): 1397–1405; Fields, "Slavery, Race, and Ideology in the United States of America," *New Left Review* (May–June 1990): 95–118; Fields, "Ideology and Race in American History," in *Region, Race and Reconstruction: Essays in Honor of C. Vann Woodward,* ed. J. Morgan Kousser and James M. McPherson (New York: Oxford University Press, 1982), 143–77. Building on Fields's formulations, Martha Hodes astutely argues that "power lies within the ability of legal, economic, and social authorities to assign and reassign racial categories to oppressive ends." See Hodes, "The Mercurial Nature and Abiding Power of Race: A Transnational Family Story," *American Historical Review* (February 2003): 85.

10. See, for example, Jennifer Morgan, *Laboring Women: Reproduction and Gender in New World Slavery* (Philadelphia: University of Pennsylvania Press, 2004); and Kathleen M. Brown, *Good Wives, Nasty Wenches, and Anxious Patriarchs: Gender, Race, and Power in Colonial Virginia* (Chapel Hill: University of North Carolina Press, 1996).

11. The most famous case that illustrates this point is the story of Thomas Jefferson, his mistress Sally Hemings, and their descendants. See Annette Gordon-Reed, *Hemingses of Monticello: An American Family* (New York: Norton, 2009).

12. Winthrop D. Jordan, *White over Black: American Attitudes toward the Negro, 1550–1812* (Chapel Hill: University of North Carolina Press, 1968).

13. On runaway ads, see *Virginia Gazette*, May 9, September 26, and October 17, 1751, and January 24, 1752. On manumission laws in Pennsylvania, see, for example, John Bayard, "An Act for the Gradual Abolition of Slavery," March 1, 1780. For manumission laws in New York, see A. Leon Higginbotham, *In the Matter of Color: Race and the American Legal Process* (New York: Oxford University Press, 1978), 128–30. For a brilliant discussion of color in eighteenth-century prison records in Pennsylvania, see Jennifer Manion, "Women's Crime and Prison Reform in Early Pennsylvania, 1786–1829" (Ph.D. diss., Rutgers University, 2008).

14. Mississippi Black Codes, 1865, sec. 1–6. For black codes in Florida, see W. E. B. Du Bois, *Black Reconstruction in America, 1860–1880* (1935; repr., New York: Free Press, 1992), 172. On contracts, see, for example, "Testimony of a New Orleans Free Man of Color before the American Freedmen's Inquiry Commission," February 9, 1864, as quoted in *Wartime Genesis of Free Labor: The Lower South*, ser. 1, ed. Berlin et al. (New York: Cambridge University Press, 1990), 3:521. Many census recorders drew a distinction between "black" and "mulatto" in the 1870 census. It is important to note that these census writers did not see the category of "color," which is listed on the census, as being synonymous with "race." See, for instance, 1870 Federal Census, "Black and Mulatto Households," Barbour County, Ala.; 1870 Federal Census, Charlottesville and Esmont, Va.; Anderson County, Tenn. For an incisive analysis of the use of color in the nineteenth-century census, see Martha Hodes, "Fractions and Fictions in the United States Census of 1890," in *Haunted by Empire: Geographies of Intimacy in North American History*, ed. Ann Stoler (Durham, N.C.: Duke University Press, 2006), 240–70.

15. There are countless marriage records that detail the color of the married couple as well as their parents. The most accessible records are available online. See Freedmen's Marriage Certificates, 1861–69. Tennessee, Bureau Refugees, Freedmen, and Abandoned Land. http://freedmensbureau.com/tennessee/marriages/tennmarrs2.htm.

16. "From the Negroes of the District of Columbia Receive Their Promised Emancipation," *New York Tribune*, April 19, 1862, for *Chicago Tribune* (1860–72); April 19, 1862; *American Freedmen* 2.11 (February 1868); Robert Sargent Holland, ed., *Laura Matilda Towne, Letters and Diary of Laura M. Towne Written from the Sea Islands of South Carolina, 1862–1884* (New York: Negro Universities Press, 1969).

17. Complexion, along with age, birthplace, names of parents, employer, and the plantation where the person labored, appeared as critical and required markers of identification for bank patrons. The Freedmen's Savings and Trust Company records are all available through a CD-ROM. For a general history of the bank, see Carl R. Osthaus, *Freedmen, Philanthropy, and Fraud: A History of the Freedman's Savings Bank* (Urbana: University of Illinois Press, 1976).

18. Fields, "Slavery, Race, and Ideology."

19. See Hodes, "The Mercurial Nature and Abiding Power of Race: A Transnational Family Story," *American Historical Review* (February 2003): 85.

20. As quoted in Lawrence Tenzer and A. D. Powell, "White Slavery, Maternal Descent, and the Politics of Slavery in the Antebellum United States," *Multiracial Activist* (July–August 2004).

21. For a brilliant account of how a dependent labor class developed in the postwar South and also in other parts of the Atlantic world, see Eric Foner, *Nothing but Freedom: Emancipation and Its Legacy* (Baton Rouge: Louisiana State University Press, 1984).

22. Certainly, there were many places in both the antebellum North and even in parts of the South where white and black lived within proximity, yet my point is to draw attention to the ways in which emancipation represented a profound change in the United States because of the movement of black people to various corners of the nation. For more on black communities, see Julie Winch's excellent study on black people in Philadelphia before the war, *Philadelphia's Black Elite: Activism, Accommodation, and the Struggle for Autonomy, 1787–1848* (Philadelphia: Temple University Press, 1993)

23. Part of the reason that *Uncle Tom's Cabin* became an overnight success story was that there were few published books that attempted to provide an interior view of slave life, let alone an elaborate discussion on the gradations of color among enslaved people. For more on *Uncle Tom's Cabin*, see Henry Louis Gates Jr., *The Annotated Uncle Tom's Cabin* (New York: Norton, 2006).

24. "Camp Lee and the Freedmen's Bureau," *Debow's Review, Agricultural, Commercial Industrial Progress and Resources* 2.4 (October 1866): 346–55.

25. See Morgan, *Laboring Women.*

26. "How the Negroes of the District of Columbia Receive Their Promised Emancipation," *Chicago Tribune,* April 19, 1862.

27. "Prof. Sturgise and His Panorama," *Christian Recorder,* April 10, 1873.

28. Over the years literary critics have done an impressive job of unpacking what this system of designation meant, but for historians it has been an otherwise unexplored territory. As many literary critics have pointed out, lighter color often referred to intelligence or aptitude, whereas darker color referred to the exact opposite. See, for instance, Werner Sollors, *Neither Black nor White yet Both: Thematic Explorations of Interracial Literature* (Cambridge, Mass.: Harvard University Press, 1999).

29. "Victims of a Handsome Quadroon," *Cleveland Gazette,* April 16, 1887, 4.

30. Bobby Newcomb, "The Charming Gay Quadroon" (New York: C. H. Ditson & Co., ca. 1868).

31. The identification of "gay" seems to stem from the nineteenth-century definition of *gay* as a synonym for *happy,* which seems to corroborate with the other reference of the character as "charming." See *OED,* "1842 *New World* 18 June 393/3: The combination of refined enjoyment, and gay abandon, which throws such a charm over the audience." That being said, the location of San Francisco, which by the twentieth century had developed as a central hub of homosexual life and culture, is fascinating. The question of whether the term *gay* in this minstrel title refers to a more contemporary meaning of the term can

only be answered by future historians who investigate the social and cultural life of the city during the nineteenth century.

32. See, for example, Charles Rosenberg, *The Cholera Years: The United States in 1839, 1849, and 1866* (Chicago: University of Chicago Press, 1987); Mary Shaw, Helena Tunstall, and George Davey Smith, "Seeing Social Position: Visualizing Class in Life and Death, *International Journal of Epidemiology* 32.3 (June 2003): 332–35.

33. Winthrop Jordan, "American Chiaroscuro: The Status and Definition of Mulattoes in the British Colonies," *William and Mary Quarterly*, 3d ser., 19.2 (April 1962): 186. While Jordan describes mulattoes in the colonial period, he does not make a distinction about how the idea of mulattoes changed in the nineteenth century; more to the point, he seems to imply that this was an attitude that seeped into the nineteenth century. I am arguing not only for an investigation of how the term *mulatto* changed over time, but I am also, more significantly, claiming that seeing the deployment of these terms as only markers of status is a limiting interpretation, which misses the larger context of why these terms are used in the first place.

34. Throughout the early years of Reconstruction, erstwhile abolitionists in the North and Republicans in Washington, D.C., committed to the enfranchisement of former slaves, struggled over how to respond to the political, social, and economic questions that arose as a result of the emancipation of four million people. For some, the antebellum political campaign for colonization remained a viable solution, while others conducted social experiments that involved freedpeople, benevolent reformers, and military officials working side by side in places such as the Sea Islands off the coast of South Carolina or in villages in Arlington and Alexandria, Virginia. See James Mitchell to Abraham Lincoln, December 13, 1861, Abraham Lincoln Papers, Library of Congress; "What Shall We Do with the Blacks?" *Chicago Tribune*, August 25, 1862. For more on the social experiments relating to Reconstruction, see Willie Lee Rose, *Rehearsal for Reconstruction: The Port Royal Experiment* (Athens: University of Georgia Press, 1998). On the government's creation of communities for former slaves, see Joseph P. Reidy, "Coming from the Shadow of the Past: The Transition from Slavery to Freedom at Freedmen's Village, 1863–1869," *Virginia Magazine of History and Biography* 95.4 (October 1987): 403–28.

35. Robert Dale Owen, James McKaye, and Saml. G. Howe to E. M. Stanton, June 30, 1863, "Preliminary Report," American Freedmen's Inquiry Commission Papers, Houghton Library, Harvard University.

36. Robert Dale Owen, J. McKaye, and Samuel G. Howe to Hon. Edwin M. Stanton, May 15, 1864, Final Report of the American Freedmen's Inquiry Commission to the Secretary of War, "Chapter III—The Future in the United States of the African Race," Library of Congress.

37. Owen, McKaye, and Howe to Stanton, "Preliminary Report."

38. The three men who authored the report, Robert Dale Owen, James McKaye, and Samuel Howe, were committed abolitionists and social reformers before the Civil War. As the war unfolded, Stanton hired them to spearhead this organization due to their commitment to the cause of black uplift.

39. Owen, McKaye, and Howe to Stanton, "Preliminary Report."

40. Throughout the domestic slave trade, slaveholders and buyers placed a higher monetary value on enslaved women who were marked as mixed-race. Moreover, Harriet A. Jacobs, author of *Incidents in the Life of a Slave Girl: Written by Herself* (1861), describes in detail the extreme perils and sexual threats that mixed-race enslaved women faced. See Jacobs, *Incidents in the Life of a Slave Girl*, ed. L. Maria Child (Cambridge, Mass.: Harvard University Press, 1987). For more on the domestic slave trade, see Johnson, *Soul by Soul*.

41. S. G. Howe, *The Refugees from Slavery in Canada West: Report to the Freedman's Inquiry Commission* (1864; repr., New York: Arno Press, 1969). Also see George M. Fredrickson, *The Black Image in the White Mind: The Debate on Afro-American Character and Destiny, 1817–1914* (New York: Harper and Row, 1971), 161–64.

42. J. C. Nott, "The Mulatto a Hybrid—Probable Extermination of the Two Races if the Whites and Blacks Are Allowed to Intermarry," *Boston Medical and Surgical Journal* 29.2, August 16, 1843.

43. There was not an oppositional discourse to these ideas as prominent as what had existed during the prewar decades—in large part because Radical Republicans, the most vociferous opponents to such claims, did not yield much political power in 1865. Radical Republican Charles Sumner, for example, was caught in the throes of a congressional debate about the employment of former slaves, a debate that he ultimately lost. By 1866–67 this would certainly change, and Radical Republicans would gain prominence in Congress, but in the immediate aftermath of the war their voices were not heard. Additionally, former abolitionists, another group whose members refuted claims about black inferiority, were beleaguered during this period, attending to the reality of former slaves sick and dying due to the biological effects of the war. Indeed, black people themselves responded both informally and formally to such accusations of inferiority throughout the nineteenth century and beyond. See, for example, Mia Bay, *The White Image in the Black Mind: African-American Ideas about White People, 1830–1925* (New York: Oxford University Press, 2000), 65–69. On Sumner, see Louis Gerteis, *From Contraband to Freedmen: Federal Policy toward Southern Blacks, 1861–1865* (Westport, Conn.: Greenwood Press, 1973), 184. For an authoritative overview of Reconstruction politics, see Eric Foner, *Reconstruction: America's Unfinished Revolution, 1863–1877* (New York: Harper and Row, 1988). On abolitionists tending to sick freedpeople, see Jim Downs, "The Other Side of Freedom: Destitution, Disease, and Dependency among Freedwomen and Their Children during and after the Civil War," in *Battle Scars: Gender and Sexuality in the American Civil War*, ed. Catherine Clinton and Nina Silber (New York: Oxford University Press, 2006), 78–103.

44. *Congressional Globe*, 38th Cong., 1st sess., 709; Samuel Cox, *Eight Years in Congress, from 1857 to 1865* (New York: D. Appleton and Co., 1865), 353.

45. It is also unclear how widely read and circulated these articles were, whereas when the federal government makes these distinctions based on color, the implications are much greater, having had the capacity of being read by nineteenth-century Americans as "official."

46. Benjamin Apthorp Gould, *Investigations in the Military and Anthropological Statistics of American Soldiers* (New York: Published for the U.S. Sanitary Commission, by Hurd and Houghton, 1869), 347–48, 465, 471, 478–79; Army Medical Museum (U.S.), *Catalogue of*

*the Medical and Microscopical Sections of the United States Army Medical Museum, Prepared under the Direction of the Surgeon General, U.S. Army* (Washington, D.C.: GPO, 1867, 53, 62.

47. While the first use of the term in the United States remains unknown, one of the earliest accounts appears in the seventeenth-century Chesapeake. See "Anonymous Testimony before Virginia Magistrates about a Sexual Assault Complaint Made by a White Woman against a Mulatto Man, 1681," as quoted in Kenneth Morgan, *Slavery and America: A Reader and Guide* (Athens: University of Georgia Press, 2005), 94.

48. For a smart analysis of color in global context, see Clarence Walker, *Mongrel Nation: The America Begotten by Thomas Jefferson and Sally Hemings* (Charlottesville: University of Virginia Press, 2009). For a wonderfully comprehensive article on color in the Americas, see Donald L. Horowitz, "Color Differentiation in the American Systems of Slavery," *Journal of Interdisciplinary History* 3.3 (Winter 1973): 509–41.

49. Iole A. Apicella, "Adventure in the Caribbean Effects of the Discovery of Haiti-Martinique and Guadeloupe," Yale-New Haven Teacher's Institute, 2007. For more on the mixed-race population in Martinique, see Katherine E. Browne, "Creole Economics and the Débrouillard: From Slave-Based Adaptations to the Informal Economy in Martinique," *Ethnohistory* 49.2 (Spring 2002): 373–403.

50. Charles H. Wesley, "The Emancipation of the Free Color Population in the British Empire," *Journal of Negro History* 19.2 (April 1934): 143.

51. John Baptista Philip, *An Address to the Right Hon. Earl Bathurst . . . Relative to the Claims which the Coloured Population of Trinidad Have to the Same Civil and Political Privileges with Their White Fellow-Subjects: By a Free Mulatto of the Island* (London: Printed for J. Hatchard and Son, 1824).

52. Carl Ludwig Lokke, "Malouet and the St. Domingue Mulatto Question in 1793," *Journal of Negro History* 24.4 (October 1939): 381–89.

53. Charles H. Wesley, "The Emancipation of the Free Color Population in the British Empire," *Journal of Negro History* 19.2 (April 1934): 144; Aline Helg, "Race and Black Mobilization in Colonial and Early Independent Cuba: A Comparative Perspective," *Ethnohistory* 44.1 (Winter 1997): 53–56.

54. *Pennsylvania Gazette*, June 1, 1796.

55. Mary Hassal to Aaron Burr, 1802, in *Secret History; or, the Horrors of St. Domingo, in a Series of Letters Written by a Lady at Cape Francois, to Colonel Burr, Late Vice-President of the United States, Principally during the Command of General Rochambeau* (Philadelphia: Bradford & Inskeep, 1808), 225.

56. Ibid.

57. For a fascinating social history on the ways in which the events in the Caribbean shaped the American Civil War, see Edward Bartlett Rugemer, *The Problem of Emancipation: The Caribbean Roots of the American Civil War* (Baton Rouge: Louisiana State University Press, 2009).

58. Alexander Hamilton, "Will the Blacks Fight?" *New York Evening Post*, July 10, 1862.

59. Diary of Charlotte L. Forten Grimké, November 1862, in *The Journal of Charlotte Forten: A Free Negro in the Slave Era*, ed. Ray Allen Billington (New York: Dryden Press, 1953), 248.

60. Helg, "Race and Black Mobilization," 55.

61. Leonard Broom, "The Social Differentiation of Jamaica," *American Sociological Review* 19.2 (April 1954): 116.

62. Bryan Edwards, *The History, Civil and Commercial of the British Colonies in the West Indies*, vol. 2, as quoted in Broom, "Social Differentiation of Jamaica," 116.

63. Helg, "Race and Black Mobilization," 54.

64. James Mitchell to Abraham Lincoln, December 13, 1861, Abraham Lincoln Papers, Library of Congress.

65. Angelina Emily Grimké Weld to Thomas Grimké, 1832, in *The Grimké Sisters: Sarah and Angelina Grimké, the First American Women Advocates of Abolition and Woman's Rights*, ed. Catherine H. Birney (Boston: Lee & Shepard Publishers, 1885), 319.

66. Priv. Charles R. Pratt to Brig. Genl. L. Thomas, August 3, 1864, P-276 1864, Letters Received, ser. 360, Colored Troops Division, RG 94 [B-55], as quoted in Ira Berlin, Joseph P. Reidy, and Leslie S. Rowland, *The Black Military Experience*, Freedom Series, vol. 2 (Cambridge: Cambridge University Press, 1982).

67. See, for example, Frances Ellen Watkins Harper's novel *Iola Leroy* (1892), which highlights how the characters embrace rather than reject their African heritage.

68. *Chicago Tribune*, August 7, 1866.

69. *American Law Register (1852–1891)*, 14.12, n.s. 5 (October 1866): 721–32.

# Abjection and White Trash Autobiography

DAVID A. DAVIS

In the eyes of many people, I grew up white trash. Until I was six years old, my family lived in a trailer beside the railroad tracks in a small southern county seat. My mother's father was the county sheriff, so her family had a claim to middle-class legitimacy, but my father was in prison, which effectively negated that claim. We were poor, below the poverty line, but we were never hungry, and we had the stuff we needed, but it was rarely new and usually didn't match. Unless my grandmother took us shopping, our clothes were secondhand, and most of our furniture was cast off from friends or relatives. My grandfather's status offered us some protection, but I distinctly remember feeling self-conscious. Because we lived in an extremely small town, everyone knew my family, so everyone knew that we were poor and that my father was in jail. I remember the awkwardness this caused, the charity we received, the teasing I endured, and the resentment I felt. My childhood certainly wasn't ideal, and it didn't meet the material standards of middle-class America, but it wasn't altogether unhappy or even abnormal. It would have been fine, I think, if not for the shame.

I tell this story about my background not because I think one must have experience being white trash in order to understand white trash autobiography nor because I believe that having been poor gives me special status as a critic of white trash autobiography. Instead, I mean to highlight what I see as the crucial aspect of white trash identity, the self-consciousness of secondary status. Perhaps my own experience makes me more sensitive to it, but white trash autobiography clearly reeks of shame. Autobiography critics have analyzed how autobiographers deliberately construct identity in texts, and the identity politics of race and gender have often been important considerations in these studies. Here I intend to focus attention on class and self-representation. In the fairly recent past, several white southern writers have written their own life stories, portraying their experience growing up poor and white in the South: Dorothy Allison's *Two or Three Things I Know for Sure* (1995), Rick Bragg's *All Over but the Shoutin'* (1997), Harry Crews's *A Childhood: The Biography of a Place* (1978), and Janisse Ray's *Ecology of a Cracker Childhood* (1999). These autobiographies demonstrate a peculiar type of narrative involving the firsthand rhetorical construction of the poor white self. I'm keying on this identity in autobiography because white trash has been a common stereotype in southern literature, often portrayed as ignorant, lazy, and malicious. White trash autobiographies confront those characterizations, but, curiously, they do not exactly overturn them. These autobiographies humanize the often caricatured figures, but they bear out many of their stereotypical characteristics. Even white trash autobiographers portray themselves and their families as, well, white trash. I find this aspect of the narratives more interesting than frustrating because, in my own experience, I understand that white trash people are often equally proud of and ashamed of their identity.

Consequently, people who grow up white trash tend to feel their identity development to be disturbed or unsettled, disrupted by the self-conscious awareness of poverty. In *Powers of Horror: An Essay on Abjection*, Julia Kristeva describes this effect as abjection. The abject, according to her theory, is the detritus of life, such as waste, excrement, or the corpse, that impinges upon the conditions of daily life and disrupts identity, system, or order. In some cases an individual may come to see his or her own self as abject. "The abjection of self," she writes, "would be the culminating form of that experience of the subject to which it is revealed that all its objects are based merely on the inaugural *loss* that laid the foundations of its own being. There is nothing like abjection of self to show that all abjection is in fact recognition of the *want* on which any being, meaning, language, or desire is founded."[1] The recognition of the self as white trash, I contend, initiates this sense of loss. For my purposes, the phrase *white trash* is essential because it signifies the disruption of self, the recognition of the self as simultaneously white within a social system that privileges whiteness and as rejected from that white privilege. I am thus inclined to see the representation of the self as trash that characterizes poor white autobiography as a form of abjection.

Within the United States, being southern, in and of itself, may be a form of abjection. Leigh Anne Duck makes this case in *The Nation's Region*. She argues that modern America projects backwardness onto the South because the enduring legacy of agrarianism, segregation, and poverty marks the region as out of sync with the progressive, industrial nation. She sees a form of nationalistic abjection represented in the work of Erskine Caldwell, whose degraded southern families in *Tobacco Road* and *God's Little Acre* inspire feelings of disruption and disgust. Caldwell's abject depiction of poor whites during the Great Depression, Duck explains, "provoked anxiety concerning both the status of the nation and that of the white race."[2] His popular novels and long-running stage productions contributed to an image of poor white southerners as pathetic and sinister, and works by many other authors, such as Faulkner's *As I Lay Dying*, along with the photographs of poor southerners by the Farm Security Administration, ingrained the notion of poor white southerners as human detritus in the American imagination. That image resonated in popular culture through the twentieth century, reinforced by works such as James Dickey's novel *Deliverance* and movies such as *Gator*.

I think the idea of abject poor white southerners as an imaginative construct is easy to understand, but almost all of these images are projections, either the work of a middle-class southerner depicting class hierarchy or the work of a nonsoutherner portraying preexisting stereotypes. In white trash autobiography, however, poor white southerners speak for themselves, effectively constructing their own abjection. Southern autobiography, according to Lewis Simpson, has an inherent aspect of inferiority. In "The Autobiographical Impulse in the South" he contends that there are no great southern autobiographies because "southerners have no choice but to identify with the great political and social failure of the South."[3] Fred Hobson nonetheless notes that southerners have a compulsion, born from guilt or pride, to interpret their own region, which he describes as the "rage to explain."[4] White trash autobiographies, while demonstrating a rage of their own, complicate the tradition of southern autobiography in some respects. These narratives have a sense of failure, but they follow a consistent pattern of class uplift, and poor southerners are less likely to apologize for their racial attitudes. So this is a different form of southern autobiography.

These recent autobiographies coincide with the emergence of white trash studies as an area of intellectual inquiry. Annalee Newitz and Matthew Wray collaborated on the topic, publishing the essay "What Is 'White Trash'?" and editing the collection *White Trash*. Their central contention is that "the term *white trash* points up the hatred and fear undergirding the American myth of classlessness. Yoking a classist epithet to a racist one, as white trash does, reminds us how often racism is in fact directly related to economic differences. As a stereotype, white trash calls our attention to the way that discourses of class and race difference tend to bleed into one another, especially in the way that they pathologize and lay waste to their 'others.'"[5] I want to underscore their use of the term *pathologize* because it indicates the sense of abject identity as a form of contamination. When used as a projection, the term *white trash* signifies social detritus, but when used in the first person as an identifier, it takes on a much more complex and nuanced meaning. In other words, saying "I am white trash" means more than saying "you are white trash." To own the identity means to find pride in shame, to find beauty in ugliness, and to speak as someone usually spoken for.

*Speaking for Ourselves*

Customarily, white trash people have not written their own stories. Generations of poverty and illiteracy trapped most mute, inglorious poor white southerners into illiteracy, so representations of poor southerners, extending at least as far back as William Byrd's characterization of lubberland in *The History of the Dividing Line* (1733) and Frederick Law Olmsted's *Journeys and Explorations in the Cotton Kingdom* (1861), were written by upper- or middle-class southerners or by visiting travel writers. Characterizations of poor whites have frequently been exaggerated, biased, or—in some cases—romanticized. John C. Inscoe actually sees the middle-class apprehension of poverty as a consistent feature in southern autobiography through the middle of the twentieth century.[6] At the end of the century, however, white trash authors appeared in the literary marketplace publishing books that represented their own experiences. This phenomenon may have a great deal to do with the end of the South's primarily agricultural economy and with the spread of compulsory public education, conditions that made literacy more readily achievable for poor whites.

The fact that these texts were written is unsurprising. It is, I think, more surprising that these stories have found a mainstream audience. Take Dorothy Allison's *Bastard Out of Carolina* (1992), possibly the key text of white trash literature, as an example. The story has been a best seller, won several prestigious awards, and been made into a film, but the book bears an unmistakable sense of class apprehension. The protagonist, Ruth Anne "Bone" Boatwright, describes her family as trash, and the tension between poor whites and their middle-class counterparts drives much of the plot. The apprehension of class in texts such as this, I think, invites comparisons to the apprehension of race in many works of African American literature, such as Ralph Ellison's *Invisible Man* or Richard Wright's *Black Boy*. All of these texts have in common the urge to speak for the self and in so doing to seize the power of self-definition. As a result, these first-person texts present to the mainstream audience a more nuanced and more complex portrayal of marginalized groups. In the case of white trash narratives, audiences typically find a combination of shame and defiance.

The significant difference, however, between poor white autobiography and African American autobiography is the tension between agency and self-definition. African American autobiographies have a long literary tradition that encompasses accounts of antebellum slavery, postbellum racial uplift, and twentieth-century racial confrontation. William L. Andrews explains that "one way to chart the development of African-American autobiography is to track the gradual replacement of a discourse of distrust and self-restraint that relies on white-authored prefaces and appendices to authenticate and authorize black writing by a discourse that avows frank self-expression as a sign of authenticity and independent self-authorization."[7] Making a claim to white trash identity is itself a sign of authenticity. Although white trash autobiographies have a significantly shorter tradition, they also document a form of identity that is in opposition to the cultural mainstream.

Dorothy Allison's autobiography *Two or Three Things I Know for Sure*, for example, begins with a description of her family: "My sisters' faces were thin and sharp, with high cheekbones and restless eyes, like my mama's face, my aunt Dot's, my own. Peasants, that's what we are and always have been. Call us the lower orders, the great unwashed, the working class, the poor, proletariat, trash, lowlife and scum. I can make a story out of it, out of us."[8] Her linkage of class and storytelling marks the definitive characteristic of white trash autobiography.

The stories told in white trash autobiographies are often based on memories of poverty. Harry Crews tells a story, for example, of how his family's first and only milch cow died because his father had to choose between saving the cow or taking his son to the doctor. After his mother left his alcoholic stepfather, they lived in a shanty among the poor white section of Jacksonville, and his mother worked for almost nothing in the King Edward Cigar factory. In *All Over but the Shoutin'*, Rick Bragg tells stories of scavenging at the city dump, of eating free school lunches, and of receiving welfare. At one point the welfare checks were cut off, so his mother pulled him and his brothers in a wagon along the highway to a store where they could buy groceries on credit. "In the Deep South," he explains, "you ride, and if you don't have something to ride in, you must be trash."[9] Although this was a difficult experience, Bragg makes an important point about his own recollection: "You lose a lot in your memory, over so many years. But I distinctly remember, before I was old enough to cover myself in what my mother called false pride, that there was some happiness there. While I was often frightened and troubled by the drastic changes in our life, because of our father, I was too damn little and too damn stupid to be miserable" (42). Growing up white trash is not inherently traumatic. A person can in fact grow up poor and happy, but poverty exposes a person to privation, which can lead to difficult, perhaps even traumatic, experiences.

The most common negative experience related in these autobiographies is the sense of shame. Poverty almost inexorably leads white trash people to feel diminished self-worth and to believe that the feeling is deserved. Dorothy Allison describes her self-concept in an autobiographical essay, "A Question of Class," published in 1994. "What may be the central fact of my life," she writes, "is that I was born in 1949 in Greenville, South Carolina, the bastard daughter of a white woman from a desperately poor family. . . . That fact, the inescapable impact of being born in a condition of poverty that this society finds shameful, contemptible, and somehow deserved, has had dominion over me to such an extent that I have spent my life trying to overcome or deny it."[10] Shame, the internalized feeling of abjection, defines the experience of being white trash.[11] This response, the burden of shame, is the significant difference between writing about white trash and writing as white trash.

C. Vann Woodward's notion of southern history as a burden attempts to explain southerners' conflicted attitudes toward southern identity. The bulldozer revolution that he prophesied in "The Search for Southern Identity" in 1958 has come to pass, yet southern identity remains intact, largely because poor white southerners continue to embody many of the negative traits of regional distinctiveness.[12] At this point in history southern identity has somewhat eroded for middle-class white southerners and black southerners. As James Cobb explains in *Away Down South: A History of Southern Identity,* they can both ally themselves with respective nationalized mainstream populations and thus participate in dominant cultural forms, or they can choose to portray an affected regional identity.[13] Poor white southerners, however, are less likely to participate in the cultural mainstream and are thus consistently marginalized. Even when poor white identity appears to be culturally ascendant, as Peter Applebome's *Dixie Rising* indicates, it is characterized as an invasion into mainstream American culture, which underscores the burden of white trash identity.[14]

Janisse Ray grew up in a poor, fundamentalist family in rural Georgia. Considering that almost everyone in that time and place shared those characteristics, she had no real basis for self-consciousness. Yet she felt a sense of shame; she even titles a chapter of her autobiography, *Ecology of a Cracker Childhood,* "Shame." She explains that "away from home we were ashamed of the junkyard. Our daddy was a junk dealer, but when we filled out his occupation on forms from school we wrote 'salesman.' . . . We knew nobody else lived like we did, but we didn't know how they lived. We knew they were wasteful and threw perfectly good things in the garbage, which ended up at our house. We thought that meant they were better than we were."[15] For Ray and the other white trash autobiographers, the home and the family serve as a defensive shield against judgment, a sanctuary against shame. But that sanctuary can also be a primary source of shame, as Ray's shame of her father and home in front of outsiders demonstrates.

The corollary to shame in this case is pride. White trash autobiographers evidently are proud enough of themselves and their families to own their identities and publish their stories, and many feel a sense of defiant pride. Rick Bragg, for example, subjected his potential girlfriends to a test of their class prejudice. If they reacted negatively when he brought them home for the first time, he dumped them. He learned class awareness from his elementary school teachers, who separated the students by their social class and gave the well-off students special treatment. He learned class shame from his mother. He explains that he realized years later that the reason she rarely left home was "because she was afraid we might be ashamed of her" (74). She called his feeling of shame or defiant self-consciousness "false pride" (73).

The pride Bragg feels is actually a form of sublimated anger that is entirely consistent with the experience of shame. Class awareness for all of these autobiographers produces a form of tension born of class antagonism. As the writers internalized their class identity, they developed a set of outward behaviors designed to keep people of other classes at a distance. Bragg's mother not going into public is one example, and Dorothy Allison's gruesome storytelling is another. This is because the sense of shame becomes most acute in the presence—or under the gaze—of a middle-class person. Middle-class encounters in the books tend to be contained, and middle-class characters tend to be objectified in a mode that seems to invert Inscoe's description of working-class encounters in autobiographies by middle-class southerners. While middle-class southerners seem to romanticize "downward mobility," to use Inscoe's phrase (147), white trash autobiographers tend to describe their visits to middle-class family members as visits to a strange land where they feel ill at ease, and they tend to describe other middle-class people—bosses, teachers, shopkeepers, and extended family—as hostile and threatening, rarely as sympathetic or understanding.

Considering poor whites' sense of secondary status, one might expect them to be more sympathetic toward other oppressed people, but poor whites tend to be racist, even in their autobiographies. Poor whites have often been accused of being the key source of southern racial antagonism, but it is impossible to place the blame for racism on any particular group.[16] White trash autobiographers, however, are much less likely to apologize for their racism than their middle-class counterparts.[17] Harry Crews's closest playmate was the son of a black sharecropper, Willalee Bookatee, and he recalls that Willalee was crucial to his racial attitudes. "There was a part of me in which it did not matter at all that they were black," he remembers, "but there was another part of me in which it had to matter because it mattered to the world I lived in. It mattered to my blood."[18] Crews and his brothers harassed Willalee mercilessly, often beyond the point of tears. The other autobiographers portray blackness as a mostly distant issue. Rick Bragg, for example, only mentions race when he discusses poor whites' response to the civil rights movement. He explains that he "had no contact with black people beyond a wave, now and then" (58). Since poor whites did not employ servants, they lived mostly separate lives, except for when they worked together in menial labor, but poor whites greatly resented the notion that black people wanted to break down that separation.

White trash autobiographies bear out some of the characteristics of the class stereotype, particularly poverty, shame, and racism. Telling their own stories allows the autobiographers to construct their identity, but they must contend with an essentialist version of southern white trash that implicitly intervenes on their narratives. Janisse Ray explains, "It didn't take me many years to realize I was a Southerner, a slow, dumb, redneck hick, a hayseed, inbred and racist, come from poverty, condemned to poverty" (30). The extent to which a person born white trash can change their identity is open to discussion. Faulkner's Flem Snopes pulled himself from poverty, maliciously if not miraculously, but he never changed his class identity, so Faulkner's fictional projection suggests that one cannot cease to be white trash.[19] All of the autobiographers made their way through higher education, which afforded them the opportunity at least to try to change their class identity. Ray tried to "lose [her] identity with the junkyard, and [her] Southernness" (31). She hides her accent and mingles with intellectuals, but she never feels authentic in this version of her identity, so over time she deliberately recovers her white trash identity. "Turning back to embrace the past has been a long, slow lesson not only in self-esteem but in patriotism—pride in homeland, heritage," she writes. "It has taken a decade to whip the shame, to mispronounce words and shun grammar when mispronunciation and misspeaking are part of my dialect, to own my bad blood. What I come from has made me who I am" (32–33). This self-conscious realization, I argue, is the fundamental marker of white trash autobiography. When one owns their white trash identity, then a person can see the beauty in a junkyard.

### Awful Loveliness: The Aesthetics of Trash

Ugliness has a peculiar beauty. In the 1930s the federal government created the Farm Security Administration, a domestic propaganda unit whose objective was to document graphically the conditions of poverty as a means of developing public support for New Deal programs. The agency produced thousands of photographs of squalor, especially of the living conditions of poor southerners.[20] Pictures of poor southerners appeared in popular media, and the symbolism of shacks, overalls, mules, and general dirtiness became directly associated with white trash. Although the subjects of these photographs were definitively ugly, the photographs themselves are frequently beautiful. But they are beautiful because they accentuate ugliness. A similar effect occurs in white trash autobiographies; ugliness sometimes means beauty.

"Beauty is a hard thing," Dorothy Allison writes. "Beauty is a mean story. Beauty is slender girls who die young, fine-featured delicate creatures about whom men write poems." These stereotypical versions of beauty, however, do not apply to white trash. "We were not beautiful. We were hard and ugly and trying to be proud of it. The poor are plain, virtuous if humble and hardworking, but mostly ugly. Almost always ugly" (37). Allison accentuates the depiction of ugliness in her autobiography by including photographs, and these images enhance the story by providing graphic evidence of her family's ugliness.[21] But it isn't exactly true that her family is ugly. Her mother, in fact, was quite beautiful as a young girl, but her beauty faded rapidly through overwork and worry exacerbated by poverty. The shift from beautiful to ugly, and the wastage this shift indicates, embodies the aesthetics of abjection.

White trash bodies tend to be ugly, damaged, and exhausted. Although capable of beauty, the bodies more often delineate where beauty could have been or used to be. A picture of Rick Bragg's mother, young and lovely, appears on the cover of *All Over but the Shoutin'*, but he describes her as toothless, poorly dressed, and overworked. Harry Crews, meanwhile, found the Sears Roebuck catalog fascinating because "all the people in its pages were perfect." The people he knew in real life, however, were not perfect. "Nearly everybody I knew had something missing," he explains, "a finger cut off, a toe split, an ear half-chewed away, an eye clouded with blindness from a glancing fence staple. And if they didn't have something missing, they were carrying scars from barbed wire, or knives, or fishhooks." The people in the catalog also appear happy, "looks that [he] never saw much of in the faces of the people around [him]" (58).

Just as white trash bodies tend to be wasted, the landscape in white trash autobiographies tends to show signs of disruption—pollution, decay, and erosion—but writers more commonly attribute signs of actual beauty to the landscape. Rick Bragg calls the Appalachian foothills of north Alabama "the most beautiful place on earth" (3). Dorothy Allison sees the putrescence mingled among the beauty—like the cloying pungency of a rotting magnolia blossom—in Greenville, South Carolina. "That country was beautiful, I swear to you the most beautiful place I've ever been," she claims. "It is the country of my dreams and the country of my nightmares: a pure pink and blue sky, red dirt, white clay, and all that endless green—willows and dogwood and firs going on for miles" (7). Harry Crews audaciously describes the monotonous landscape of south Georgia, miles of sand, wiregrass, pines, and scrub oak, as "lovely in its ugliness" (17). The physical landscape where it is undisrupted by people shows signs of actual beauty, and it may be the distinction between the disturbed land and the undisturbed land that best illustrates the aesthetics or poverty, the wastage and the abjection.

Janisse Ray explains how poverty, which wastes the bodies of white trash people, leads to the disruption of the landscape.

> In the rural South, the land of the longleaf pine, these were the pictures travelers remembered: tarpaper tobacco shanties; bent-over women in the cotton fields; shoeless schoolchildren; chain gangs; bathrooms for whites only; Saturday afternoon towns spangled with mule farmers in faded and patched overalls and not a dime in their pockets. Passing through my homeland it was easy to see that Crackers, although fiercely rooted in the land and willing to defend it to the death, hadn't had the means, the education, or the ease to care particularly about its natural communities. Our relationship with the

land wasn't one of give and return. The land itself has been the victim of social dilemmas—racial injustice, lack of education, and dire poverty. It was overtilled; eroded; cut; littered; polluted; treated as a commodity, sometimes the only one, and not as a living thing. Most people worried about getting by, and when getting by meant using the land, we used it. When getting by meant ignoring the land, we ignored it. (164–65)

Survival, not beauty, dictates the ecology of poverty, but the expediency of immediate survival leads to waste.[22] Yet although poor whites waste resources in their struggle to survive, they do not waste consumer goods or other resources, as middle- or upper-class whites do, largely because they can't.

Survival for white trash people tends to be precarious, and their lives are often nasty, brutish, and short. Bad things happen to poor whites, largely because poverty limits their agency and access to resources, so they are completely vulnerable. They are often victims of labor exploitation, they are often subject to violence, and they are often sad. I don't mean to overly generalize or to necessarily equate poverty with sorrow. In fact, all of the white trash autobiographies recount moments of genuine happiness and relationships based on love. But misfortune and victimization drive the narrative tension in these texts, and that characteristic is entirely consistent with the aesthetics of abjection. In cases of aesthetic judgment, abjection means the waste, disruption, or decay of actual beauty. The bodies of white trash people and the landscapes of white trash settings show signs of that waste, and the narratives of white trash autobiographies show signs of disruption and decay.

Harry Crews tells a series of stories about spectacular accidents. As a child, he endured infantile paralysis that left him bedridden, and then he fell into a washtub of boiling water at a hog killin' that left him bedridden again. He recovered from these injuries, but he endured the experiences with an alcoholic father, juvenile delinquency, and poverty that are characteristic of white trash autobiographies. Perhaps the most fantastic story he tells is of a man who walks into a butcher shop where he is working, asks for a knife, and pounds it into his chest. His stories, disturbing though they may be, are fairly representative of the experiences found in all of the books. Dorothy Allison endures sexual and physical abuse, Janisse Ray's father suffers from a serious mental illness, and Rick Bragg's father is a violent drunk. For poor whites these evidently are the ordinary conditions of everyday life.

In white trash autobiographies poverty drives the self-representation. The events, the settings, and the characters all show outward signs of abject poverty, and the narrators' voices evidence their awareness of shame. Tension thus develops in the stories between self-definition and victimization. The narrators typically resist the urge to portray themselves as helpless or hopeless, but they clearly feel a sense of forces at work beyond their control. These forces disrupt their identity, leaving them with a sense of loss, which, according to Kristeva's theory, is the definition of *abjection*. Aesthetically, this loss appears as wastage in the form of scarred bodies, landscapes, and lives. Because of the damage, ugliness appears where beauty could have or should have been.

## Consuming Trash

Ugly as they are, white trash people have long had a significant place in the literary marketplace, usually as outlandish characters in books by middle-class writers. The recent white trash autobiographies trade in part on the tangible value of bootstrap narratives that reaffirm the American Dream of class mobility, but this version of white trash self-determination is a fairly new product. Historically, stories about poor whites—as opposed to stories by poor whites—have been a standard item in southern fiction. Sylvia Cook argues in *From Tobacco Road to Route 66* that poor whites in literature are defined "in terms of the moral, emotional, and intellectual incongruity."[23] Because they are portrayed as depraved, shiftless, and ignorant, they have functioned primarily as either comic or malicious characters, as in Faulkner's *As I Lay Dying* or Caldwell's *Tobacco Road*. They occasionally appeared in the proletariat fiction of the 1930s as redeeming characters, as in Elizabeth Madox Roberts's *Time of Man*, but those depictions are unusual. Writers have sold stories about white trash for literally centuries, but only recently have white trash profited on their own stories.

White trash spectacle has material value. Dina Smith asks an important question about the way white trash have been portrayed: "Does the spectacular figure of the rickety-limbed, saggy-breasted poor white in [*The Mind of the South* by W. J.] Cash and [*The Southern Poor White from Lubberland to Tobacco Road* by Shields] McIlwane express a utopian desire to remake the South (or a Southern "agrarian identity") by drawing attention to the abject plight or white working-class Southern populations, the extension of a defeated, non-unionized South? Or is it an expression of class/racial violence, an apology for white Southern privilege that inevitably still privileges whiteness through the location of white victimhood?"[24] Given the choices, the latter option is more likely, but let me stress that Smith has in mind texts that project white trash identity—that is, texts by middle-class writers that trade on poor white stereotypes. In almost all of these texts the white trash character operates at a remove from the reader, separated by intellectual, emotional, or moral incongruity. As a result, "writers, high and low, have made 'white trash' into a sleazy, porn-loving, peanut-butter-chewing, consumable identity, one attractive to a middle-class desiring such fatty substances" (385).

White trash autobiographies repurpose this identity, examining the forces that create the stereotype in ways that complicate the typically two-dimensional portrayal. This more nuanced version of the identity evidently has its own material value. Harry Crews has become a cult figure in contemporary southern literature. Janisse Ray's *Ecology of a Cracker Childhood* won several awards, including the American Book Award. Dorothy Allison's novel based on her life, *Bastard Out of Carolina,* is one of the classics of contemporary writing, and her memoir complements the novel. Rick Bragg's *All Over but the Shoutin'* has become a best seller in its own right.

These books have clearly found an audience, but to go back to Dina Smith's questions, what purpose do these stories serve? The answer to that question is different for the producers and the consumers. Readers of white trash autobiography expecting to find the sleazy, fatty identity could easily find their preconceptions confirmed and their social superiority affirmed, or they could find an uplifting narrative that alters their preconceptions. But the consumers' perspective is not nearly as interesting, in my opinion, as the producers' perspective. Rick Bragg explains the autobiographical compulsion to counter the misconception that poor people do not long for the things they do not have. "The only thing poverty does," he explains, "is grind down your nerve endings to a point that you can work harder and stoop lower than most people are willing to. It chips away a person's dreams to the point that the hopelessness shows through, and the dreamer accepts that hard work and borrowed houses are all this life will ever be. While my mother will stare you dead in the eye and say she never thought of herself as poor, do not believe for one second that she did not see the rest of the world, the better world, spinning around her, out of reach" (25). One could conclude, thus, that white trash autobiographies are a form of communication between these two separate worlds, a way of sharing the experience of abjection.

Although poor whites occupy the same space, roughly, as middle-class people, their lives tend to be as thoroughly separated as if they lived in different worlds. White trash autobiographers personally experience a sense of living in between these two worlds. They tend to be different from most poor whites because of their intellectual curiosity—all of the autobiographers were voracious readers—but they are different from middle-class people because of their poverty. For them education was both a means of class uplift and a personal struggle. None followed traditional paths through school, and all worked menial jobs to support their education. Dorothy Allison and Janisse Ray both describe feeling ashamed of their white trash identity while in college, and they attempted to separate themselves from their background. I did exactly the same thing in college, trying to identify with the middle class and hiding my working-class background.

As a material artifact, the autobiography mediates between these class differences. It is the result of a complicated and disoriented process of identity ambiguity on the part of the autobiographer. Kristeva describes this process as "jouissance," the cacophony of inhabiting multiple identities at once. "When I *seek* (myself), *lose* (myself), or experience *jouissance*—then 'I' is *heterogeneous*," she explains. "Discomfort, unease, dizziness, stemming from an ambiguity that, through the violence of a revolt *against*, demarcates a space out of which signs and objects arise. Thus braided, woven, ambivalent, a heterogeneous flux marks out a territory that I can call my own because the Other, having dwelt in me as *alter ego*, points it out to me through loathing" (10). Undergoing this process does not mean overcoming abjection; instead, it means recognizing abjection within oneself and hating it. When Harry Crews returned to Bacon County, Georgia, after three years in the U.S. Marines, he committed a sin in the eyes of poor whites that demonstrates the feeling of jouissance. After working in the field on a hot day, he cursed the sun. "To curse [the sun, the rain, or the land] is an ultimate blasphemy," he writes. "I had known that three years ago, but in three years I had somehow managed to forget it. I stood there feeling how much I had left this place and these people, and at the same time knowing that it would be impossible to leave them completely. Wherever I might go in the world, they would go with me" (182).

This raises another important question. If the autobiographers feel consciously disconnected from their white trash identity, can their autobiographies authentically be white trash texts? As a person who has also made the transition from white trash to intellectual, I doubt that I can give an authentic answer, but it is a relevant issue. Scott Romine has examined the issue of authenticity in southern culture more broadly construed in the "age of cultural reproduction," when satellite communication, interstate highways, international corporate capitalism, and mass population flows have changed southern distinctiveness. He argues that the "fake South," that is, the commercialized version of southern stereotypes, "becomes the real South through the intervention of narrative."[25] What people think of as authentic, in other words, is itself an imaginary construction. As a narrative form, then, white trash autobiographies make an intervention, but that does not necessarily mean that they are authentic artifacts in the strictest sense.

The production—and the cultural reproduction—of white trash autobiographies indicates a market for consumable versions of white trash identity, a market that also fits such products as the films *Deliverance* and *Searching for the Wrong-Eyed Jesus*. The spectacle of poor whites, whether they speak for themselves or whether they are the subjects of class projection, continues to resonate in contemporary culture. White trash autobiographies complicate the persistent stereotypes, giving a voice and a sense of beauty to an abject population. But this is a relatively new phenomenon, for a common projection of poverty and ignorance—the embodiment of human trash—to find its own voice and to tell its own story.

NOTES

1. Julia Kristeva, *The Powers of Horror: An Essay on Abjection*, trans. Leon S. Roudiez (New York: Columbia University Press, 1982), 5.

2. Leigh Anne Duck, *The Nation's Region: Southern Modernism, Segregation, and U.S. Nationalism* (Athens: University of Georgia Press, 2006), 95.

3. Lewis P. Simpson, "The Autobiographical Impulse in the South," in *Home Ground: Southern Autobiography*, ed. J. Bill Berry (Columbia: University of Missouri Press, 1991), 66.

4. Fred Hobson, *Tell About the South: The Southern Rage to Explain* (Baton Rouge: Louisiana State University Press, 1983), 3.

5. Annalee Newitz and Matthew Wray, "What Is 'White Trash'? Stereotypes and Economic Conditions of Poor Whites in the United States," in *Whiteness: A Critical Reader*, ed. Mike Hill (New York: New York University Press, 1997), 169. Newitz and Wray also collaborated on the collection *White Trash: Race and Class in America* (New York: Routledge, 1997).

6. John Inscoe, "'All Manner of Defeated, Shiftless, Shifty, Pathetic, and Interesting Good People': Autobiographical Encounters with Southern Poverty," in *Reading Southern Poverty between the Wars, 1918–1939*, ed. Richard Godden and Martin Crawford (Athens: University of Georgia Press, 2006), 143–62.

7. William L. Andrews, "Richard Wright and the African American Autobiography Tradition," *Style* 27. 2 (Summer 1993): 272.

8. Dorothy Allison, *Two or Three Things I Know for Sure* (New York: Dutton, 1995), 1.

9. Rick Bragg, *All Over but the Shoutin'* (New York: Vintage, 1997), 65.

10. Dorothy Allison, "A Question of Class," in *Skin: Talking about Sex, Class & Literature* (Ithaca, N.Y.: Firebrand Books, 1994), 15.

11. J. Brooks Bouson explores the fictional representation of shame in "'You Nothing but Trash': White Trash Shame in Dorothy Allison's *Bastard Out of Carolina*," *Southern Literary Journal* 34.1 (Fall 2001): 101–23.

12. C. Vann Woodward, "The Search for Southern Identity," in *The Burden of Southern History*, 3d ed. (1960; repr., Baton Rouge: Louisiana State University Press, 1993), 3–25.

13. James C. Cobb, *Away Down South: A History of Southern Identity* (New York: Oxford University Press, 2007).

14. Peter Applebome, *Dixie Rising: How the South Is Shaping American Values, Politics, and Culture* (New York: Harvest, 1997).

15. Janisse Ray, *Ecology of a Cracker Childhood* (Minneapolis: Milkweed Editions, 1999), 29.

16. Both W. J. Cash, in *The Mind of the South* (New York: Knopf, 1941), and Lillian Smith, in *Killers of the Dream* (New York: Norton, 1961), specifically attribute racism to poor white southerners.

17. Fred Hobson analyzes this tendency in *But Now I See: The White Southern Racial Conversion Narrative* (Baton Rouge: Louisiana State University Press, 1999). For a pair of recent examples, see Tim Tyson, *Blood Done Sign My Name* (New York: Three Rivers Press,

2004); and Melton McLaurin, *Separate Pasts: Growing Up White in the Segregated South* (Athens: University of Georgia Press, 1998).

18. Harry Crews, *A Childhood: The Biography of a Place* (Athens: University of Georgia Press, 1995), 62.

19. Brannon Costello explains Flem's class struggle in *Plantation Airs: Racial Paternalism and the Transformations of Class in Southern Fiction, 1945–1971* (Baton Rouge: Louisiana State University Press, 2008).

20. The entire catalog of FSA photographs can be found at the Library of Congress website at http://memory.loc.gov/ammem/fsahtml/. For analyses of the agency, see William Stott, *Documentary Expression and Thirties America* (Chicago: University of Chicago Press, 1986); and Stuart Kidd, *Farm Security Administration Photography, the Rural South, and the Dynamics of Image-Making, 1935–1943* (Lewiston, N.Y.: Edwin Mellen Press, 2004).

21. Timothy Dow Adams explains how Allison employs pictures to tell her story in "Telling Stories in Dorothy Allison's *Two or Three Things I Know for Sure*," *Southern Literary Journal* 36.2 (Spring 2004): 82–99. Katherine Henninger argues that she also uses fictional representations of photographs to tell a story in *Bastard Out of Carolina* in the essay "Claiming Access: Controlling Images in Dorothy Allison," *Arizona Quarterly* 60.3 (Fall 2004): 83–104.

22. Jay Watson offers an ecocritical reading of *The Ecology of a Cracker Childhood* in "Economics of a Cracker Landscape: Poverty as an Environmental Issue in Two Southern Writers," *Mississippi Quarterly* 55.4 (Fall 2002): 497–513.

23. Sylvia Cook, *From Tobacco Road to Route 66: The Southern Poor White in Fiction* (Chapel Hill: University of North Carolina Press, 1976), 5. Cook's book responds to Shields McIlwaine, *The Southern Poor-White: From Lubberland to Tobacco Road* (Norman: University of Oklahoma Press, 1939).

24. Dina Smith, "Cultural Studies' Misfit: White Trash Studies," *Mississippi Quarterly* 57.3 (Summer 2004): 369–87.

25. Scott Romine, *The Real South: Southern Narrative in the Age of Cultural Reproduction* (Baton Rouge: Louisiana State University Press, 2008), 9.

# The Professional Southerner and the Twenty-First Century

ROBERT JACKSON

W hen the Dude flirts with Bunny in *The Big Lebowski* (1998), she tells him not to worry about the large man passed out on a raft in the nearby swimming pool. "Uli doesn't care about anything," she says. "He's a nihilist." To which the Dude responds perceptively, "Ah, that must be exhausting." Indeed, Uli Kunkel, alias Karl Hungus, and his fellow nihilists spend an exorbitant amount of time and effort believing in nothing. But they are all too human, repeatedly revealing a less than fervent faith in the absence of any objective grounding of truth itself as well as in the senselessness of traditional values, and they end up worse than exhausted: the Dude's best friend, Vietnam veteran and enforcer of boundaries Walter Sobchak, authoritatively beats them down in a bowling alley parking lot. Among its many other lessons *The Big Lebowski* instills a deep skepticism at the idea of transforming something as abstract as nihilism into a full-time job. The Dude himself is no nihilist, though with his passive-voice humanism he too has scant success in finding a respectable profession. In fact, most of the people who do hold down regular jobs—and this pattern runs through all of the films of Joel and Ethan Coen—turn out to be frauds of one sort or another. Work itself is never an indicator of virtue, nor is any profession a repository of constructive personal or social values. The Dude's laconic estimation of the fatigue of nihilism might offer an instructive model for measuring the returns paid, here in the early years of the twenty-first century, by the existential investment of another vocation: not the professional nihilist but the professional southerner.

My first conscious encounter with the phrase *professional southerner* in print was its mention in Russell Merritt's essay "Dixon, Griffith, and the Southern Legend," originally published in *Cinema Journal* in 1972. In his discussion of the D. W. Griffith's epic film *The Birth of a Nation* (1915), Merritt writes: "Griffith's immediate source was the notorious Reconstruction melodrama, *The Clansman*, a prime specimen of the skid row depths to which the Southern romance had sunk. Its author was Thomas Dixon, Jr., from North Carolina, a professional Southerner, sometime preacher, novelist, and fervent Negrophobe."[1] When I came across this essay in 2000 or so, it struck me that being a professional southerner would be a particularly unfortunate career choice. Merritt's language implies associations with inferior literary artistry, rabid racism, and, in the phrase *sometime preacher,* an expedient and disingenuous religious mask. The professional southerner was clearly little more than a false prophet—a troubling conclusion to reach in consideration of the fact that Dixon was wildly successful in many of his endeavors and enjoyed popular acclaim as well as the friendship of President Woodrow Wilson.

Some time later I read W. E. B. Du Bois's review of *The Birth of a Nation* (he refers to it as *The Clansman,* the film's original working title) in the May 1915 issue of the *Crisis,* and it struck me that Merritt might well have picked up the phrase from Du Bois. "Several years ago," Du Bois begins, "a 'professional southerner' named Dixon wrote a sensational and melodramatic novel which has been widely read." Rejecting the film's suggestion that the northern abolitionist politician modeled on Thaddeus Stevens "was induced to give the Negroes the right to vote and secretly rejoice in Lincoln's assassination because of his infatuation for a mulatto mistress," Du Bois anticipates Merritt's later charge that Dixon is a mere poetaster. "Small wonder that a man who can thus brutally falsify history has never been able to do a single piece of literary work that has brought the slightest attention, except when he seeks to capitalize burning race antagonisms."[2] Du Bois, of course, was not primarily a film critic or scholar and had surprisingly little to say about motion pictures despite the medium's huge influence on popular culture and public opinion, including racial attitudes, in the first half of the twentieth century. His review focuses more on the NAACP's efforts to ban the film in New York City than on the film itself—though he does admit that the film's portrayal of the Civil War includes "a number of marvelously good war pictures." His invocation of the professional southerner points to a broad conception, beyond literature and film, of Thomas Dixon's persona in American public life. The phrase is not defined carefully here but is presented with the assumption that readers will easily recognize a familiar type.

From the perspective of the early twenty-first century, what might we say about this type? Is the professional southerner as familiar and typical as Du Bois and Merritt would have us believe? More pragmatically, does the category continue to offer a legitimate career option for the leisured classes, for those scouring the employment pages during an economic recession, or, indeed, for those confronting the academic job market? For the professional southerner is a cultural icon whose history offers much more than a simple appendix of individuals such as Dixon but something closer to a narrative of ideas and changing attitudes about southern history and culture and about the ways the South has presented itself and been presented to the rest of the world for more than a century. What began as an expression of my own mild curiosity about the phrase itself eventually turned into a more pressing and sustained—not to say exhausting—quest that implicated my own work and self-conception as a scholar interested in the history and culture of the South, leading me to a sense of how varied and vague, how strange, the professional southerner's career has been.

During the winter of 2009 I conducted an unscientific survey whose results were interesting. I asked a number of distinguished scholars of southern history, literature, and culture what a professional southerner was and who might qualify on a short list. This innocent query whipped up a good deal of anxiety, fear, and insecurity among respondents, many of whom were, and are, leading lights in their fields. "A professional southerner is someone who seizes on and exaggerates a southern identity for the purpose of making money," one responded studiously, only to undercut his authority by adding that he was "curious to hear what the right answer is." Another offered a short list that included James Carville, Dizzy Dean, Tennessee Ernie Ford, and Hank Williams Jr. Though composed of different people, this list called to mind John Shelton Reed's 2001 list of "The Twenty Most Influential Southerners of the Twentieth

Century."[3] Reed's list begins with the likes of Martin Luther King Jr. and William Faulkner, individuals so overdetermined with historical and cultural significance that they might be seen to transcend the category, at least in the pejorative Du Boisian connotation of 1915. (Or perhaps not: racism and segregation, so central to Du Bois's thinking when he attacked Thomas Dixon, were prominent in his thoughts again nearly half a century later, in 1956, when he challenged Faulkner to debate on the courthouse steps in Sumner, Mississippi, where Emmett Till's killers recently had been acquitted; Faulkner, who had spent earlier decades cultivating his southern persona in all sorts of ways, but who in the postwar years, as a Nobel laureate and resident of a Deep South state in the throes of racial violence and a national reputation that had reached, to borrow Merritt's phrase, "skid row depths," resented being viewed as a spokesman for an entire region for which he had enormous ambivalence, declined.) John Shelton Reed himself, the compiler and theorist of the millennial "most influential southerners" list, was mentioned as a professional southerner; "EVERYthing he writes," one respondent wrote, "from poor whites to bbq, deals with the South." My respondents also mentioned Colonel Sanders for consideration as a professional southerner, raising the question whether one must be a native southerner to qualify. Sanders was born in southern Indiana in 1890, spent his first forty years elsewhere before settling in eastern Kentucky, received the honorary title of "Kentucky Colonel" from the governor of the state in the mid-1930s, and presented himself with white suit and goatee after 1950; other Kentucky Colonels include Fred Astaire, Mae West, Winston Churchill, Whoopi Goldberg, Muhammad Ali, Tiger Woods, Ronald Reagan, and Pope John Paul II.

Such an informal survey as this raises far more questions than it answers, and does virtually nothing to define the professional southerner in any helpful way. It does, however, register the ambivalence of many thinkers toward important elements of southern society—including race, politics, religion, gender, and history itself—along with their unease with the construct, the very mention, of the professional southerner. "But don't call ME a professional southerner," one respondent, a leading figure in southern studies for the last generation, implored (stopping just short of demanding the anonymity I've maintained for the entire group here). "I intensely dislike so many things about Dixie—mainly its politics and fundamentalism (and even the word Dixie)." Perhaps the professional southerner gains force exactly through this quality of danger and discomfort, through an unapologetic, headlong, passionate embrace of a region whose complex and tragic history has sobered its more serious students.

Prototypes of the professional southerner gave birth to the Lost Cause in the immediate aftermath of the Civil War. With former Confederates such as the vocal Gen. Jubal A. Early publishing memoirs as early as 1866 and ordinary white southerners, from the women who formed the United Daughters of the Confederacy (UDC) to countless others participating in Decoration Days and monument dedications each year, Confederate memory quickly emerged as a self-sustaining culture industry. "We lost nearly everything but honor," Early told Gen. Robert E. Lee, "and that should be religiously guarded."[4] Insisting to the last on the region's "honor" and, in doing so, rejecting any more nuanced view of the war that considered the moral compromise of slavery and thus the white South's own hand in the war's devastation, the Lost Cause spoke to the need of a defeated people to fashion meaning and justification for the unprecedented ravages of their society.

Within twenty years, however, the professional southerner was speaking to other audiences, and 1885 might be taken as the year such a figure had become recognized, by southerners and non-southerners alike, as a national presence. In that year Walter Hines Page's pseudonymous autobiography, *The Southerner,* included an amusing portrait of an old southern "colonel" and a New England "bishop" and the pair's negotiations of the culpability for the state of the South:

> [The Bishop's] attitude toward the South was very like Colonel Stringweather's attitude toward the North, with the difference that the Colonel was a poor man whom few knew, and the Bishop was a rich man and the companion of richer men; and he was much sought after and he talked unctuously to many 'philanthropists.' The poor old Colonel gloried in the poverty of our people. He used to say that the South was the only country left in the world where men are contented without money, believe in God, read Scott's novels, bake sweet potatoes properly, and vote the Democratic ticket. The Bishop suggested fat bank-checks of absolution—a sort of insurance fund of silence about sins near at hand.

And Page looked more closely at the colonel, seeing in him something of that definition of the professional southerner offered by one of my survey respondents, "someone who seizes on and exaggerates a southern identity for the purpose of making money."

In truth, the "professional" Southerner—the man whose capital in life is the fact that he is a Southerner—and your "professional" reformer of the South have many resemblances. Your Southerner shows his intimacy with the Deity by swearing; your reformer shows his intimacy by a condescending familiarity; and you make take your choice of them for bores. They are alike in that neither will learn anything; different only in the angle at which their complacent density misses common sense and a helpful knowledge of mankind.[5]

Scott Romine makes an interesting comparison between Page's awareness of the demand for the kind of public performance of southernness and Du Bois's "double consciousness," as articulated a few years later in *The Souls of Black Folk* (1903). But while Du Bois's insights advance from the enforced and repressive space of segregation, Page's intentions here elicit skepticism more than sympathy from Romine, who notes that Page himself was "the eminent professional southerner of his time—a self-appointed but recognized ambassador from the South to the North" (xiii). Yet even in these short passages, Page's attitude is a good deal more probing and critical of southern culture than those of earlier figures like Early and later ones like Dixon.

Page was exemplary but far from alone in representing the South to the North in the mid-1880s. The period included an explosion of popularity of southern local color fiction in national periodicals, and many white Americans hoped the end of Reconstruction would give way to a new era of regional reconciliation. The Georgia editor and orator Henry W. Grady delivered his famous speech "The New South" at a banquet of the New England Club of New York on December 21, 1886, telling his Yankee audience:

The Old South rested everything on slavery and agriculture, unconscious that these could neither give nor maintain healthy growth. The new South presents a perfect democracy, the oligarchs leading in the popular movement—a social system compact and closely knitted, less splendid on the surface, but stronger at the core—a hundred farms for every plantation, fifty homes for every palace—and a diversified industry that meets the complex needs of this complex age.[6]

Insisting, in the tradition of Jubal Early, on the "brave and simple faith" of the Confederate cause, Grady nevertheless expressed approval "that the omniscient God held the balance of battle in His Almighty hand and that human slavery was swept forever from American soil" (39–40). In making this concession, and even more explicitly in his conclusion, Grady's appeal revealed that he viewed New England, not the South itself, as his audience:

> Now, what answer has New England to this message? Will she permit the prejudice of war to remain in the hearts of the conquerors, when it has died in the hearts of the conquered? Will she transmit this prejudice to the next generation, that in their hearts which never felt the generous ardor of conflict it may perpetuate itself? Will she withhold, save in strained courtesy, the hand which straight from his soldier's heart Grant offered to Lee at Appomattox? Will she make the vision of a restored and happy people, which gathered above the couch of your dying captain, filling his heart with grace, touching his lips with praise, and glorifying his path to the grave—will she make this vision on which the last sigh of his expiring soul breathed a benediction, a cheat and delusion? (40–41)

Grady's New South vision was, as Page satirically anticipated, more Chamber of Commerce than UDC. His rhetorical achievement was to meld the two, promising a white southern paternal stewardship of free blacks even as he imagined a modernized South that sustained strong connections to the rest of the world through capital flows, communication networks, and the ideal, if not the practice, of free labor.

The same year Grady spoke to the New England Club, Henry James published *The Bostonians,* a novel featuring Basil Ransom, a veteran of the war and conservative Mississippi lawyer who has settled in New York and visits his relatives in Boston regularly. Ransom's audience with New Englanders provides a central dramatic tension in the novel because he finds himself in competition with his feminist cousin Olive Chancellor for the affection of her young protégée, Verena Tarrant. For Mrs. Luna, a wealthy widow who enjoys nothing more than imagining the defeated South's exotic chivalry, Ransom takes up the role willingly:

> He abounded in conversation, till at last he took up his hat in earnest; he talked about the state of the South, its social peculiarities, the ruin wrought

by the war, the dilapidated gentry, the queer types of superannuated fire-eaters, ragged and unreconciled, all the pathos and all the comedy of it, making her laugh at one moment, almost cry at another, and say to herself throughout that when he took it into his head there was no one who could make a lady's evening pass so pleasantly.[7]

James did not know southern culture particularly well and was insecure about developing a character like Basil Ransom. His strategy, apparent in this passage, was to portray the South not in any empirical way, but as a figment of his characters' imaginations. This is the South of the New England drawing room, the South offered by a particular sort of professional southerner to a particularly receptive northern, and implicitly female, audience. In a sense it is a postcolonial South, exotic and mythic, conquered and soulful. James seems to be commenting on the popular South of local color, exposing the fraudulence of the national audience that devoured the romance of the region at the end of the nineteenth century. He does this even as he endows Basil Ransom with a complexity of character that transcends the simplistic typecasting of the professional southerner, whether of Early's Lost Cause vintage or of Grady's New South assembly line model.

How did the New South's professional southerner fare in the early twentieth century? The figure seemed to be in many places at once, and the term was in wide circulation. At the annual "Dixie Dinner" of the New York Southern Society, held on February 22, 1910, at the Hotel Astor on Broadway and 44th Street, the Baltimore-born artist and author F. Hopkinson Smith delivered a withering critique of New York, calling it "the most insolent city on the face of the globe" and lamenting the all-consuming quest for money that had frayed the bonds of affection between men. "Let's get back to our traditions, let's be courteous to women, true to our friends—in a word, the Southern blood." Following this successful speech, Judge Charles F. Moore offered insights into the influence that southerners had on the city and the influence of the city on southerners.

Southerners in New York are divided into two classes—the real and the professional Southerner. There is the Southerner who lives in New York and the Southerner who infests New York. Some of them do a lot and say nothing and others talk a lot and do nothing. If you want your history to be known go and do something. Dig a tunnel under the North River so that the benighted individuals in Jersey can get home easily or write a story like "Col. Carter of Cartersville" [a popular novel by Smith, first published in 1891]. The true Southerner and the man who does the most for the South is the one who does something and who by the integrity of his life wins the admiration of the world. New York has been eminently generous to the Southern man and has held nothing back.

The evening also included a performance by "a negro quartet of the Fisk Jubilee Singers," whose rendition of "Dixie" was met with "wild applause mingled with cheers."[8]

News of the banquet and its speeches soon migrated south in the person of Archibald R. Watson, a Mississippi lawyer whose career went rather more smoothly than Basil Ransom's. Speaking at a meeting of the Louisiana State Bar Association on May 21, 1910, Watson, who had been appointed to the position of Corporation Counsel for New York City by Mayor William Jay Gaynor, dismissed the professional southerner as a figment of the imagination. He told the story of responding to a journalist's question regarding the mythic figure:

I said I had never met but one "Professional Southerner" in New York, and that was some years ago. He cultivated the accent and pronunciation of the cotton-field darkey, discoursed upon the former wealth and influence of his family, grew excited over discussions of the Civil War, the thought of which would drive him to drink if some one else would pay the bartender; got money from me to visit an aunt, declared to be at the point of death in Richmond, Va.—and as a subsequent investigation proved, had been born and reared in the State of Connecticut.

This is the only professional Southerner I ever met in New York.[9]

Even as he rejected the idea that the professional southerner even existed, however, the circumstances of Watson's speech suggest that he was acting the part himself, attempting to trade on his bona fides as a Mississippian to advance the fortunes of his political mentor in New York. As the *New York Times* reported the next day, "It is thought that Mr. Watson's object was to bring Mr. Gaynor's name before Southern Democrats in such a way that they would consider him in their discussions of the Presidential candidate for 1912." In a paradoxical reversal, Watson's speech defended New York, not the South, from what he saw as unfair criticism and prejudice against its people and culture in order to present the reformist mayor in the best possible light. The *Times* story concluded by noting that "Mr. Watson vigorously answered criticisms of F. Hopkinson Smith of New York's alleged insolence and wickedness. He declared that New York was hospitable to those who deserved hospitality, and that its wickedness was far overbalanced by its good."[10]

A decade later, the February 1920 issue of *The Red Book Magazine* included J. F. Natteford's short story "A Professional Southerner." Natteford had a prolific screenwriting career in his future, racking up more than one hundred film and television credits during the half-century between World War I and Vietnam. He was best known for Westerns but revealed an interest in regional cultures that also included the South, as in the opening lines of "A Professional Southerner":

> Judge Stephenson Shelby—"Judge" by self-appointment—was a professional southerner. During long years of residence in New York he had discovered that a nicely pointed white goatee is to some men the unfailing outward manifestation of Southern honor, and that among impressionable women of means, an accent as soft, thick and honeyed as molasses is a guarantee of warm-hearted Southern chivalry. These facts he consciously capitalized in his profession. To put it baldly, he was a salesman of worthless stocks and an unashamed pirate of Liberty bonds.
>
> But the Judge was not wholly without character, as is attested by the fact that any imputation of his poker ethics, unless followed by prompt apology, was certain to be wiped out by personal violence. Even the mildest of men, not choleric and not Kentuckians, may lose their tempers at an accusation touching their only remaining virtue.[11]

Judge Shelby lives in a noirish urban world, and his values reflect the competitiveness and ruthlessness—the "insolence," Smith would say—of the city, yet he ultimately puts his dishonesty in the service of a childhood acquaintance from Kentucky who came to the city seeking medical treatment but was quickly swindled out of his life savings. Shelby wins a thousand dollars from unwitting provincials (not southerners but rubes from Indiana) in a crooked poker game, and gives the money to his friend and his daughter so that they might buy their family farm back before the aging man dies and the girl is reduced to prostitution. In the end the hard-boiled Shelby lives up to an honor code that transcends his profession as a confidence man, as the final lines of the story attest: "Turning, then, he bade them farewell and strode off hungrily down the street, one hand clutching his hickory-knot cane as he walked, the other in an empty pocket" (104). Natteford's professional southerner is, by the perverse logic of the naked city, a constructive, redeeming figure, marked not by racism or headlong defense of the South—indeed, Shelby distinctly recalls the many failings, from intolerance to fundamentalism, that drove him from his native region in the first place—but by a sense of loyalty to the ideal of a nurturing South to which his bedridden friend may yet return.

By the time of the Great Depression, the professional southerner had entered a slow decline that would last through the middle third of the twentieth century. In Nashville a group of intellectuals known as the Agrarians, heirs to the 1920s Fugitive group based at Vanderbilt University, published *I'll Take My Stand* (1930), in which traditional southern values, exemplified by the belief that "the culture of the soil is the best and most sensitive of vocations," were advocated in reaction to the accelerating pace and all-consuming appetite of modern industrial development. These thinkers, most of them poets and scholars and a very few of them actual farmers in any sense of the term, feared the political and economic implications of industrialism but had little by way of viable alternatives beyond their cherished "principles," which, they admitted, "do not intend to be very specific in proposing any practical measures."[12] Some members of the group later published a follow-up volume, *Who Owns America?* (1936), even as others, including the young Robert Penn Warren, sought to distance themselves from their earlier views.

The Agrarians had competition from a Chapel Hill group more inclined to positivism, social science research, and a kind of expert management of southern political and especially economic affairs that owed much to the New Deal. Led by University of North Carolina sociologist Howard Odum, these men had little patience for the lyrical flights of the Nashville cohort—a sentiment more in line with mainstream American views of the time. By 1942, when Virginius Dabney, editor of the *Richmond Times-Dispatch* and an important regional spokesman himself, published *Below the Potomac*, the professional southerner seemed to be in marked retreat. Dabney dismissed the figure as a decidedly minor nuisance in the mid-twentieth-century South:

Our reference to that obnoxious species of Southern fauna, the professional Southerner, leads to the question whether he is ubiquitous as some believe. There are still parochial and unreconstructed Southerners among us, but they are gradually growing less articulate, and also less numerous. Fewer inhabitants of the former Confederacy spend their time in uncritical ravings anent the splendors of ante-bellum and post-bellum civilization, in full-throated ululations alleging the superiority of Southern horses, women, dogs, oboe-players, fly-fishermen, and flagpole-sitters over those of any other section of the globe.

The professional Southerner is, of course, a sentimental and narrow-minded person who is congenitally incapable of seeing anything bad in the South or anything good in the North. He is the sort of individual who is largely responsible for the backwardness of the South in certain fields, for the region's excessive sensitiveness to criticism, and for an occasional propensity on the part of Southerners to regard even the most valid Northern demurrers to Southern attitudes and mores as nefarious plots hatched by descendants of William Lloyd Garrison.[13]

World War II and the Cold War led some to predict the imminent extinction of Dabney's kind of reactionary professional southerner, even as the civil rights movement generated new opportunities for some white southerners, including political figures such as Orval Faubus and George Wallace, business and community groups such as the Mississippi-based Citizens' Councils of America, and print and television pundits such as James J. Kilpatrick, to fashion careers as opponents of desegregation and defenders of a "southern way of life" they claimed had always existed. Ralph McGill, a longtime editorialist for the *Atlanta Constitution*, wrote in 1963 that he had seen the last of the professional southerner on the night of May 17, 1954, as he contemplated the news of the U.S. Supreme Court's decision in *Brown v. Board of Education:*

> It came to me also that almost without comment the professional Southerner had all but disappeared and that I had not really noted his going.
>
> He was a pleasant fellow, or lady, who cultivated a drawl and emphasized good manners. These Southerners made really superior weekend guests in the twenties. In the roof gardens, and, later, the nightclubs, they could be very picturesque by covertly requesting the band to play "Dixie" and then giving the rebel yell when the gallop swing of it began. At college they were more often viewed as charming, rather than bores. These professional Southerners passed with the depression, and it was a pity, really, because they worked very

hard at learning the role they played. But, of a sudden, there was no more demand of it.[14]

These observations are situated in McGill's larger reverie about the tragic sweep of southern history from slavery to the mid-twentieth century, beginning with Eli Whitney and ending with a brief exchange between Theodore Bilbo and himself in the corridor outside a Senate Chamber in 1940 (the Mississippi demagogue had once called McGill "limiculous," and McGill wanted to know where he had learned the word). The aging, now seemingly harmless Bilbo stands in for the passing of the segregationist South, as a kind of sinister doppelgänger to McGill's congenial professional southerner, whose passing McGill also dates to the Depression. McGill doesn't seem to make the connection consciously, and for all his perceptiveness, courage, and early commitment to racial justice, he fails to discern that these two visages—one flashing a charming smile, the other baring fangs—had been as inseparable and complementary as the two faces of Janus.

As later segregationists including Faubus and Wallace would discover, the civil rights movement and the legal dissolution of racial segregation in the South simply shifted the political terrain in ways that invited new incarnations of the professional southerner. But in the last decades of the twentieth century, too, it was not simply racists who sought to wield this figure's evasive but very real influence. Antiracists did too. During a period in which blacks steadily migrated from the urban North to the South, demonstrating a relationship to the region that existed quite independently of white needs, desires, or expectations, the political consultant James Carville and his overachieving charge, Bill Clinton, embraced central elements of the professional southerner's appeal and adapted them to a new political era. Clinton's success in the 1992 presidential election, even more than that of Jimmy Carter in 1976, demonstrated how effectively the professional southerner could be rebranded, and proved once again, just as such various figures as Henry Grady, Booker T. Washington, Dizzy Dean, Margaret Mitchell, Martin Luther King Jr., Dolly Parton, and Billy Graham had shown for more than a century, how smoothly he—and she—could travel and charm and win converts beyond the geographic boundaries of the South. At the end of the century, the professional southerner was as adept as ever at evolving to face new historical conditions, new political, economic, and cultural realities. And if the professional southerner remained, most of the time, a white person, Clinton did what he could to blur even that boundary, prompting the likes of Toni Morrison to report African Americans' oft-murmured belief that "this is our first black President."[15]

The stakes of this role playing in the era of our second black president continue to be high, whether in Arkansas, Washington, New York, Hollywood, or the academic profession. Probably no better example of this exists than that of Clinton himself, who, after assiduously crafting his own image in such matters over the course of a long political career, failed to escape the tenacious valences of the professional southerner in the early twentieth century. During the interminable Democratic primary in advance of the general election of 2008, Clinton's reference to then-Senator Barack Obama as a "kid," along with a separate remark regarding the "fairy tale" of Obama's professed good judgment on several key issues, triggered a backlash that accused Clinton of practicing the same race-baiting rhetoric that had characterized generations of white southern politicians before and since the civil rights movement. "I don't know why he didn't just call him 'boy' and get it over with," Rep. James E. Clyburn of South Carolina was told by another black congressman after Clinton's statements. "Clinton was using code words that most of us in the South can recognize when we hear that kind of stuff," Clyburn told the *New York Times* (in yet another remarkable instance of a self-identified southerner playing the role of interpreter of the subtle, distinct culture of the South for a northern audience).[16] Despite a lifetime of support for antiracist policies, Clinton found himself in the rather hopeless position of denying that he was, in fact, a racist. Whether this episode points to the sort of world evoked in Philip Roth's novel *The Human Stain* (2000), in which a college professor's career and life are destroyed by his use of a single word judged, probably unfairly in its context, to have racial overtones, or represents a legitimate contestation of the arrogance of white paternalism, it seems clear that the professional southerner relies as much on narrow and selective memory as on a memory that is long, precise, and faithful. And the performative arena of politics seems perhaps a better place for these forces to play and compete than anywhere else. This professional southerner is, to be sure, an opportunist.

Returning from this bruising culture to the academy, which is not without its own internecine warfare, its own ideological impurities, and its own horizon of opportunities, I continue to ruminate on the implications of the strange career of the professional southerner for the field of southern studies. I think they are important to consider not just in terms of what they reveal about the field's past but also for what they might suggest about its future. This concern returns me to the late Clintonian era, to a pair of books whose writers, Gary W. Gallagher and Grace Elizabeth Hale, are, I acknowledge by way of confession, former teachers and current friends of mine.

For decades, scholars in the field have faced criticism on the grounds that their work is pitched to audiences more ideological than intellectual, and more commercial than legitimately scholarly. Historians Fred Rippy and E. Merton Coulter, for example, complained that C. Vann Woodward had written the rampant *Origins of the New South, 1877–1913* (1951) "to please Gunnar Myrdal, the Civil Rights advocates and all the Northern Left-Wingers," and groused that the book "put C. Vann on the pinnacle in Yankeeland."[17] Such remarks reveal the ever-present danger in being associated with the professional southerner—a career path that may lead to riches, the sectionalist and segregationist Rippy and Coulter acknowledge, but at the price of one's soul. In the introduction to *The Confederate War* (1997) Gallagher seems to be attempting to inoculate himself from any such comparable *ad hominem* attacks—coming from the reverse direction—by pointing to his distance from the subject of his study:

> Any historian who argues that the Confederate people demonstrated robust devotion to their slave-based republic, possessed feelings of national community, and sacrificed more than any other segment of white society in United States history runs the risk of being labeled a neo-Confederate. As a native of Los Angeles who grew up on a farm in southern Colorado, I can claim complete freedom from any pro-Confederate special pleading during my formative years. Moreover, not a single ancestor fought in the war, a fact I lamented as a boy reading books by Bruce Catton and Douglas Southall Freeman and wanting desperately to have some direct connection to the events that fascinated me. In reaching my conclusions, I have gone where the sources led me.[18]

Does this recourse to distance, geographic and familial, augment Gallagher's authority? Would being a native Virginian or New Englander with ancestors in the war compromise his credibility—at least, with one or another region's readers, to say nothing of a reader in, say, Tehran? And where does this gesture to establish his scholarly perspective at a remove from the risk of "special pleading" fit with his acknowledged lifelong enthusiasm for the subject and adolescent desire for closer proximity to it? These are troubling questions, not least because they problematize the historian's most fundamental asset, his voice, without which he would no longer be himself. "I have gone where the sources led me" is thus not just a statement about the primary and secondary material Gallagher has evaluated; it is, at the same time, an existential assertion, a declaration that his identity as a historian exists not based on ideological commitments or social debts but on purer motives.

Hale's *Making Whiteness* (1998) takes an altogether different approach to the problem of authority. In her introduction Hale explicitly inserts herself into the tumultuous history of southern segregation in order to establish a more compelling historian's voice. She insists on the need to search out insights not from the distant perspective adopted by Gallagher but "from within our history now":

> American history in its broadest sense—what has happened, how we have represented to ourselves what has happened, and how we will continue in this intersecting of making and telling—is vitally important here. If we understand the past as always having been only white and black, what will be the catalyst that makes the future different? The epiphany that erases the bloody divisions? The revelation that makes tomorrow, any time, whole? If we cannot imagine less racially binary pasts or raceless futures, who will? If we cannot craft a dance of time to do more than deepen and elaborate racial difference—and set the hued fragments in motion until the jig reveals the pattern and the colors blur—who will make this time? Integration, created from within our history now, is our only future.[19]

Evoking the antiracist energy of civil rights activism, Hale takes on a prophetic voice here, as though her task as a historian is to lead the way to a promised land of more humane racial imaginings.

Near the end of *Making Whiteness*, after several hundred pages of devastating exposure and criticism of many of the guises of segregation—in the academy, in domestic spaces, in consumer culture, in racial violence, and elsewhere—Hale's voice and vision change from critic's to apologist's, blending with those of Lillian Smith, a heroic opponent of segregation during its heyday. Unleashing a relentless attack on Jim Crow from atop Old Screamer, her mountain in north Georgia, Smith is like Moses here,, and Hale, fusing her voice as a historian with Smith's voice as a prophet, seamlessly ventriloquizes the message of integration: "And yet Smith's shout from the mountain was not a voice crying alone in the wilderness. Segregation, by law at least, did end within Smith's lifetime, and her own deep courage helped destroy this one great wall within humanity. But Smith had also imagined segregation as a culture larger than law, as southern and even American whiteness itself, as all the categories that excluded others and ordered power. Integration, she understood, was the only future" (278).

This summary variation on Hale's introductory claim that "integration, created from within our history now, is our only future," invites the same existential query posed to Gallagher's purportedly disinterested detective-historian: where is this voice coming from? Hale intentionally perceives her earlier insight anew, and does so through the eyes of Lillian Smith, in order to reinforce the idea that her argument's authority is derived not from any detached vantage point but from the very cauldron of racial repression and injustice that gave birth to a woman like Lillian Smith, who apprehended both the mass psychosis of southern segregation and the possibilities for a more humane, egalitarian future. The authorial voice in *Making Whiteness* thus becomes a curious amalgam of Lillian Smith in the 1940s and Hale at the end of the century.

Despite these starkly divergent methods, Gallagher and Hale share an awareness of the looming shadow of the professional southerner in their discipline. And in the very structure of their writings these historians of the South demonstrate constructive attempts to respond to such a presence. Each writer clearly recognizes its dangers, and each works on several levels to turn them to advantages, generating complex texts that speak in informed ways not only to the southern past but also to the challenges of representing that past in ways that satisfy the ever-shifting demands of the present.

Is all this sophistication really necessary? If their efforts are any indication, Gallagher and Hale clearly believe it is. I suppose that such reflexivity, which has become an extraordinarily powerful tool and one of the defining features in our contemporary efforts to narrate the southern past in ways that transcend, from the earth up, the exhausted empire-building narrative history of the old days, whenever those may have been, does have its uses. And what about me? Are my early discovery of the professional southerner's existence, my quixotic search for the secrets of this chameleonic icon, my disclosure of mentorship and friendship with residing geniuses, some named and others kept secret, not also useful, instructive, revelatory? Are these not, too, marks of the professional? I won't deny it. From another perspective, however, going to such lengths to ensure one's own authority seems altogether too cynical, a concession to the disingenuousness or outright ignorance of one's audience, or an admission of the supremacy of a political correctness that has approached McCarthyism in its demand for reassurance of the historian's proper credentials and loyalties. Must we name names, even if, at long last, they include our own?

So these questions are open, and yours, and ours, to field. Amid the uncertainty, though, I think the history of the professional southerner illuminates the terrain of southern studies in a way that seeks less to demoralize our sense of the state of the profession than to animate and deepen our imagination of the future. For the professional southerner, evasive and indefinable in his and her endlessly performative self-conceptions, finally has less to do with authors, speakers, fictional characters, and political actors than with those observing and listening and responding to them. He and she, and we, have the opportunity, through this insight, to remake our narrative as one of call-and-response, in the southern style. Whether galvanizing Confederate memory, reaching north for reconciliation and its financial payout, posing as a confidence man or demagogue, insisting on rights denied and privileges deserved, preaching from the mountaintop with Georgia accents and allusions biblical and literary, sacred and secular, the question is always the same, always asked in the present tense, and always poised with expectation.

What will we do next?

NOTES

1. Russell Merritt, "Dixon, Griffith, and the Southern Legend," *Cinema Journal* 12.1 (Autumn 1972): 31.

2. W. E. B. Du Bois, "The Clansman," *Crisis* 10.1 (May 1915): 33. For an excellent case study of the American film industry's need for interpreters of southern culture, see Matthew H.

Bernstein, "A 'Professional Southerner' in the Hollywood Studio System: Lamar Trotti at Work, 1925–1952," in *American Cinema and the Southern Imaginary,* ed. Deborah E. Barker and Kathryn McKee (Athens: University of Georgia Press, 2011), 122–47. Bernstein derives his use of the term *professional southerner* from the work of film historian Thomas Cripps and defines the figure as "an expert by birth whom the Hollywood studios came to rely on for an understanding of southern culture, mores, and attitudes" (143).

3. John Shelton Reed, "The Twenty Most Influential Southerners of the Twentieth Century," *Southern Cultures* 7.1 (2001): 96–100.

4. Gary W. Gallagher, *The Confederate War: How Popular Will, Nationalism, and Military Strategy Could Not Stave Off Defeat* (Cambridge, Mass.: Harvard University Press, 1997), 169.

5. Walter Hines Page, *The Southerner,* ed. Scott Romine (1885; repr., Columbia: University of South Carolina Press, 2008), 388.

6. Henry Woodfin Grady, *The New South and Other Addresses* (New York: Haskell House, 1969), 37–38.

7. Henry James, *The Bostonians* (1886; repr., New York: Oxford University Press, 1998), 197.

8. "Harsh Criticism for New York City," *New York Times,* February 23, 1910.

9. *Report of the Louisiana State Bar Association* (New Orleans: Louisiana State Bar Association, 1910), 100.

10. "Gaynor Is Boomed by Watson in South," *New York Times,* May 22, 1910.

11. J. F. Natteford, "A Professional Southerner," *Red Book Magazine* 34.4 (February 1920): 49+.

12. Twelve Southerners, *I'll Take My Stand: The South and the Agrarian Tradition* (1930; repr., Baton Rouge: Louisiana State University Press, 1977), xlvii. For a withering critique of this intellectual tradition's influence within the academy, see Paul Bové, "Agriculture and Academe: America's Southern Question," *Boundary 2* 14.3 (Spring 1986): 169–96. Bové identifies and labels the "Professional Southernist" as "a monumental historian and an antiquarian" who reproduces, "in the form of explanation and apology, the tragic image of the Agrarians and their allies as failed prophets, bearers of refused alternatives, preservers of a better way, and guides to spiritual, imaginative renewal" (172).

13. Virginius Dabney, *Below the Potomac: A Book about the South* (New York: D. Appleton-Century, 1942), 12–13.

14. Ralph McGill, *The South and the Southerner* (Boston: Little, Brown, 1963), 24.

15. Toni Morrison, "Talk of the Town: Comment," *New Yorker,* October 5, 1998.

16. "The Long Road to a Clinton Exit," *New York Times,* June 8, 2008.

17. James M. Cobb, "On the Pinnacle in Yankeeland," in *Origins of the New South Fifty Years Later: The Continuing Influence of a Historical Classic,* ed. John B. Boles and Bethany L. Johnson (Baton Rouge: Louisiana State University Press, 2003), 161.

18. Gallagher, *Confederate War,* 13.

19. Grace Elizabeth Hale, *Making Whiteness: The Culture of Segregation in the South, 1890–1940* (New York: Pantheon, 1998), 10–11.

# CONTRIBUTORS

IAN BINNINGTON teaches nineteenth-century American history at Allegheny College. He is completing his first book, *Confederate Visions: Nationalism, Symbolism, and the Imagined South in the Civil War.*

ORVILLE VERNON BURTON is distinguished professor of humanities and the director of the Clemson University CyberInstitute. He is emeritus University Distinguished Teacher/Scholar and professor of history, African American studies, and sociology at the University of Illinois and the author of *The Age of Lincoln* and *In My Father's House Are Many Mansions: Family and Community in Edgefield, South Carolina.*

DAVID A. DAVIS is assistant professor of English and southern studies at Mercer University in Macon, Georgia. He has published numerous essays on southern literature and culture, edited reprints of Victor Daly's *Not Only War* and John L. Spivak's *Hard Times on the Southern Chain Gang*, and is writing a book about World War I and southern modernism.

JIM DOWNS is assistant professor of history at Connecticut College. He is the author of *Sick from Freedom*, a book about the health conditions of former slaves during and after the American Civil War. He is the editor of two anthologies, *Taking Back the Academy* and *Why We Write.*

ROBERT JACKSON is assistant professor of English at the University of Tulsa. He works at the intersection of modern American literature, history, and media studies and currently is writing a book about early cinema and the U.S. South. He is the author of *Seeking the Region in American Literature and Culture: Modernity, Dissidence, Innovation* and *Meet Me in St. Louis: A Trip to the 1904 World's Fair.*

ANNE MARSHALL is associate professor of history at Mississippi State University. She is the author of *Creating a Confederate Kentucky: The Lost Cause and Civil War Memory in a Border State.*

FARRELL O'GORMAN is professor of English at Belmont Abbey College and former associate professor of Catholic studies at DePaul University. He is the author of *Peculiar Crossroads: Flannery O'Connor, Walker Percy, and Catholic Vision in Postwar Southern Fiction.*

JASON PHILLIPS is associate professor of history at Mississippi State University. He is the author of *Diehard Rebels: The Confederate Culture of Invincibility.*

K. STEPHEN PRINCE is an assistant professor of history at the University of South Florida. His book, *Stories of the South: The Cultural Retreat from Reconstruction,* is forthcoming from the University of North Carolina Press.

JEWEL L. SPANGLER is associate professor of history at the University of Calgary in Alberta, Canada. She is the author of *Virginians Reborn: Anglican Monopoly, Evangelical Dissent, and the Rise of the Baptists in the Late Eighteenth Century.*

BERTRAM WYATT-BROWN was the Richard J. Milbauer Professor Emeritus, University of Florida, and a visiting scholar at Johns Hopkins University. His books include *Southern Honor: Ethics and Behavior in the Old South; The Shaping of Southern Culture: Honor, Grace, and War, 1760s–1890s;* and *Lewis Tappan and the Evangelical War against Slavery.*